Literature
for
Children

Literature
for
Children

A Short Introduction

DAVID L. RUSSELL
Ferris State University

Longman
New York & London

Literature for Children: A Short Introduction

Longman, 95 Church Street, White Plains, N.Y. 10601

Associated companies:
Longman Group Ltd., London
Longman Cheshire Pty., Melbourne
Longman Paul Pty., Auckland
Copp Clark Pitman, Toronto

Senior editor: Naomi Silverman
Production editor: Ann P. Kearns
Cover design: Susan J. Moore
Cover illustration: "Picture Books in Winter," *A Child's Garden of Verses,* by Robert Louis Stevenson,
New York: Scribner's (Scribner's Illustrated Classics), 1905.

Library of Congress Cataloging-in-Publication Data

Russell, David L., 1946–
   Literature for children : a short introduction / David L. Russell.
      p.   cm.
   Includes bibliographical references and index.
   ISBN 0-8013-0673-6
   1. Children—Books and reading. 2. Children's literature—History and criticism. I. Title.
   Z1037.A1R89   1991
   028.5—dc20   90-40862
                                                                          CIP

ABCDEFGHIJ—AL—99 98 97 96 95 94 93 92 91 90

Contents

Preface

The purpose of this little book is to provide both students of children's literature and the general reader with an introduction to the study of the field. My premise is that literature written for children should adhere to standards as demanding and exacting as any imposed on literature for adults. The academic study of literature for children is a phenomenon of recent times and, if no longer in its infancy, is at least in its adolescence. From time to time it exhibits the usual growing pains, the doubts and uncertainties, the awkward self-consciousness associated with adolescence. But its importance is at last being realized by all but the most pretentious of schools, and it is becoming a respected part of numerous curricula.

Courses on children's literature are found variously in the English Literature Department, the Education Department, or the Library Science Department. Consequently, the approaches to the study differ widely from place to place, being at times extremely academic and at times eminently practical. The danger of the former is that it can devolve into an esoteric discussion that ignores the child's involvement in the literature. The danger of the latter is that it can devolve into pedagogical methodology that disregards the exploration of ideas or literary quality. Of course, both aspects are important, and as students of children's literature, we should take advantage of the tension between these two extremes, which helps to keep this a lively and meaningful field of study.

I have tried to address both the literary aspects and the pedagogy in this text, although this is decidedly not a methods text for language arts. The book is divided into two parts, the first addressing the context within which we view literature for young people (including a brief historical survey, theories of child development, and instructional methods of sharing literature) and the second examining the principal literary genres and the necessary critical apparatus to read and evaluate literature. It is evident from the relative lengths of the two parts that my principal thrust is the consideration of the literature itself. This reflects my personal conviction that educational methodology must be the handmaiden to content knowledge and not the other way around. I hope that this text provides the essential content knowledge, so that the readers may depart with a richer and deeper understanding of what children's literature is all about.

In my own teaching, I find that college students often have not read many works that were once considered almost standard childhood fare—*Alice's Adventures in Wonderland, The Wind in the Willows, The Adventures of Tom Sawyer, Treasure Island*—and many are not much better versed in the more recent contributions to the field (those of C. S. Lewis, Robert Cormier, Katherine Paterson, Madeleine L'Engle, and so on). As a result, I believe it important that students be exposed to some of these primary sources, which form the basic texts in my classes. However, in addition to the reading of the literature itself, I have found it desirable that they have some small supplemental text that will give them a foundation for their reading. That is the motivation behind the book. It is not intended to be a definitive survey of children's literature, but only a beginning—a preface—to further reading.

Since many colleges and universities do not distinguish sufficiently between children's and adolescent (or young adult) literature, making a single course suffice, I have elected to take "children's literature" in its broadest possible sense. My discussions include books for infants as well as for teenagers. Additionally, in providing this overview I have not filled the pages with plot summaries of selected works. These are already available in numerous places, and my intention is to give the readers the necessary critical apparatus to read and judge books for themselves—not to relieve them of the necessity for reading those books.

Each chapter concludes with a bibliography of critical works, and, when appropriate, the chapters also conclude with a list of selected works of literature. These booklists are to be taken as suggestive and by no means exhaustive. I have tried to include the most important works in all cases, as well as some of my own personal favorites. Ultimately, every serious student of children's literature should probably create his or her own bibliography of primary works.

It is my hope that my readers will come away with a renewed interest in and healthy respect for children's literature, with an understanding of the complexities of the literature, and with an appreciation of the importance of the literature in the lives of young people. Reading is unquestionably the most fundamental of all academic skills, and the love of reading is among the richest gifts we can bestow upon our children. Our justification has been eloquently pronounced by the writer of Ecclesiasticus:

> If thou hast gathered nothing in thy youth,
> how canst thou find anything in thine age?

PART I
The Contexts of Children's Literature

CHAPTER 1

The History of Children's Literature

THE BEGINNINGS

The earliest children's literature was the oral tale passed on by word of mouth from elder to child—a practice reaching beyond antiquity. We may imagine flickering hearth fires, guarding against the chill of night, around which storytellers shared their tales of gods and heroes, princes and dragons, foolish peasants and clever animals, tales of thrilling journeys, noble quests, mighty battles, and tender love. Of course, no one thought of these as children's literature nor were they specifically intended for children; children just happened to be in the audience and happened to enjoy hearing these stories. And this would be the condition of children's literature for centuries, the children adopting what they liked from the storehouse of adult literature. Hence, the young of ancient Greece enjoyed Homer's *Iliad* and *Odyssey,* and those of ancient Rome turned to Virgil's *Aeneid* and Ovid's *Metamorphoses.* Much of this ancient literature had a universal appeal that transcended the limitations imposed by youth.

By medieval times (from roughly 500 to 1500 A.D.) little had changed in this regard. Writers simply did not think to create a literature especially for children. In part, this was natural because childhood itself was largely ignored; it was kept as brief as possible, the object being for the child to reach adulthood as quickly as possible and thus become a contributing member of society. Children were seen as miniature adults (a fact easily observed in medieval paintings where children are depicted as little more than very short grown-ups). There was virtually no understanding of child development, and education (which was reserved primarily for the clergy and the nobility) was extremely unenlightened. And even among the aristocracy, the ability to read was often quite rare. (The practice of affixing an official seal to a document was actually necessitated by the fact that often even kings could neither read nor write—Charlemagne is one example.) Given these circumstances, it is not surprising that ancient and medieval writers were reluctant to expend their talents and energies writing for children—it was no way to ensure literary immortality.

So for centuries, children had to be content to cull favorite stories from the available adult literature. However, this still left much for them to enjoy. As with ancient literature, medieval literature still preserved a universal quality, aimed at a broadly based audience and containing much that appealed to young and old alike. Medieval children found delight in the romantic adventures of noble knights, such as those of King Arthur's Round Table or of Charlemagne's court. In the British Isles, which is our proper domain in this study, children heard the tales of Robin Hood, an early antihero, in fact an outlaw. The Middle Ages being an intensely religious period, it is only natural that biblical tales and stories of the lives of saints would be popular fare. There were also local legends, celebrating the great deeds of some half-real, half-mythical hero of the neighborhood. The lively medieval imagination drew no clear distinction—as we do today—between fantasy and realism. For many medieval people, magic, enchantment, and miracles were as real as taxes. This may be one of the reasons medieval children were so content simply to borrow the literature of their parents. (We must remember, too, that in medieval society, the population was considerably younger than that of today; even in the 1700s fifty was considered a relatively advanced age.)

In the fifteenth century, all this began to change. At that time movable type was introduced into Europe, and that soon led to widespread book publication. Prior to this, every book had to be laboriously copied by hand, which made books extremely rare and prohibitively expensive. (Monastic and university libraries often chained their books to tables to prevent theft—forget about checking a book out for the weekend.) Consequently, few people bothered to learn to read. But the new printing methods made books cheaper and more plentiful. Additionally, Europe was growing prosperous as a result of several factors: (1) The Crusades opened up trade routes with the East; (2) strong central monarchies began to harness warring feudal lords and to encourage the growth of peaceful commerce and industry; (3) the European discovery of the New World brought untold wealth to some and opportunity to many. This growing wealth saw the rise of a middle class. Whereas peasants could not afford to educate their children and had no reason to anyway, the new middle class valued education and needed to read and write in order to carry on trade. By the end of the seventeenth century, social changes were well under way that would clear the path for a genuine literature for children.

THE DISCOVERY OF CHILDHOOD: THE PURITANS AND JOHN LOCKE

In the late seventeenth and early eighteenth centuries, English children continued to adopt certain adult works of literature. They were especially drawn to the fanciful allegory in John Bunyan's *Pilgrim's Progress* (the story of a man's journey to Heaven, although children particularly delighted in the horrific monsters that plague him on the trip). Perhaps even more popular was Jonathan Swift's satirical allegory *Gulliver's Travels* (a work that is still retold from time to time for children and that has been the subject of several movies for young people). The moral and ethical messages of these works did not concern the youthful readers, who were simply after a good tale. Both of these works are built around the idea of a dangerous journey, which is one of the oldest motifs in literature and dates back as far as Homer's *Odyssey*. It is also one of the most successful of literary patterns, and the excitement and adventure it provides undoubtedly account for its continued popularity among young people.

However, also by this time, significant changes in the social concept of childhood were taking place. As mentioned above, it was really the rise of the middle class that encouraged the distinction between childhood and adulthood and subsequently a distinction in the literature for each. The Puritans especially, with their concern for education and their focus on the family's responsibility to ensure the salvation of the children's souls, were a major influence. As might be expected, the first books for children were *didactic* books—that is, they were intended to instruct children. John Comenius' *Orbis Sensualium Pictus* (1657) is generally regarded as the earliest children's illustrated book. It was, in fact, a Latin vocabulary book—a sort of "Latin through pictures." Other early schoolbooks included the so-called hornbooks. Commonly found in New England, these consisted of simple wooden slabs, usually with a handle, on which were attached parchment containing rudimentary language lessons (the alphabet, numerals, and so on). The slabs were then covered with transparent horn (from cattle, sheep, goats), which served as a primitive form of lamination. These books proved to be very durable.

One of the great influences on early children's literature during this period was the English philosopher John Locke, who, in 1693, wrote a celebrated essay entitled *Thoughts concerning Education*. In this work, he formulated his notion that the minds of young children were similar to blank slates, just waiting to be written upon and thus instructed. Locke effectively discounted the influence of heredity by suggesting that every child possessed the capacity for learning. Moreover, Locke felt, it was the responsibility of adults to see to the proper education of children. The Puritans were interested in childhood for religious reasons, whereas Locke stressed the importance of childhood for intellectual reasons. So it was that the idea of books for children received the considerable support of both religion and philosophy.

THE EIGHTEENTH CENTURY: NEWBERY AND COMPANY

As a consequence of these influences, the serious publishing of children's books soon began. Although he may not have been the first, John Newbery, an English entrepreneur, was certainly the most successful of the early publishers of books for children. His *Little Pretty Pocket Book* (1744) is now considered a landmark in children's literature, the first significant publication for children that sought not only their edification but their enjoyment as well. This collection of songs, moral tales, and crude woodblock illustrations marked the successful beginning of a publishing phenomenon that has not yet stopped ballooning.

The French philosopher Jean-Jacques Rousseau, in the mid-eighteenth century, added yet another angle to the concept of children's reading. His ideas about education were expressed in a book called *Emile* (1762), where he emphasized the importance of *moral* development (the Puritans' concern had been spiritual; Locke's, intellectual). For Rousseau, proper moral development could be best accomplished through simplicity of living (even 200 years ago people were becoming distressed over the increasing complexity of life). It was a short jump from Rousseau's ideas to extremely didactic and moralistic books for children, books that supposedly taught them how to be good and proper human beings. (Newbery had, in fact, contributed his fair share of moralistic tales, *Little Goody Two Shoes* being the most famous.) A great many writers, most of them women (men still looked upon writing for children as an inferior occupation), churned out a great number of moralistic tales throughout the remainder of the eighteenth century and well into the nineteenth. Most of these writers, such as Maria Edgeworth, Sarah Trimmer, and Mrs. Barbauld, are largely forgotten now, and their works seem both tiresome and preachy. But their influence was tremendous, and thinly veiled didactic children's books, bent on teaching proper behavior, can still be found crowding the shelves of bookstores and libraries.

THE EARLY NINETEENTH CENTURY: FAIRY TALES REVIVED

Almost contrary to the strain of didacticism in children's literature was the resurrection and perseverance of the old folktales from the oral tradition. In 1729, *Tales of Mother Goose* by the Frenchman Charles Perrault was first translated and published in English. The tales were retellings of old folktales, including "Cinderella," "Little Red Riding Hood," "Sleeping Beauty," and so on. Perrault himself may not have intended these stories for children at all, but for the entertainment of the ladies at the French royal court. Nevertheless, children adored them—as they always have—and throughout the eighteenth century more and more retellings appeared (many originating in France, but the movement was contagious throughout Europe).

At the beginning of the nineteenth century, two German philologists, the brothers Wilhelm and Jacob Grimm, collected a great number of folktales and published them (once again, not expressly for children). These not only carried adult themes, but were often alarmingly frank and filled with violence, and as we might imagine, many adults considered them unsuitable for children. Folktales clearly went against the grain of the didactic works being published for children, but the exciting, fast-paced, and imaginative stories captivated young readers. In 1846, the Dane Hans Christian Andersen's *Fairy Tales* were first published in English and have remained popular ever since. Andersen was not only a collector and reteller, but a writer of original tales, most of which were clearly inspired by folktales and written in the folktale tradition. By the end of the nineteenth century, the collectors Joseph Jacobs and Andrew Lang were making available to English readers a wealth of folktales from the world over. Disputes still arise over the appropriateness of folktales for children's reading, but the disputes are always among adults, never among the children themselves, who continue to read and love the old tales.

THE MID- AND LATE NINETEENTH CENTURY: THE GOLDEN AGE

In 1865, Lewis Carroll (pseudonym for Charles Dodgson, a mathematics professor at Oxford University) published *Alice in Wonderland* and thus began a new era in children's literature. *Alice* is the first significant publication for children that abandoned all pretense of instruction and was offered purely for enjoyment. It was this book that broke the bonds of didacticism that had so long gripped children's literature, and thus were opened the gates for a wealth of imaginative writing, in both England and America. Perhaps the richest store of literature for young people during this period can be found in the field of *fantasy,* including George MacDonald's *The Princess and Curdie* (1877), L. Frank Baum's *The Wizard of Oz* (1900), and Kenneth Grahame's *The Wind in the Willows* (1908). The fantasies are widely varied, ranging from Grahame's animal fantasy to MacDonald's fairy stories to Baum's fanciful journey. These early works have continued to inspire fantasy writers to the present day.

Also especially popular in the nineteenth century were *adventure stories* for boys, of which Robert Louis Stevenson's *Treasure Island* (1881 and 1883) and Mark Twain's *The Adventures of Tom Sawyer* (1876) and *The Adventures of Huckleberry Finn* (1884) are the most enduring. But thousands of (mostly mediocre) books were published by popular writers of adventure stories. British children seemed to prefer stories set in faraway and unfamiliar places, whereas American boys found satisfactory adventure in stories set in their native land, often in the romantic past of their still young nation. Also, we cannot ignore those writers in the vein of Horatio Alger, Jr., whose immensely popular success stories have made his name virtually a household word to this day, long after people have ceased to read his books. Alger's heroes were always downtrodden boys who struggled for fortune and respectability, both of which they ultimately gained, not necessarily because of their hard work but rather because of their moral uprightness. Also primarily for boys was the so-called *school story,* about the antics of boys at boarding schools (Thomas Hughes's *Tom Brown's School Days,* 1857, is a prototype of this sort of fiction).

For girls of this period, there were the popular *domestic stories,* tales of home and family life focusing on the activities of a virtuous heroine, usually suffering dire straits but eventually achieving good fortune and a happy marriage. (If both the Alger stories and the domestic stories sound vaguely familiar, they should—they are essentially old folktales transmuted into nineteenth-century forms.) Many of the domestic novels sank into maudlin sentimentality (Martha Finley's *Elsie Dinsmore* series was at once the most popular and the most sentimental, with Elsie shedding enough tears in the course of a book to flood the Great Plains). But Louisa May Alcott's *Little Women* (1868) and L. N. Montgomery's *Anne of Green Gables* (1908), both domestic novels, rank among the minor classics of children's literature.

Also of importance during this period were advances in printing techniques, which produced full-color printing by the latter half of the nineteenth century. These advances encouraged first-rate artists such as Randolph Caldecott, Walter Crane, and Kate Greenaway to enter the field of children's books. By the end of the nineteenth century, stunningly illustrated children's books were available at reasonable prices, and by the first quarter of the twentieth century libraries were at last designating children's rooms (or at least children's shelves).

THE TWENTIETH CENTURY: WIDENING WORLDS

Children's books of extraordinary quality have appeared with great consistency throughout the twentieth century. The charming works of Beatrix Potter (*The Tale of Peter Rabbit,* 1901; *The Tale of Benjamin Bunny,* 1904) and of Wanda Gág (*Millions of Cats,* 1927) helped to lay the groundwork for the unified picture storybook for the very young. *Millions of Cats* is considered the first true American picture-book. Prior to its appearance, American children had to rely on English reprints or meager and crudely illustrated books produced on cheap paper. With the 1930s the flood of high quality picture-books began—a fact recognized in 1936 when the American Library Association began awarding the Caldecott Medal for the most distinguished American picture-book. This tradition has been expertly continued by such illustrators as Robert McCloskey, Marcia Brown, and Maurice Sendak, and such storytellers as Margaret Wise Brown and Robert Lawson.

Modern fantasy has proved itself the equal of its great Victorian forebears. A. A. Milne's toy fantasy, *Winnie-the-Pooh* (1926), has become a staple of childhood culture. The fantasies of P. L. Travers (*Mary Poppins,* 1934), C. S. Lewis (*The Chronicles of Narnia* series, 1950–56), E. B. White (*Charlotte's Web,* 1952), Philippa Pearce (*Tom's Midnight Garden,* 1959), and Ursula Le Guin (*A Wizard of Earthsea,* 1968) only begin to scratch the surface of outstanding modern classics. Many modern fantasies explore complex psychological, sociological, and even moral issues. The field of science fiction (fathered by the nineteenth-century French writer Jules Verne) has come into its own in the twentieth century, the best works squarely confronting some of the important human issues of our day.

Modern realism has taken several directions, and the best of it has been characterized by an adherence to truth and a rejection of sentimentality (an unwarranted and self-indulgent wallowing in emotion). Laura Ingalls Wilder's *Little House in the Big Woods* (1932) and its sequels, and Esther Forbes's *Johnny Tremain* (1943), are outstanding examples of historical realism. The contemporary realism of Virginia Hamilton (*M. C. Higgins, the Great,* 1974), Robert Cormier (*The Chocolate War,* 1974), Katherine Paterson (*The Great Gilly Hopkins,* 1977), and Cynthia Voigt (*Homecoming,* 1982) again only suggests the variety of the broad selection of quality books for young people available today. Virtually no topic, from gang violence to premarital pregnancy to homosexuality, is taboo from modern realistic works.

We should not forget the considerable work being done in the area of nonfiction—biography, history, science, art, technology, and so on. Gifted writers such as Millicent Selsam, Russell Freedman, David Macaulay, Leonard Everett Fisher, and Milton Meltzer have brought great distinction to the writing of informational literature for young readers. Children and adolescents now have at their disposal very fine biographies, reliable and interesting histories, accurate and clear science books. And adults are beginning to realize the importance that excellent nonfiction plays in stimulating children to pursue intellectual explorations.

But, of course, with this virtual avalanche of children's books (and it grows every year) we might logically suspect that a great number of these are not of the highest quality. In the face of so large a selection, it can be very confusing and distressing to try to separate the wheat from the chaff. This will be a major consideration for the remainder of this book; our point here is only to suggest the diversity and quality that have emerged in today's writing for young people. Literature for both children and adolescents has in this century enjoyed the talents of some of the best storytellers and writers. Authors need no longer feel diffident or apologetic about writing for children, nor artists about drawing for children. And we are all richer for that.

THE WRITERS OF BOOKS FOR YOUNG PEOPLE

Unfortunately, there is still a mistaken attitude among many readers and some writers that books for children are relatively effortless to write, that anyone with marginal talent can whip out a "kids' book" in no time. We noted above that early children's books were written chiefly by women—a sign of eighteenth-century chauvinism, the male writers saving themselves for what they believed to be the more lofty calling of writing serious books for adults. Despite the appearance of enduring children's classics such as *Alice in Wonderland, The Adventures of Tom Sawyer, Treasure Island, The Wind in the Willows,* and *Charlotte's Web,* we have not entirely escaped that condescending attitude, and many writers of children's books occasionally find themselves in the awkward position of defending their profession.

Speaking to this unfortunate condescension toward children's books, C. S. Lewis tells us: "When I was ten, I read fairy tales in secret and would have been ashamed if I had been found doing so. Now that I am fifty I read them openly. When I became a man I put away childish things, including the fear of childishness and the desire to be very grownup" (1980, 210). He further reminds us that growth, maturation, actually consists not of putting away old pleasures, but of adding new ones.

> I now enjoy Tolstoy and Jane Austen and Trollope as well as fairy tales and I call that growth;
> if I had had to lose the fairy tales in order to acquire the novelists, I would not say that
> I had grown but only that I had changed. A tree grows because it adds rings; a train doesn't
> grow by leaving one station behind and puffing on to the next. (211)

The general public is surprisingly uneducated about children's literature. Contrary to popular belief, having once been a child and having read some of the childhood classics does not qualify one as an authority on children's books. It has only been in the past few decades that a serious study of children's literature has emerged. We should take heart that at last the field is being acknowledged as worthy of consideration. The study of children's literature is the study of childhood, of human aesthetic development, of human intellectual development, of social development. The purpose of children's literature and its study is to bring the advantages and the joys of reading to all children, for without reading, the ideas of the past would be lost forever, and we would be forced naked into the world. The more that we, as adults, know about children's literature, the better equipped will we be to help children discover these advantages and these joys.

Surely it will not do for us to adopt a snobbish attitude toward children's books, insisting that children read only those that we perceive as the best. On the other hand, thousands of new children's books appear each year—and not every one is a classic. We ought to prepare ourselves to provide intelligent guidance for young people in their reading. The most important thing, in the final analysis, is that young people are *reading*. Through reading, young people expand their ideas, develop their tastes, and ready themselves for their contributions to society and civilization. As adults, perhaps the best we can do for young readers is to expose them to as many books as possible, on as many subjects as possible. And we may hope that they will find the universe a place of exciting challenges and extraordinary beauty.

BIBLIOGRAPHY OF CRITICAL STUDIES

Aiken, Joan. "On Imagination." *The Horn Book* 60 (November/December 1984): 735–741.

Aries, Philippe. *Centuries of Childhood: A Social History of Family Life.* New York: Knopf, 1962.

Bator, Robert, comp. *Signposts to Criticism of Children's Literature.* Chicago: American Library Association, 1983.

Coody, Betty. *Using Literature with Young Children.* 2d ed. Dubuque, IA: Brown, 1979.

Cott, Jonathan. *Pipers at the Gates of Dawn: The Wisdom of Children's Literature.* New York: Random House, 1981.

Darton, F. J. Harvey. *Children's Books in England, Five Centuries of Social Life.* Cambridge, U. K.: Cambridge University Press, 1966.

Egoff, Sheila A., ed. *Only Connect: Readings on Children's Literature.* 2d ed. Toronto: Oxford University Press, 1980.

———. *Thursday's Child: Trends and Patterns in Contemporary Children's Literature.* Chicago: American Library Association, 1981.

Fraser, James H., ed. *Society and Children's Literature.* Boston: Godine, 1978.

Harrison, Barbara, and Gregory Maguire, comps. and eds. *Innocence & Experience: Essays & Conversations on Children's Literature.* New York: Lothrop, 1987.

Haviland, Virginia, ed. *Children and Literature: Views and Reviews.* Glenview, IL: Scott, Foresman, 1973.

Hazard, Paul. *Books, Children, and Men.* Boston: The Horn Book, 1983.

Hunter, Mollie. *Talent Is Not Enough.* New York: Harper, 1976.

Inglis, Fred. *The Promise of Happiness: Meaning and Value in Children's Fiction.* Cambridge: Cambridge University Press, 1981.

Lewis, C. S. "On Three Ways of Writing for Children." In *Only Connect,* edited by Sheila Egoff. 2d ed., 207–220. New York: Oxford University Press, 1980.

Meek, Margaret, Aidan Warlow, and Griselda Barton. *The Cool Web: The Patterns of Children's Reading.* New York: Atheneum, 1978.

Meigs, Cornelia, Elizabeth Nesbitt, Anne Thaxter Eaton, and Ruth Hill. *A Critical History of Children's Literature: A Survey of Children's Books in English.* New York: Macmillan, 1969.

Sadker, Myra Pollack, and David Miller Sadker. *Now Upon a Time: A Contemporary View of Children's Literature.* New York: Harper, 1977.

Thwaite, Mary F. *From Primer to Pleasure in Reading: An Introduction to the History of Children's Books in England.* Boston: The Horn Book, 1972.

Townsend, John Rowe. *Written for Children.* Boston: The Horn Book, 1974.

Trelease, Jim. *The Read-Aloud Handbook.* New York: Penguin Books, 1982.

CHAPTER 2

Children and Literature

THE IMPORTANCE OF LITERATURE

If we lost the ability to read, our civilization would disappear in a single generation, and our species would of necessity return to its agrarian and hunting beginnings. And although some might think they would find the life of peasant simplicity preferable to the modern rat race, we must remember what else we would be sacrificing. Man's advances in medicine, art, music, philosophy, theater, technology, and the like are largely made possible because we are able to record our knowledge and thus pass it on to others. Writing has made our civilization possible.

Yet we discover an alarming number of adults in the United States to be functionally illiterate—people unable to read newspapers, food labels, job applications, or election ballots, and thus unable to live successfully in society and to make significant contributions to it. Many other people can read but don't, people who never develop a love of belletristic reading (that is, novels, poems, plays, and short stories). Much as we might desire that all young people not only learn to read but also to appreciate literature, that is just not feasible. This should not overly concern us, nor should it dissuade us from trying to instill such appreciation. The ability to read is perhaps the most important educational skill an individual can acquire. Reading immeasurably enriches our lives by (1) broadening our awareness, (2) deepening our understanding, (3) stimulating our imagination, and (4) refining our sensibilities. In a civilized society, illiteracy is the ultimate intellectual deprivation.

THEORIES OF CHILD DEVELOPMENT

Before we go on to consider some of the methods of sharing literature with children, it is important to examine some of the current thinking about the growth and development of children. The greater our knowledge of children, the better our understanding of their books and their relationship to books. Child development studies have revealed that children are psychologically more complex than originally believed. And although there is no single theory with which everyone feels comfortable, a knowledge of the more prominent theories can help us discover more meaningful ways of bringing books and children together.

Piaget's Cognitive Theory of Development

The Cognitive Theory of development, devised by the Swiss psychologist Jean Piaget, is perhaps the most famous of the theories. Piaget saw a person's intellectual or mental development as occurring in steps, each building on the previous one. He outlined four major periods of intellectual development, some of which he subdivided into stages. The first period Piaget identified is the Sensorimotor Period (from birth to about two years), during which the child is incapable of establishing object permanence—in other words, infants and toddlers do not realize that objects continue to exist even if they cannot be seen. Consequently, the infant's world is entirely egocentric, and what matters most is sensory experience, including the development of coordination. During this period, the most important thing for our consideration is to plant the seed of reading, to encourage the handling of books, to establish story times. Brief works, such as the nursery rhymes, picture concept books, and tactile books that offer young readers opportunities to feel textures (such as Dorothy Kunhardt's *Pat the Bunny*), are particularly suited to short attention spans.

Once children have established the concept of object permanence, they move into the second period, the Preoperational Period, between the ages of two and seven. Piaget further subdivided this period into two stages. During the first two to three years, children are in what he termed the Preconceptual Stage, characterized by a very subjective logic. These children tend to classify things according to changing criteria, for example, or they infer relationships on the basis of a single attribute, and they interpret movement as an indication of life (thus inanimate objects may take on human characteristics). At this stage, children are better able to follow a story line, and the simple plots of folktales acquire new meaning for them. Animal stories and fantasies readily fit into their system of thought. About the age of four they arrive at what Piaget termed the Intuitive Stage. They are developing language skills and increasing awareness of the world around them; consequently, they are becoming less egocentric. Now stories about human relationships carry new meaning as do stories that explore inner emotions—Maurice Sendak's popular *Where the Wild Things Are* (1963) has been successful because it so pointedly addresses the needs of its intended audience. This is an extremely important stage for children's reading, since it is a stage of exploration and a time when children discover hidden interests. A wide variety of books on many different topics can help them during this discovery process.

The third period—the Period of Concrete Operations—covers roughly the ages of seven to eleven. This is when children begin to use rudimentary logic and problem solving. They begin to understand time and spatial relationships. The so-called problem novels of such writers as Judy Blume and M. E. Kerr are popular during this period, because of the young readers' own growing experiences. Historical fiction becomes more meaningful during this period, since the children now have a grasp of the passage of time. Laura Ingalls Wilder's *Little House* series has been a staple for readers in these years. Additionally, stories about other lands, such as Meindert DeJong's story of the Netherlands, *The Wheel on the School* (1954), become appealing for them as their world becomes still less egocentric.

Finally is the Period of Formal Operations, beginning around the age of eleven and concluding at about fifteen (when full cognitive maturity, according to Piaget, can be said to be established). During this period young people become capable of using formal logic, engaging in a true exchange of ideas, comprehending the viewpoints of others, and essentially understanding the world as a social phenomenon requiring human interaction. At this period, readers have few restrictions on them in terms of what they can understand, although it has only been in the past few decades that adult writers have provided them with a full gamut of relevant subjects in their books. Examples of topics found in books for this age group include inner-city gang wars (S. E. Hinton's *The Outsiders*), homosexuality (John Donovan's *I'll Get There, It Better Be Worth the Trip* and Sandra Scoppettone's *Trying Hard to Hear You*), racial prejudice (Mildred Taylor's *Roll of Thunder, Hear My Cry*), premarital sex (Judy Blume's *Then Again, Maybe I Won't*), just to name a few. The works of Robert Cormier (*I Am the Cheese, The Bumblebee Flies Anyway,* and others) have raised much controversy among adults about the appropriateness of the subject matter for adolescents (*I Am the Cheese* deals with a violently corrupt government engaged in mind control, for example). Yet, despite the overall negative tone of these works, they remain popular among a significant segment of the young reading population. Once we understand something about Piaget's discoveries concerning cognitive development, we adults may not be so surprised by the appeal some of these works have for teenagers.

Erikson's Psychosocial Development Theory

Erik Erikson sees maturation as a series of psychosocial conflicts, each of which must be resolved before one can move on to the next, in much the same way that Piaget sees successive levels in cognitive development. Erikson's theory includes five principal stages of development throughout childhood. The first stage, from birth to roughly eighteen months, is focused on the conflict of Trust versus Mistrust; this is when children most require security (chiefly provided through creature comforts and affection). At least part of the success of nursery rhymes is due to repetition; these simple verses are usually repeated night after night and thereby provide a reassuring order to life. Margaret Wise Brown's classic, *Good Night Moon,* has long been popular as a story for early childhood because it exudes a familiar warmth: We observe a little bunny saying good night to all his favorite possessions in the comfort of his womblike bedroom.

Erikson's second stage, Autonomy versus Doubt, from eighteen months to about three years, is when children become aware of others around them, especially their care givers and siblings. At this time they must try to establish their own individual identities, and, as a result, this is a period of exploration. Beatrix Potter's *The Tale of Peter Rabbit* beautifully illustrates the moral dilemma that faces children at this stage: The protagonist must choose between acting on his own will and obeying the authority of his mother.

The third stage, Initiative versus Guilt, occurring between the ages of three and six, is when children begin to realize their own responsibilities and to understand interpersonal conflicts; consequently, they can now experience guilt. In Ezra Jack Keats's *Peter's Chair* (1967), Peter comes to regret his selfish motives in refusing to share his baby things with his infant sister, and he finally offers them to her of his own free will. Peter has arrived at a higher stage of social development than his rabbit counterpart in Beatrix Potter's tale, which is demonstrated by his resolve to alter his behavior.

The fourth stage, Industry versus Inferiority, taking place between the ages of seven and eleven, is characterized by a determination to achieve success, often working in concert with others. At the same time, however, children have a tendency to measure themselves up against their peers and find themselves wanting. Beverly Cleary's *Ramona* books wonderfully demonstrate these feelings; young readers view Ramona with a sympathetic eye as she strives for acceptance among her peers.

The fifth stage is achieved at adolescence and that is Identity versus Role Diffusion. Perhaps the great crisis of adolescence is the discovery of identity, not only personal identity, but cultural and social identity as well. These issues are explored in realistic novels such as those by Virginia Hamilton (*M. C. Higgins, the Great*) and Katherine Paterson (*The Great Gilly Hopkins*), and also in fantasies such as Ursula Le Guin's *Earthsea* tetralogy.

There are probably as many developmental theories as there are developmental psychologists to devise them. Nevertheless there is considerable agreement that human beings develop in stages, that these stages can only be roughly approximated in terms of years, that there is much overlapping in these stages, and that there may be occasional regression or a temporary going backward as children develop. Many of the finest writers are likely oblivious to the names assigned to these stages and may not even be aware of an organized theory of development. Instead, they write intuitively and know human beings from personal observation and not from classroom instructions.

SHARING LITERATURE WITH CHILDREN

Important as it is to understand something about child development, to help us to select more appropriate books for our children's ages and interests, it is equally important to be aware of exciting and interesting ways to share books, poems, and tales with children. Literature must be read if it is to be of any value or to have any meaningful impact. Perhaps the principal responsibility of adults in this regard is simply to make sure that children and books come together—often—and that, when they do, the experience is a pleasurable and stimulating one. This is how good reading habits are formed, both at school and at home.

Sharing Books in Schools

In our schools today, too much use is made of textbooks and too little of the fine literature—fiction, poetry, and nonfiction—that is currently available for young people. Library time is too often used as a reward or as a time filler, when it ought to be an integral part of the educational program. Students should be taught from the beginning how to use the library for information and enjoyment. The library should represent not a silent, awesome sepulcher for books, but a busy, exciting marketplace of ideas and entertainment, a place where students can browse for luxuries or shop for necessities for the mind and spirit.

Every classroom should have plenty of books on hand, both fiction and nonfiction. Ample time for sharing books, reading aloud, and silent reading should be scheduled. (And this goes for junior and senior high schools as well.) Simply put, books should be seen as an inseparable part of education, an invaluable part of life.

Sharing Books at Home

To nurture in children a healthy attitude toward reading requires above all good role models in adults. If they never see their parents reading, children can hardly be expected to pick up the habit—and it is a habit. A family reading time can be an effective way of instilling that habit. Reading engenders more reading, as ideas and pleasures in one book encourage us to seek others. To establish the reading habit in children, it is important for adults to provide an atmosphere free from the persistent interference of television cartoons, sit-com reruns, and other mindless distractions. It is not a bad idea for every home to start its own modest library. Inexpensive books can still be found on the sale tables in bookstores, and many schools sponsor book swaps and participate in paperback book clubs. Parents should not rely on teachers to acquaint their children with books. Family visits to the public library on a frequent and regular schedule do much to instill respect for books and to keep the idea of reading alive in young minds—excellent supplements to reading experiences at home and in school. In short, much of the responsibility for a child's attitude toward reading and books lies in the home. In the following pages, we will examine some of the ways adults can use to give children enjoyable and thought-provoking adventures in reading. This is in no way an exhaustive list, but rather a suggestive one. We are limited only by our own imaginations.

Reading Aloud

From the parent's gentle singing of a lullaby while rocking an infant to sleep to the reading of such childhood classics as *Alice in Wonderland* or *Pinocchio,* sharing literature with children orally can be one of the most fulfilling of human experiences. The relaxing moments of story time with two-, three-, and four-year-olds are among the most cherished of parenthood. But the times are equally magical when young children want to read the stories aloud themselves. Jim Trelease's *Read-Aloud Handbook* is an excellent resource for adults who wish to cultivate the skill of effective reading aloud. And, as Trelease points out, reading aloud need not stop when children acquire the ability to read for themselves. Many of us can remember those pleasurable times when a beloved teacher read to us in elementary school. It is unfortunate that more more reading aloud is not done in the upper grades—no one, not even college students, is too old to enjoy a good story read aloud effectively.

Of course, "effectively" is a key word here. Reading aloud entails something more than simply pronouncing the words on the page. The proper inflections, the correct tone, the meaningful pause—all these help to make the experience more rewarding for reader and listener alike. However, reading aloud is not acting, and exaggerated theatrics may actually detract from the story itself and defeat the entire purpose. Generally, the best reading is slow and deliberate (listening audiences miss a great deal of what is said to them anyway, and reading too rapidly only increases the chances of their becoming lost or confused). Effective reading is also carefully enunciated, with a natural voice that suits inflection, cadence, and pace to the story. If the book is a picture-book, then the illustrations must be shared with the audience. This is easy enough when reading to one or two children, but somewhat more difficult when the reader must share a picture-book with a classroom of thirty. Then, of course, it is important to make sure that the illustrations can be easily seen by everyone. (Beatrix Potter's small books are clearly intended for an intimate story time, not for sharing with large groups.) It is possible to buy "giant" books now, books in very large format for kindergarten and first grade classes; however, the selection is limited, and we should not feel that standard-sized books are inadequate for groups. An alternative is to break larger classes into small groups for story sharing.

The story ought to be one that is enjoyed by the reader as well as the listener, because it is not easy to pretend to like a book, and the reader risks passing on his or her distaste, intentionally or not.

Reading aloud is most helpful for the very young when it is a daily activity. It is one of the best means of instilling the habit of reading in young children, as well as showing them the kind of feeling that lies close to the surface of a good book.

Finally, nothing beats rehearsing the story ahead of time.

Storytelling

Storytelling, the art of narrating a tale from memory, is one of the oldest of all art forms—undoubtedly reaching back to prehistoric times. Through storytellers virtually all the traditional folktales were preserved for centuries, having only been committed to paper in the past two or three centuries. To be an effective storyteller, one must be something of a performer, for the delivery is crucial and requires considerable preparation and rehearsal. But the reward in the form of wide eyes and broad smiles of delight is generally worth the effort.

Folktales are natural sources for storytellers. They include easily memorized patterns, ample dialogue enlivening the story, and they are brief enough to be relayed in a single setting. Also, they lend themselves well to adaptation, so the storyteller can adjust the tale to the audience. Of course, a rich, mellifluous voice is an asset to any would-be storyteller, but few of us are so blessed. However, this means only that we need to develop some other asset—effective body movement, eye contact, clear enunciation, meaningful inflection, and appropriate pauses. And with practice (particularly with deep breathing from the diaphragm), it is possible to develop a greater vocal range and a voice that will project. Much of the storyteller's skill derives from knowing how to pace the telling, when to slow down, when to speed up, when to talk in near whispers, when to shout, and so on. Additionally, natural body gestures and direct eye contact help to engage the audience.

At least part of the success of storytelling lies in the choice of an effective story. Action and dialogue are usually preferable to lengthy description or exposition; consequently, the fast pace of folktales makes them particularly suitable. The inclusion of regional speech patterns or dialect can be very effective, but this places a further burden on the storyteller to accomplish the pronunciation convincingly. A good storytelling narrative builds up to a climax and then ends quickly while the audience's interest is still at a peak. It is important that the narrator tell stories that he or she finds thoroughly enjoyable, for delight is contagious.

It is not important that all young people become storytellers themselves; that is not the point. What is important is that they have known the joy of hearing a good story told well, and that may encourage them to seek out other good stories to read on their own.

Book Discussions

One of the most common classroom approaches to literature is the book discussion, which should go beyond a series of questions from the teacher accompanied by the "correct" response from the students. A good book discussion evolves and metamorphoses as it proceeds, stimulates and provokes thought. To ensure that it does this, the leader of the discussion needs to be prepared.

What kinds of questions should he or she ask? If they require only that the respondent regurgitate facts from the story, little discussion (and less thinking) will occur. To obtain a lively exchange of ideas, appropriate questions must be asked in the appropriate order. Educators have identified many different levels of questions, but for most practical purposes these can be reduced to three levels based on reading comprehension.

Memory or literal questions ask the audience to recall facts from the story or poem: plot incidents, character identifications, details of the setting, and so on. It is good to begin a discussion with memory questions, for they can help determine if the readers understood the basic elements of the work. Additionally, memory questions tend to be the easiest type of questions, and they can help to loosen up the audience by giving early positive reinforcement. Memory questions tend to focus on matters of plot and setting, but they should direct our attention to significant points and not to minor details, and require something beyond "yes" or "no" responses. Unfortunately, some discussion leaders seldom get beyond these factual questions.

The second level of questioning consists of *interpretation questions,* questions requiring the readers to make inferences and draw conclusions from the facts of the story or poem, or to discover relationships between elements in a story. These questions may require analysis (lifting individual facts from the story and examining them carefully) or synthesis (putting together disparate facts in a new way) or perhaps application (relating fictional events to real life). In any case, it is important that readers understand that any conclusions they draw be based soundly on the evidence found in the work itself. Simple personal opinions are not adequate if they cannot be supported by the hard facts of the story. Interpretation questions focus on matters of character, motivation, and theme.

The third and most sophisticated level of questioning is that of *evaluation.* These questions ask the readers to judge the literature as a work of art; they focus on matters of style, imagery, symbolism, and so on. Evaluation must be based on generally agreed upon standards (such as those discussed in Chapter 7). Very young children will not be well enough equipped with a critical apparatus to handle evaluation effectively, although it is interesting to learn what they find enjoyable and why. The more we read, the better we are able to make judgments about what we read.

To illustrate how these various levels of questions might be employed, we may use E. B. White's classic *Charlotte's Web.* We may begin a discussion with memory or literal questions: Why was Wilbur's life in danger? How did Fern save Wilbur? How did Charlotte save Wilbur? How did Wilbur repay Charlotte? All these questions can be answered factually from a reading of the book, and all have some thematic significance focusing on the relationships between the various characters. There is no virtue in memory questions that seem designed to trick even the most careful reader, and if we can think of no good reason for asking a question it probably should not be asked.

Memory questions may then be followed up by interpretation questions, asking the readers to weigh and consider the facts. We might ask such things as these: Explain how the relationship between Fern and Wilbur changes over the course of the book. How does Wilbur's character change from the beginning to the end of the book? In what ways do Templeton, Charlotte, and Wilbur remind you of people you know? Interpretation questions should ultimately help us to see the relationships between literature and life, and should, when possible, ask us to draw on our own experience.

Finally, we may turn to the critical evaluation questions: Compare this animal fantasy with Kenneth Grahame's *Wind in the Willows* or with Robert Lawson's *Rabbit Hill.* How are they alike? How are they different? Which is most believable? Compare *Charlotte's Web* with another of E. B. White's fantasies: *Stuart Little* or *Trumpet of the Swan.* What similarities and differences do you find? If you prefer one over another, why? Asking young readers which of two books they prefer is only useful if we can get them to articulate their reasons and thereby help them to understand their own tastes a little better. It is good to remember that with many interpretation and evaluation questions, there are no clear wrong or right answers, only answers that are more convincingly supported than others.

Writing Experiences

As early as second grade, most children are capable of responding to literature through writing, and certainly by the time they reach the middle elementary grades, children should be writing as a regular part of their total curriculum. Keeping journals in which they are free to record their feelings without fear of a recriminating grade can be a very effective way of helping children to become more thoughtful readers. When we have to commit our ideas to writing, we are compelled to think them through more thoroughly and to impose more order on them than when these ideas are freely (and perhaps aimlessly) floating about in our heads. Writing, in other words, can help us to analyze and evaluate our thoughts. Journal writing is only effective, however, if it becomes habitual and if the individual entries are reasonably lengthy. (An entry of fewer than 150 words may have little value as an exploration of ideas.)

Other writing exercises might include reader response essays, in which young readers are asked to consider particular aspects of a book, such as character, plot, setting, theme, and so on. A specific topic for response may be assigned, or children may be allowed to choose. With reader response essays, young readers ought to be encouraged to draw on concrete examples from the reading to support their ideas. The reader response essays can be good exercises in preparing children for more formal critical analyses in later years.

Another interesting writing experiment is to have young readers write a preliminary essay in preparation for a reading assignment. For example, prior to reading Natalie Babbitt's *Tuck Everlasting,* middle school students might be asked to write on the following topic: "If you discovered the fountain of immortality, would you drink from it? Why or why not?" Then, once the students have read the book, in which such a question is actually posed to the protagonist, they might be asked to write a follow-up essay reconsidering the same issue but with the new light shed by the novel. A comparison of the two responses—before and after—can be quite interesting.

There are countless imaginative exercises available to replace the old book report. Children may enjoy making up their own endings to stories, for example, or writing new episodes with their favorite characters (Peggy Parrish's *Amelia Bedelia* series or Beverly Cleary's *Ramona* books provide wonderful starting points for younger readers). Creating their own books complete with illustrations and covers is a particularly rewarding activity for children of all ages. Newspaper stories based on events in books can be also be fun to write (Roald Dahl's *James and the Giant Peach* or *Charlie and the Chocolate Factory* offer some delightful opportunities here). Some children may enjoy reading and writing about a favorite author's life. Writing an imaginary diary of a fictional character, such as Laura from Laura Ingalls Wilder's *Little House* series, can help children understand the concept of point of view. Having children create a story from their own life experiences can help them gain firsthand knowledge of plot. Script writing, in which children must devise dialogue for characters, can enrich their understanding of language differences, characterization, and setting.

Whatever the project may be, writing ought to be integrated into the reading program, for writing and reading ought not to be divorced. A good writer must necessarily be a good reader.

Dramatic Responses to Literature

Dramatic responses to literature include a wide range of activities, from oral interpretation (a one-person performance of a piece of literature) to creative dramatics and role-playing (which are really impromptu inventions of the actors). We will briefly consider a few of these approaches.

Oral Interpretation. Oral interpretation typically involves a one-person performance of a poem or brief prose passage—usually, but not necessarily, memorized. The effectiveness of oral interpretation lies in the performer's vocal talents and meaningful gestures. It is very much like storytelling, except that oral interpretation does not allow for variants in its material. Faithful adherence to the words of the literary piece is an absolute necessity. For all these reasons, oral interpretation is generally not suitable for use with young children, but some of the techniques of oral interpretation and storytelling can be effectively employed in some of the activities below.

Story Theater. Story theater is simply a pantomime accompanied by a narrator who reads or tells the story. Since even inanimate objects (such as a tree) might be portrayed by an actor, story theater allows for a very flexible number of performers and can be as simple or elaborate as the means dictate. Pantomime does not require line memorizing, making it one of the least threatening dramatic forms for diffident children. The best stories for a story theater presentation are those with plenty of action; otherwise the pantomimers would be little more than furniture.

Reader's Theater. Reader's theater, as the name implies, involves the reading of a script as opposed to acting it out. The participants assume various speaking roles in a story, usually one reader for each speaking character and one narrator to read the exposition. True reader's theater is traditionally performed without any action whatever, with the readers sitting on chairs and using only their voices to convey meaning. Even the readers' clothing should be subdued and not suggestive of costuming (uniform dress, usually in black and white, is preferred). Since no memorization, physical movement, scenery, or properties are involved, reader's theater provides a ready outlet for self-expression. Stories with several speaking parts and ample dialogue work best for reader's theater presentations.

Creative Dramatics. Creative dramatics is the dramatization of a story with improvised dialogue. This allows children to perform their own versions of stories without strict adherence to script (although in creative dramatics, the actors are expected to remain faithful to the story line). This activity requires considerable preparation and may be as elaborate in setting, properties, and theatrical accoutrements as the director desires. Creative dramatics can be less threatening than a more traditional play since there is no need for memorization. And, since the actors must have a firm grasp of plot and character, this exercise can result in a more meaningful consideration of character, plot, and theme. One of the great advantages to creative dramatics is that many folktales and other short stories or even chapters from favorite books (*Winnie-the-Pooh* or *The Wind in the Willows* comes to mind) can be readily adapted to the form.

Role-Playing. Role-playing is similar to creative dramatics, but it removes us one step farther from the literary source, for the actors assume specific character roles and are expected to invent not only the dialogue but the action as they proceed. Typically, a problem is posed, and through the role-playing exercise, the children arrive at a solution. Consequently, the experience of role-playing allows them to examine the issues through the eyes of others. Role-playing is only marginally connected with literature, but is a widely used and effective method of exploring personal and social values. And, of course, since these values are usually a part of literature, role-playing can be adapted as a response to literature. Children, for example, could be assigned the roles of various characters (such as those from Cleary's *Ramona* books), and they could then be presented with a dilemma to solve. The important element in a successful role-playing exercise is to be sure that each assigned role is a distinct personality who will respond appropriately as the personality suggests.

Art and Literature

Another popular means of extending literature is through art. As soon as they can handle a crayon or pencil, even the youngest children can be asked to draw pictures in response to a story. The means by which art can enrich the literary experience are limited only by the imaginations of those involved. A few of the more widely used methods will be discussed here.

The Graphic Arts. Children love working with paints, watercolors, crayons, and pencil. These are usually the simplest art projects, requiring little individual instruction, and they allow for a great deal of originality. Even having young children draw pictures suggested by picture storybooks can be a means of getting them to explore different artistic styles as they try to imitate Sendak's impressionistic style in Zolotow's *Mr. Rabbit and the Lovely Present,* or Potter's delicate representational style in *The Tale of Peter Rabbit,* or the expressionistic style of Ludwig Bemelmans in *Madeline.* The most highly individualistic creation, however, is provided by allowing children to draw pictures suggested by the stories read to them and then showing them another artist's interpretation.

Collage, not technically a "graphic" method except that it can make use of pens, pencils, and other drawing instruments, is a picture created from nonpainterly materials (cloth, wood, cotton, leaves, rocks, and so on). This was the favorite method of Ezra Jack Keats (*The Snowy Day, Peter's Chair,* and many other fine picture-books) and Leo Lionni (*Frederick* and *Inch by Inch,* among others). Creating a collage is especially appealing for young children, since it does not require highly developed drawing skills, and its three-dimensional character and texture provide added interest.

Similar to the collage is the *montage,* which is a collection of pictures arranged into a single composite. Both the collage and the montage can be used as responses to literature. Children can be asked to create a poster, for example, that reflects their feelings about a particular work. Doing this, young readers focus on a specific aspect of the literature— usually either character or theme. This is the great advantage of incorporating artwork into the literature program, for the readers are encouraged to distill all their thoughts on a story into a single visual image. The result may be that they understand the work's plot or theme or characterization a little bit better than when they began.

The Plastic Arts. The plastic arts include the three-dimensional, nonpainterly works, such as sculpture. The *diorama* is a three-dimensional scene easily created from a shoebox or other carton and decorated with cardboard cutouts, plastic figures, or any other suitable objects. It is really a sort of primitive doll house and can be seen as an extension of the montage and collage in that it requires the maker to focus on a single thematic idea. By a further extension of the diorama, children can create miniature stages and puppet figures with which to reenact a story, thus combining an artistic and a dramatic response to literature. A natural development of the miniature stage is for the children to create stories of their own to dramatize.

Mobiles are free forms, usually cut from paper or cardboard, interconnected and suspended by string or wire so that when hung they turn freely in the breeze. These are popular with children from infancy, and many babies enjoy some form of mobile hung over their cribs. *Stabiles* are similar to mobiles in that they are abstract sculptural forms, but stationary. Modeling with clay or working with other craft materials, such as the ubiquitous Popsicle sticks, can provide further imaginative outlets as responses to stories or poems.

Other Artistic Media. *Puppetry* is an elaborate and time-honored art form, and puppets can be very simple (a sock on a hand or decorated paper bag) or very complex (a marionette with movable hands, feet, eyes, and mouth). Puppetry, however, soon brings us back to the dramatic response to literature, for once the puppet is made, the truly meaningful part of the experience begins. Behind the mask of the puppet, many shy children have found an exhilarating outlet for their deepest feelings.

A recently popularized extension to literature is cooking, with some children's books including recipes suitable for children, and there are, in fact, some very fine cookbooks written for children (Virginia Ellison's *Pooh's Cookbook* is for the very young).

Regardless of the art project, it is important to remember that, if the art is seen as a true extension of the literature, it should not be regarded as the end itself. In other words, we arc not reading *Pinocchio* for the purpose of making our own puppet after we are finished reading. Moreover, if the art is to be a true extension of the literature, it should not be simply gratuitous: Now that we have read *Pinocchio,* let's all draw a picture of his nose. If the art project cannot become a meaningful part of the study of the literature, helping children to focus closely on the concept of character, plot, setting, theme, tone, and so on, it is of little literary use. A relationship between the art and the literature should not be fabricated extraneously. Both, after all, are valuable in their own right, and neither should be regarded as a handmaiden to the other.

Children on Their Own

Our success in introducing children to books can only be measured when the children are grown and on their own. Have we provided them with the necessary tools so that they are able to read with competence? Have we instilled in them a love for books, so that they want to keep on reading and learning? Have we allowed them the necessary opportunity to discover the joy of reading? Whether as parents, teachers, or interested adults, we have these challenges before us. Books have long been feared by bigots and tyrants, the two principal book burners. Their fear is justified, for indeed, in the knowledge and the beauty they impart, books can make us both wise and free.

BIBLIOGRAPHY OF CRITICAL STUDIES AND EDUCATIONAL AIDS

Aquino, John. *Fantasy in Literature.* Washington, DC: National Education Association, 1977.
Bauer, Caroline Feller. *This Way to Books.* Bronx, NY: Wilson, 1982.
Bosma, Betty. *Fairy Tales, Fables, Legends, and Myths: Using Folk Literature in Your Classroom.* New York: Teachers' College Press, 1987.

Chambers, Aidan. *Introducing Books to Children.* 2d ed. Boston: The Horn Book, 1983.
———. *The Reluctant Reader.* Elmsford, NY: Pergamon Press, 1969.
Cioni, Alfred J., ed. *Motivating Reluctant Readers.* Newark, DE: International Reading Association, 1981.
Coody, Betty. *Using Literature with Young Children.* 2d ed. Dubuque, IA: Brown, 1979.
Cook, Elizabeth. *The Ordinary and the Fabulous: An Introduction to Myths, Legends and Fairy Tales.* 2d ed. New York: Cambridge University Press, 1969.
Cullinan, Bernice. *Literature and the Child.* 2d ed. San Diego: Harcourt Brace Jovanovich, 1989.
Currell, David. *The Complete Book of Puppetry.* Boston: Plays, 1975.
Donelson, Kenneth L., and Alleen Pace Nilsen. *Literature for Today's Young Adults.* 2d ed. Glenview, IL: Scott, Foresman, 1985.
Gillies, Emily. *Creative Dramatics for All Children.* Wheaton, MD: Association for Childhood Education International, 1973.
Huck, Charlotte S., Susan Hepler, and Janet Hickman. *Children's Literature in the Elementary School.* 4th ed. New York: Holt, Rinehart and Winston, 1987.
Hurst, Carol. "What to Do with a Poem." *Early Years* (February 1980): 28–29, 68.
Leonard, Charlotte. *Tied Together: Topics and Thoughts for Introducing Children's Books.* Metuchen, NJ: Scarecrow Press, 1980.
Pellowski, Ann. *World of Storytelling.* Ann Arbor, MI: Bowker, 1977.
Sawyer, Ruth. *The Way of the Storyteller.* New York: Penguin Books, 1942.
Shapiro, Jon E., ed. *Using Literature & Poetry Affectively.* Newark, DE: International Reading Association, 1971.
Shedlock, Marie. *The Art of the Storyteller.* 1915. New York: Dover, 1951.
Trelease, Jim. *The Read-Aloud Handbook.* Rev. ed. New York: Penguin Books, 1985.
Troeger, Virginia Bergen. "Student Storytelling." *Teaching K–8* (March 1990): 41–43.

PART II
The Genres of Children's Literature

CHAPTER 3

The Picture Storybook

DEFINITION

Few things in life are more rewarding than sharing a good picture-book with a wide-eyed young child. The picture-book—a collaboration of the talents of the writer and the artist—has the power to shape a child's lifelong tastes and attitudes toward reading.

The *picture-book* is best defined as a book in which the text and pictures are equally important, as opposed to an *illustrated book* in which the text is primary. Many books for adults—including this textbook—are "illustrated," that is, they include pictures. But in a true picture-book, the pictures tell the story along with the text, and the result can be described as a happy marriage between the text and pictures. There are very fine examples of *wordless picture books*—books containing only pictures—and there is much controversy over whether these works actually constitute "literature." They surely cannot be evaluated according to the same criteria as a book with a written text. On the other hand, many wordless picture-books (Mitsumasa Anno's *Anno's Journey* and Lynd Ward's *The Silver Pony* for example) do tell stories and include points of view, themes, character studies, settings, tones—all literary elements we recognize in written texts. (See the essays by Cianciolo [1984] and Groff [1984], for two different viewpoints on the value of wordless picture-books.) In this chapter we will consider the picture storybook. Concept and other informational books will be addressed in later chapters.

THE STORY

Varieties of Narrative

Today, few subjects are taboo in children's picture-books. Modern works in particular often deal with such social and psychological issues as death, divorce, sibling rivalry, and other social and psychological adjustments facing children. The emergence of these topics in picture-books may suggest the faith that writers place in today's children and their ability to handle the complexities of our world. But picture-books are not primarily tools for helping children cope with their problems. Instead, literature is meant chiefly for enjoyment, and our first thought ought to be for a book's potential for entertaining the reader.

Picture storybooks are of essentially four major types:

1. Folktales, Legends, and Myths. These remain age-old favorites, the familiar stories that have been passed down through the generations. They adhere to the traditional story-telling patterns (usually beginning with "Once upon a time" and ending with the hero or heroine living "happily ever after"), and they typically take place in some never-never land where magic is commonplace. Innumerable versions of "Cinderella," "Little Red Riding Hood," and "The Three Little Pigs" are available at any one time (and they make for interesting comparisons, incidentally). Folktales are also the basis for many modern fantasies (James Thurber's *Many Moons* comes to mind).

2. Modern Fantasy Stories. These include those tales, usually with modern settings, that employ magic as a principal feature. Unlike the folktales, the modern fantasies can be ascribed to specific authors, and therefore do not appear in different versions. Maurice Sendak's classic *Where the Wild Things Are* fits into this category, as do Chris Van Allsburg's Christmas enchantment *The Polar Express* and Crockett Johnson's wonderfully imaginative tale *Harold and the Purple Crayon*. As with folktales, modern fantasies build on the child's delight in worlds of make-believe, but whereas folktales generally distance the magic through time and place, many modern fantasies bring the magic into contemporary life. In this way, they appeal to the same drive that makes a child want to believe in Santa Claus or the Tooth Fairy. (And, by the same token, most modern fantasies omit the potentially threatening forces of evil that characterize the folktales—Wicked Witches and Big Bad Wolves. This issue will be discussed at greater length in Chapter 5.)

3. Realistic Stories. These depict reality as we understand it. They may be historical, such as Brinton Turkle's warm tale of early New England, *Thy Friend, Obadiah,* or they may take on a modern setting as does Lucille Clifton's *Some of the Days of Everett Anderson,* about a contemporary African-American boy growing up in a big city. Marjorie Flack's *The Story About Ping,* concerning the escapades of a duckling on the Yangtze River in China, is a realistic story about an animal—although some may feel that Ping is given feelings that may be all too human. The appeal of realistic stories is often in their ability to depict sympathetic characters with whom young readers can identify or empathize.

4. Anthropomorphic Stories. These generally avoid magic or enchantment and have all the appearances of realistic stories except for the fact that the main character or characters are nonhuman with human traits. Anthropomorphic Stories ("anthropomorphic" means humanlike) constitute a very large portion of the popular children's picture storybooks. Talking animals are popular, such as Beatrix Potter's charming stories of rabbits, mice, ducks, and so on, or Russell Hoban's tales of Frances the Badger. Many folktales include talking animals, but the modern anthropomorphic tales typically avoid magic, create quite realistic contemporary settings, and focus on everyday issues that are of concern to young people (Frances the Badger rides to school on a school bus and prefers peanut-butter-and-jelly sandwiches for lunch). Anthropomorphic stories sometimes have as their protagonists inanimate objects such as boats (Hardie Gramatky's *Little Toot*), houses (Virginia Burton's

The Little House), or machines (Virginia Burton's *Mike Mulligan and His Steam Shovel*). Nevertheless, in nearly all cases, the story lines are (the anthropomorphism aside) realistic. Bernard Waber's Lyle the Crocodile, for example, walks on two legs, eats at the table with the human family he lives with in a house on East 88th Street in New York City (*The House on East 88th Street* and *Lyle, Lyle Crocodile*). These books give young readers early exposure to symbolism, for they see the animal or inanimate characters as symbolizing facets of human nature. Also, children have little trouble imagining animals and even machines with human traits (in fact, they may have difficulty imagining animals, especially, without human traits), and most children have a fascination with animals (pets, for instance), making anthropomorphic stories great favorites.

NARRATIVE ELEMENTS

Regardless of the nature of the story, all stories contain the principal narrative elements of storytelling—plot, character, setting, theme, and style. These will be discussed in somewhat more detail in Chapter 8, "The Nature of Fiction," but for the time being a brief overview will suffice.

Plot

The story in a good picture-book—even in the simplest—meets all the requirements of a well-told tale. It has a clearly defined beginning, middle, and ending. Whether it is through such familiar phrases as "Once upon a time" or simply establishing the setting ("In the great green room"), young children very early on learn to recognize the conventions of storytelling. Reading books teaches them very early on the distinction between fact and fiction. They readily see when something is "only a story," and this distinction allows them to enjoy a healthy fantasy world and, in fact, to lead normal lives.

The plot—which is simply the sequence of events in a story leading to a specific goal—must be clear and fairly direct. A small rabbit disobeys his mother, goes into Mr. MacGregor's garden, and after a series of adventures, barely escapes with his life. For the very young, the time frame must be simple chronology—no flashbacks, for example. (With older children, more complex plot structures—such as the intriguing parallel plots of Robert McCloskey's *Blueberries for Sal*—are suitable.) Additionally, a good story for the very young includes *action*, perhaps *suspense*—although surely not at the same level of intensity as an adult might require—and, more often than not, *humor*.

Character

Typically, the stories focus on a character—either a human (usually a child) or an animal who possesses childlike characteristics. The principal character provides someone with whom the child audience can identify. Peter Rabbit appeals to young children because most of them have encountered temptations similar to Peter's, and his desire to do the forbidden is quite familiar to them. Characterization in picture-books is usually quite simple; the stories are just not long enough to depict complex character development.

But that does not mean that the characters cannot be genuine or real. Bernard Waber's *Ira Sleeps Over* shows us the very real anxieties of a young boy spending his first night away from home. Ira's biggest worry is how he is to get through the night without Tah

Tah, his teddy bear, which he leaves home to avoid being thought silly. But he discovers that his "tough" friend, Reggie, also sleeps with a teddy bear—Foo Foo by name. Ira and Reggie exhibit human emotions typical of children their age, and young readers readily identify with and sympathize with them.

Setting

Since each page is accompanied by illustrations, most picture-book stories rely on the visual element to articulate the setting. Nevertheless, the setting remains a story element, because when and where a story happens determine a great deal about how and why things happen. Consequently, when a folktale begins with the pronouncement "Once upon a time in a kingdom far, far away" we are immediately prepared for a certain type of tale, a tale in which we might reasonably expect to encounter an ogre, a magical object, a talking animal. On the other hand, if the setting is modern suburbia, we might logically expect greater attention to realism (although magic is not necessarily ruled out). Settings in picture-books tend to be simply described (but the illustrations may be lavishly detailed). Young children, who have relatively short attention spans, desire a story with action and have little patience with detailed physical description, and it is, of course, the great advantage of the picture-book that the setting can be conveyed nonverbally. Each page or double-page spread can be considered as a sort of set piece, like the individual scenes of a motion picture, and the success of the picture-book depends heavily upon the effective selection of scenes.

Subject and Theme

The subject of a good story is one that holds meaning for a young child. A picture-book for preschoolers on the subject of toxic waste disposal would be silly, but child disobedience is not an unreasonable subject; many children will have had considerable firsthand experience of it.

This brings us to the theme of a picture-book. The theme is the principal idea that governs the story. In *The Tale of Peter Rabbit,* the theme might be something like this: Disobedience of parental authority often results in dire consequences. But we also might identify some other themes: "A mother's love is unconditional," or perhaps "The most effective punishment is that which we inflict upon ourselves." The theme itself may be quite serious, even in books for the very young. But we should not confuse theme with moral or lesson. For children, the enduring stories are those that seek first to entertain. Children are no different from adults in this respect. We usually do not choose our reading material on the basis of the moral lessons we will learn from it—we simply want a good story. Why should we expect young children to react any differently?

The theme of a good picture-book will be deftly woven into the story. Most child readers recognize Peter's actions as unwise, but we are fooling ourselves if we think that after reading *Peter Rabbit* children will become more dutifully obedient. Learning from reading is a cumulative process. We learn the wisdom of obedience in the same way that Peter does— through personal experiences, some of them harrowing. The subtle weaving of a meaningful theme into an exciting story is one of the triumphs of Potter's little masterpiece. The work would have been much less satisfying if Mrs. Rabbit had reprimanded Peter with a scolding and an "I told you so." We, as readers, know (and so does his wise mother) that Peter has learned his lesson without a sermon.

Likewise, in *Ira Sleeps Over* an implied theme is that it is not only natural but all right for a child to have fears about spending a night away from home. But the story goes beyond this and suggests that it is also all right for a young child to express affection openly, even if it is toward a stuffed animal. In other words, the story encourages sensitivity in children. But Potter and Waber get their points across without having to preach to us.

Works written primarily to teach lessons—moral or otherwise—are termed *didactic*. A prime example of didactic literature is the fable—those brief and simple animal tales that typically conclude with the formulaic phrase, "And the moral of the story is . . ." Adults often read Aesop's *Fables* to young children in the mistaken belief that the moral lessons tagged onto the stories will be taken to heart. In fact, for preschoolers and even children in the primary grades, the lessons of the fables are frequently too sophisticated and are therefore lost on the audience. Aesop is for older children. There is a place for didactic writing—this text is one example—but most adult and child readers prefer that didacticism be saved for school texts, how-to books, and Sunday sermons.

Literary Style

Boredom results from one of two things: Something is either too simple or too complicated. Readers demand books that are increasingly challenging, but not completely beyond their personal comprehension level. As children become more sophisticated in their reading, they demand more complex characters, intricate plots, serious and probing themes, broader vocabulary, and more refined sentences.

These issues bring us to the matter of style. Picture-books are typically brief—most are designed to be read in a single sitting, with 2,000 words being an average length. The vocabulary must not be so difficult as to discourage the child, and yet it must not condescend, either. Writers must not talk down to their child readers, but rather treat them with respect and as equals. The vocabulary ought to broaden the child's language experience. But it makes no sense to criticize a picture-book because it contains some words that might be unfamiliar to the child audience. (Beatrix Potter's reference to "camomile tea" comes immediately to mind, as does the "porridge" in "The Three Bears.") One of the results of our reading should be an expanded vocabulary. If the books we read contained only words we know, we all would still be talking in colorless monosyllables. Once again, the best book is one that challenges without overwhelming us.

Since picture-books are frequently written for nonreaders, one requisite is that the book read well aloud. Natural breaks should come at the turning of the pages; otherwise the sharing of the book becomes awkward. The child's ears hear one thing as the eyes behold another. Children—lovers of the sounds of language—respond enthusiastically to rhythm and rhyme. (The rollicking refrain of "Hundreds of cats, thousands of cats, millions and billions and trillions of cats" in Wanda Gag's classic, *Millions of Cats*, has delighted young audiences for over sixty years.) We also ought to demand fresh imagery and imaginative language as well as effective and convincing dialogue, when dialogue is used. Picture-books using dialogue of several characters (such as Jeffrey Allen's *Mary Alice, Operator Number Nine*) can be particularly delightful for an adult to read and a joy for the child to hear.

In short, we should expect from picture-books the same high literary standards that we apply to books for adults. In fact, young children are perhaps in some ways even more sensitive to sound and meaning than we adults are. They and their reading should be approached with the proper healthy respect.

THE ILLUSTRATIONS

Artistic Elements

Illustrations in a good picture-book are fine examples of *narrative art,* or art that tells a story. If we adults have done our job well, children soon reach a point at which they enjoy handling and looking at books by themselves. They particularly enjoy being able to look at the pictures and to tell the story on their own. A good picture storybook will enable a child to narrate a tale fairly accurately from the pictures.

Beyond their narrative quality, however, the pictures define the mood or the tone of the story—so we would not expect a simple tale of a young bunny settling down at bedtime and saying good night to various objects in his room to be depicted in bright, garish colors and wildly abstract designs.

The best illustrations exhibit the elements of good art. The finest picture-book artists are serious and talented artists. They have *not* chosen to draw for children because they lacked the talent to draw for adults. They respect their child audience. And they realize that condescension—usually in the form of "cuteness" and rounded, faceless, cuddly figures that all look alike—is insulting to children. The child audience deserves, instead, imaginative art that is both highly individualistic and skillfully executed.

The artist's work is actually the effective use of *illusion.* The artist makes us see things that are not really there—distance, depth, texture, and so on. And the magic extends even further, for the artist gives us an emotional experience as well. Illustrations can make us feel warm, happy, apprehensive, and so on. The more we understand about the artist's craft, the better able we are to judge picture-book illustrations intelligently.

An illustration is made up of several elements: line, space, shape, color, texture, composition, and perspective.

Line. Lines are used both to define objects and to suggest emotional responses. We all realize that lines outline figures and therefore give them definition or shape, but lines can also suggest movement, distance, and even feeling. Curves and circles suggest warmth, coziness, and security (perhaps recalling the safety of the womb and its circular shape). Sharp and zigzagging lines suggest excitement and rapid movement. Horizontal lines suggest calm and stability (the flat earth), whereas vertical lines suggest height and distance—figures at the top of a page appear to be farther away than those at the bottom. Imaginative use of line, such as the graceful, delicate lines in Marcia Brown's *Cinderella* or the lively ruckus created by Margot Zemach's lines in *Duffy and the Devil* (Figure 3.1), can capture the special spirit of a story.

Space. We often do not think of space—literally the empty parts of the page—as an artistic element, but in fact it is very powerful. The use of space is actually what draws our attention to specific forms depicted on the page. If a page contains very little empty space, but is instead crowded with images, our eyes are forced to examine all the forms carefully. However, if a page contains a great deal of space, our eyes are immediately drawn to the objects that are left on the page, and all of our attention is focused on them. In this way the artist gives these objects special importance. Generous use of space in a picture can suggest emptiness, loneliness, isolation. Space may also create the illusion of distance. Conversely, the lack of open space on a page may contribute to a claustrophobic feeling (see *Jumanji,* Figure 3.2) or confusion or even chaos.

Figure 3.1. Margot Zemach's illustrations for *Duffy and the Devil* (retold by Harve Zemach) capture the lively, comical nature of this Cornish Rumpelstiltskin tale. Notice how movement and chaos are suggested by the ragged lines moving in every direction.

Shape. The predominant shapes in an illustration help to elicit emotional reactions. Grouped massive shapes may suggest stability, enclosure, or confinement, or perhaps awkwardness (Figure 3.2). On the other hand, lighter, delicate shapes may suggest movement, grace, and freedom (Figure 3.3). Some illustrations consist chiefly of shapes to the exclusion of lines, as in collage. Rounded shapes may suggest emotional reactions similar to those of the curved and circular lines (Figure 3.4), and squarish, angular shapes may elicit more excitable responses.

Color. It is a misconception that children require brightly colored pictures. Some of the most enduringly popular of picture-books are in black and white or monochrome (with pictures done in a single hue, such as blue or sepia). Wanda Gág's *Millions of Cats,* Leaf and Lawson's *Ferdinand the Bull,* McCloskey's *One Morning in Maine* and *Blueberries for Sal,* and, more recently, Chris Van Allsburg's *Jumanji* are only a few of these classics. And most of these books would be far less effective if they were done in full color. When

Figure 3.2. We, the viewers, are at a child's eye level looking over the table and up at the menacing monkeys (made even more disturbing from this point of view) in this surrealistic pencil drawing from Chris Van Allsburg's *Jumanji.* The figures seem to crowd us, adding an almost claustrophobic feeling, and the whole scene appears to be a moment uncomfortably frozen in time—an appropriate mood for this story of a mysterious board game come to life.

Figure 3.3. The stone lithography of Robert McCloskey's illustrations for *One Morning in Maine* help to provide the textured appearance—the fine grain we see in the pictures is actually created by the stone surface on which the drawing was made. McCloskey's style is a fine example of Representational art; he has, in fact, used himself and his daughters as models in this true-to-life tale.

Figure 3.4. This watercolor from Beatrix Potter's *The Tale of Peter Rabbit* exudes warmth and security, appropriate after Peter's harrowing experience in Mr. MacGregor's garden. The soft, warm yellows and earthy browns are complemented by gently curved lines and rounded shapes, from the oval mass of Mrs. Rabbit bent before the embracing hearth to the little round tails of each of Peter's sisters. Peter himself, having caught cold from his mischief, is distanced to the right, but nonetheless secure under the rounded folds of his bed blankets.

an artist does choose to illustrate in black and white or monochrome, he or she usually compensates for the absence of color by the effective use of line, space, and shape. Color, in fact, can often detract from a text, particularly if the color is overpowering or inappropriate. Remember, we said that a picture-book is the happy marriage between text and illustrations—one must not outdo the other.

Surprisingly, color is one of the least imaginatively used of artistic elements in children's picture-books. Color is chiefly used in a conventional fashion—skies are blue, grass is green, and so on. Children have been found to be acutely aware of subtle variations in hues, and they certainly do not demand bold, bright colors. (Donnarae MacCann and Olga Richard tell us of a seven-year-old who used thirty-two shades of blue in a painting and asked for the names of each separate color. Of course, most of us are not quite that sensitive to color variations.) Colors do have the ability to evoke emotional responses—as opposed to driving children to distraction or boredom. Psychologists tell us that reds and yellows are warm or hot colors and suggest excitement, whereas blues and greens are cool or cold colors and suggest calm or quiet. There are also certain conventional responses to color—purple signifying royalty, green envy or illness, blue depression, yellow cowardice, and so on. (These conventions are cultural phenomena: In imperial China, the color yellow was reserved for the emperor, and white is a traditional color of mourning throughout Asia.) Additionally, colors are used to suggest cultural distinctions. When illustrating a Navajo Indian story, *Arrow to the Sun,* Gerald McDermott used the colors of the Southwest—golds, yellows, desert browns, and oranges. In his *Anansi the Spider,* a traditional folktale of Africa, McDermott turns to the bold bright reds, greens, and sharply contrasting black to suggest West African folk culture.

Texture. One of the illusions the artist creates is to give a flat surface (the paper) the characteristics of a three-dimensional surface—the suggestion of fur, wood grain, smooth silk. We refer to this quality as texture. An artist who wants to emphasize the realistic quality of a picture may pay great attention to texture. However, less realistic styles may make use of texture to enrich the visual experience and to stimulate the viewer's imagination. (See *One Morning in Maine,* Figure 3.3.)

Composition and Perspective. The composition of an illustration refers to the arrangement of its details. Composition is important to the narrative quality of the picture as well as to its emotional impact. The artist must consider where best to place the focal point, from what angle the picture is to be viewed, and what mood is to be conveyed. One important aspect of composition is the point of view or perspective—that is, from what vantage point are we, the viewers, looking at the objects or events depicted? The closer we appear to be to the action, the more engaged we will be (see *Jumanji,* Figure 3.2, for an example of this). The farther away we seem to be, the more detached we are (see *A Peaceable Kingdom,* Figure 3.5). We may view events from a worm's-eye view or small child's perspective or a bird's-eye view or from a fish-eye view. The artist may wish to change points of view from illustration to illustration—perhaps to avoid monotony, but more probably to make us see and think about things in special ways. Good composition creates a sense of rhythm as we move from page to page—a rhythm that is suited to the nature of the narrative. Good composition also creates a sense of unity; the entire picture-book makes a satisfying whole with a predominant and effective mood.

Artistic Styles

High quality art has become the rule and not the exception in quality children's picture-books, and the illustrators are frequently consummate artists at the top of their profession. Consequently, it should not be surprising that we find in picture-books a rich variety of artistic styles, representing all the major schools of art. Of course, we need not spend inordinate amounts of time trying to determine the specific artistic style used by a picture-book artist. In fact, artists frequently combine features of more than one style, making it difficult to classify their efforts. Rather, our point here is that the art in the good children's picture-books is good art by any standards, and we are doing our children a disservice by not exposing them to the widest possible variety.

Children are very eclectic in their tastes; that is, they more readily accept unusual and varied styles. Children have not yet learned prejudice or narrow-mindedness, and are not nearly so set in their ways as are adults. There are wonderful stories of very young children going into museums and noting the similarities between the works of the great Flemish artist of the sixteenth century, Brueghel, and the popular twentieth-century children's illustrator, Richard Scarry. Children are wise enough to detect differences in artistic styles, and not yet jaded enough to reject the unfamiliar. Our task is simply to share with them a generous sampling of all that the world of picture-books has to offer. Some of the principal styles found in children's picture-books include the following.

Representationalism. Representational art seeks to present objects realistically, although not necessarily photographically. Nor need representational art depict realistic subjects. For example, Beatrix Potter (Figure 3.4) was almost fanatical in her desire to depict the little animal characters in her books realistically; nevertheless she felt compelled to clothe them in human garments. We still regard her art as representational art, and we see her

Figure 3.5. The spirit of the simple, industrious way of the Shakers, an early American religious sect, is depicted in this illustration by Alice and Martin Provensen for *A Peaceable Kingdom: The Shaker Abecedarious.* The lack of depth and the disproportionate scale (notice the woman's tiny feet and hands and the overly large katydid) are all characteristic of the folk art of rural New England, the home of the principal Shaker communities.

goal as wishing us to believe that her characters are real. On the other hand, Robert McCloskey's *One Morning in Maine* (Figure 3.3) faithfully depicts an extremely realistic tale—the adventures of an average family on a typical day at their summer vacation home. McCloskey used his own family for his models, and his attention to detail heightens the sense of immediacy and realism. Representational art deals with recognizable shapes, realistic color (if color is used), and proper perspectives and proportions. Representational art allows us to enter into the experience and readily become a part of it, but at the same time we are shown a new, fresh way of looking at the world.

Expressionism. Expressionism as a school of painting was quite specific and flourished toward the end of the nineteenth century. It was a reaction to the photographic realism of earlier styles (styles made somewhat obsolete by the invention of photography). Expressionism included deliberate distortion and exaggeration and wide-ranging experiments with line, space, color, shape, texture, and composition. Expressionism represents an emotional response to things, and the art captures the artist's subjective feeling rather than a faithful portrayal of reality. In picture-books, any artistic style in which the artist's individuality is paramount is considered a form of Expressionism, and it is most useful in books where there is no particular virtue in depicting objects realistically.

Expressionism taken to its logical end results in Abstractionism. But we seldom find complete Abstractionism in children's picture-books, since it effectively eliminates any narrative intent. But children are widely receptive to imaginative and highly unusual styles. They welcome the fascinating, distorted shapes and imaginative colors, such as those used by Ludwig Bemelmans in *Madeline* (Figure 3.6).

Impressionism. Impressionism derives from the late nineteenth-century French art movement of the same name, a movement characterized by experimentation with ways of looking at objects. Impressionistic art uses an interplay of color and light—usually created with splotches, speckles, or dots of paint as opposed to longer brush strokes—to create a dreamlike effect. Many of Maurice Sendak's illustrations for Charlotte Zolotow's *Mr. Rabbit and the Lovely Present* capture this dreamlike quality of Impressionism. Donald Carrick's delicate watercolors for Carol Carrick's *In the Moonlight, Waiting* and John Schoenherr's Caldecott-Medal-winning illustrations for Jane Yolen's *Owl Moon* both evoke the dreamlike qualities of Impressionistic art. Through Impressionistic art, we, the audience, are distanced from the action and are seldom allowed to participate fully in the action. Instead we view it from afar with detachment—and often with wonder. Impressionism is best suited to dreamlike fantasies and quiet, pensive moods or stories on the margin between fantasy and reality. It is the one artistic style that seems to demand color.

Surrealism. Surrealism, an artistic style explored most fully by the painter Salvador Dali, represents the artist's *intellectual* response to a subject (as opposed to the *emotional* response of Expressionism). In Surrealistic art, objects may be depicted quite realistically, but they are subjected to unnatural juxtapositions and bizarre incongruities. Chris Van Allsburg's *Jumanji* (Figure 3.2) is a prime example of Surrealistic art in a picture-book. The illustrations in this book, and in others employing this artistic style, project the disturbing qualities of Surrealistic art—almost nightmarish when contrasted with the more pleasant dream qualities of Impressionistic art—which may make it more appropriate for older readers.

Cartoon. Many experts see cartoon art as a form of Expressionism, although cartoons predate that art movement by many decades. Cartoon art employs gross exaggerations and distortions, always for a satiric or humorous effect. Political cartoons are still a regular feature in newspapers and magazines, lampooning public figures and representing abstractions with symbols (Uncle Sam, the Russian bear). Because of their broad humor and easily grasped symbolism, cartoons are particularly appealing to young children. Cartoon art avoids subtlety, and instead relies on solid lines and absence of shading for its distinctive style. If color is used, it is almost always bold and never exhibits off-hues. Dr. Seuss's beloved books display his own special brand of cartoon art—and the cartoon style is particularly suited to his rollicking, comical tales.

Folk Art. One of the most commonly used styles is Folk Art. Folk Art is the most widely varied of art forms and sometimes the most difficult to pinpoint. Folk Art is based upon the designs and images peculiar to a specific culture (Native American, Eastern European, Middle Eastern, African, and so on). There are as many different folk styles as there are

Figure 3.6. Ludwig Bemelmans's popular picture storybook *Madeline* is a delightful comedy about a spunky little girl in a Parisian convent school. The illustrations are interesting examples of Expressionistic art. Notice the angularity of the figures and the exaggerated height of the nun, Miss Clavel, accompanying the twelve little girls who walk, as we are told, in "two straight lines" (surely a commentary on convent school discipline). The trees are more like ideas of trees; there is no attempt at realistic depiction. There is a carefree jocularity in these pictures that aptly characterizes the mood of the story.

folk cultures, making it difficult to make meaningful generalizations about Folk Art. Alice and Martin Provensen's *Peaceable Kingdom: The Shaker Abecedarius* (Figure 3.5) and Margot Zemach's lively depiction of the Cornish folktale *Duffy and the Devil* (Figure 3.1) demonstrate two widely varied versions of Folk Art. Leo and Diane Dillon's illustrations for Margaret Musgrove's *Ashanti to Zulu: A Swahili Alphabet Book* are exquisite art works capturing the flavor of native African culture. In spite of the great differences in these illustrations, all attempt to re-create the atmosphere or the pervasive mood of a specific culture. Almost by definition, Folk Art recalls an earlier, simpler time and a predominantly agrarian society. Consequently, Folk Art is particularly suited to the illustration of folktales, in which the artist wishes to express the ingenuous flavor of the ethnic or regional culture that inspired the tales.

Minor Schools. The bold, black lines, richly contrasting colors, and almost vibrating lines of John Steptoe's *Daddy Is a Monster . . . Sometimes* (Figure 3.7) suggest stained-glass windows, a characteristic of a specific offshoot of Expressionism termed *Les Fauves* ("the

Figure 3.7. A child of Expressionism, Les Fauves art includes distinctive strong, black lines separating parts of the picture—much like the lines made by the lead framing in stained-glass windows. Also characteristic of this artistic style is a certain vibrance of line that suggests motion—and emotion—as in this illustration from John Steptoe's *Daddy is a Monster . . . Sometimes,* a story of parent/child relationships.

Wild Beasts" in French). The influence of the Art Deco movement of the 1930s can be seen in some of the illustrations in Rachel Isadora's *Ben's Trumpet,* with their bold, sleek designs and sharp contrast. *Brian Wildsmith's 1, 2, 3* is an example of Cubism, an early offshoot of Expressionistic art that relies principally on the juxtaposition of various geometric shapes. There are, of course, many other styles, and artists of great talent often create their own highly individualized styles, drawing their inspiration from various schools and sources. As pointed out above, many artists combine features of more than one style or school to achieve their ends.

Artistic Media

An artist, in addition to deciding the style of an illustration, must also decide upon the method of producing that illustration: Shall it be drawn with pencil or ink? Shall it be painted in oils or watercolors or tempera? Shall it be cut out on a block of wood or linoleum? Each illustration may represent an artistic style, but the illustration was accomplished through a specific medium. By *medium* we mean essentially the tool (or tools, hence the plural *media*) the artist chooses to work with. We can group media generally into the following four broad categories.

Painterly Techniques. Painterly techniques refer to art using paint as its primary medium. Paint itself consists of pigment (usually powdered) mixed with some liquid or paste to make it spreadable. A multitude of variations are possible, depending upon the medium used to mix with the pigment. Tempera is made by mixing pigments with egg yolk—or some other albuminous substance. Watercolors, as their name implies, use water as the medium, resulting in typically soft, delicate pictures as in Potter's *The Tale of Peter Rabbit.* Gouache is a powdered paint mixed with a white base to form an opaque water-color. Oil paints typically use linseed oil as a base. And acrylics use a kind of plastic base, a product of twentieth-century technology. Pastels differ from the rest in that they are typically applied in powdered form (often with the fingers). Pencil and ink drawings, while technically not painting, follow the same general principles as painterly techniques. Each of these media produces differing effects, and the artist must decide which is most suited to the story being illustrated.

Graphic Techniques. Graphic techniques refer to those techniques in which the artist prepares blocks or plates that are then inked and imprinted upon paper. The very first printed book illustrations—dating from the late middle ages—were made from blocks of wood, on which the artist carved away all the areas that were not to be printed. Today, woodcut carving is an artistic or illustrator's technique. Ed Emberley's stylized woodblock illustrations for *Drummer Hoff* are good examples of the special character of woodblock art. Linocuts are similar to woodblocks in principle, but the artist uses blocks of linoleum rather than wood. In scratchboard illustration, the artist paints black ink over a smooth board (called, not surprisingly, a scratchboard) and then, when the ink dries, scratches the design onto the surface with a sharp instrument; the result is an illustration created by white lines on a black background. Stone lithography is a complex process involving the drawing of a design with a grease mixture onto a flat stone, treating the stone with chemicals and oils so that the ungreased areas repel water. Then water and ink are successively applied, the greased areas absorb the ink, but repel the water, and when paper is pressed onto the stone, an impression is made from the greased, inked areas. (Robert McCloskey's *One Morning in Maine,* Figure 3.3, is a fine example of stone lithography; if you look closely at the illustration, you can detect the grainy surface of the stone imprinted on the paper.)

Montage and Collage. Montage (the collection and assembling of a variety of different pictures or designs to create a single picture) and collage (similar to montage, but employing materials in addition to pictures—string, cotton, weeds, anything that will work—to create a single picture) have been styles effectively used by Ezra Jack Keats in *The Snowy Day* and its sequels and by Leo Lionni in such works as *Frederick* and *Fish Is Fish.*

Photography. Photography may be considered an artistic style as much as technique, but it is, nevertheless, an art. And the art of photography is the art of composition—of arranging objects within a frame so that the result is intellectually stimulating. In picture storybooks, we normally expect something more creative than Polaroid snaps, and when photographs are used to tell stories, it is principally for realistic ones. But in informational books, the gifted photographer comes into his or her own. Imaginatively used in black and white or color, photography can be dramatic, beautiful, and highly effective.

SOCIAL CONCERNS AND THE PICTURE STORYBOOK

Because the readers of picture storybooks are young and impressionable, it is helpful to be aware of specific ways in which these books portray and interpret society. For example, children's picture-books, particularly of the past, have been guilty of stereotyping according to such features as race, gender, age, and physical handicap. Traditionally white male heroes have dominated in children's literature, for example. Although there are notable adventurous heroines of strong character (Ludwig Bemelmans's Madeline, for example), as often as not girls have been depicted as weak, submissive, and domestic, leaving the rough and tumble adventures to the boys. A recent critical view suggests that the fault lies in our culture, which would seem to value rash and aggressive behavior (characterized by the male) over the sensible equanimity typified by fictional females. Minority groups such as African-Americans have too often been ignored or unfairly stereotyped. In the 1930s and 1940s, African-Americans were virtually absent from picture-books; by the 1950s and 1960s they were portrayed essentially as middle-class white people with brown skin (Ezra Jack Keats's *The Snowy Day,* 1962, is usually considered an example); only in the 1970s were they at last portrayed faithfully, both physically and socially, with the appearance in picture-books of inner-city African-American children proud of their heritage (Lucille Clifton's *Everett Anderson* series provides notable examples).

By and large, writers of recent fiction have become more sensitive to minority groups, and it is possible to locate books depicting strong heroines, self-confident characters from many cultures, sympathetic elderly people (Tomi da Paola's *Nana Upstairs, Nana Downstairs,* 1973), children from broken homes (Patricia MacLachlan's *Mama One, Mama Two,* 1982), and children with physical or emotional handicaps (Taro Yashima's *The Crow Boy,* 1955). Although we do not, in fact, know the extent of the impact that reading has on an individual, it is a fairly safe assumption that extensive reading will *reinforce* beliefs. It is good for us to be aware of the underlying messages in children's books precisely because children are vulnerable and impressionable. This does *not* mean that we become censors and forbid certain books to our children (censorship always has a way of backfiring), but by making a concerted effort to see that our children's reading includes a diverse selection of social attitudes, we can enrich their entire reading experience.

THE PICTURE-BOOK AND THE CHILD

It bears repeating that a good picture-book for children represents the marriage of two arts: writing and illustrating. A well-told tale with illustrations suited to the story's mood and purpose, accurately depicting the text and effectively extending it, is a special delight for young readers. If the illustrations and the text are appropriately juxtaposed (the illustration on a given page should relate directly to the text on that page or at least on the opposite page), and the text and the illustrations enjoy a sensible balance, then the book is all the more accessible and enjoyable. Of course, the experts are the children themselves—the books are for them, and they often prove much wiser than adults in their responses to what they read. However, most children rely upon us, the adults, to bring them into contact with good books. This is a great responsibility. If children do not learn to love reading and books by the time they reach the ages of five or six (and some say that even that is too late), they are in danger of growing up to be nonreaders. This is why a good picture-book is so important: It gives young children positive and rewarding experiences with books from their earliest years.

BIBLIOGRAPHY OF CRITICAL STUDIES

Alderson, Brian. *Looking at Picture Books 1973.* New York: Children's Book Council, 1974.

Bader, Barbara. *American Picturebooks from Noah's Ark to the Beast Within.* New York: Macmillan, 1976.

Cianciolo, Patricia. *Illustrations in Children's Books.* 2d ed. Dubuque, IA: Brown, 1976.

——. *Picture Books for Children.* Chicago: American Library Association, 1981.

——. "Use Wordless Picture Books to Teach Reading, Visual Literacy and to Study Literature." In *Jump Over the Moon,* edited by Pamela Barron and Jennifer Q. Burley, 139–144. New York: Holt, 1984.

Dooley, Patricia. "The Window in the Book: Conventions in the Illustrations of Children's Books." *Wilson Library Bulletin* October 1980: 108–112.

Freeman, La Verne, and Ruth Sunderlin Freeman. *The Child and His Picture Book.* New York: Century House, 1967.

Gainer, Ruth Straus. "Beyond Illustration: Information about Art in Children's Picture Books." *Art Education* (March 1982): 16–19.

Gottleib, Gerald. *Early Children's Books and Their Illustrations.* Boston: Godine, 1975.

Groff, Patrick. "Children's Literature Versus Wordless Books?" In *Jump Over the Moon,* edited by Pamela Petrick Barron and Jennifer Q. Burley, 145–154. New York: Holt, Rinehart and Winston, 1984.

Hurlimann, Bettina. *Picture-Book World.* Cleveland: World, 1969.

Kingman, Lee, ed. *The Illustrator's Notebook.* Boston: The Horn Book, 1978.

Kingman, Lee, Joanna Foster, and Ruth Giles Lontoft, compilers. *Illustrators of Children's Books, 1957–1966.* Boston: The Horn Book, 1968. (Also, *Illustrators of Children's Books, 1744–1945* and *Illustrators of Children's Books, 1946–1956.*)

Kingman, Lee, Grace Hogarth, and Harriet Quimby. *Illustrators of Children's Books, 1967–1976.* Boston: The Horn Book, 1978.

MacCann, Donnarae, and Olga Richard. *The Child's First Books.* Bronx, NY: Wilson, 1973.

Matthias, Margaret, and Graciela Italiano. "Louder Than a Thousand Words." In *Signposts of Criticism of Children's Literature,* compiled by Robert Bator. Chicago: American Library Association, 1983.

Pitz, Henry C. *Illustrating Children's Books: History, Technique, Production.* New York: Watson-Guptill, 1963.

Pritchard, David. "'Daddy, Talk!' Thoughts on Reading Early Picture Books." *The Lion and the Unicorn* 7/8 (1983/84): 64–69.

Roxburgh, Stephen. "A Picture Equals How Many Words? Narrative Theory and Picture Books for Children." *The Lion and the Unicorn* 7/8 (1983/84): 20–33.

Shulevitz, Uri. *Writing with Pictures: How to Write and Illustrate Children's Books.* New York: Watson-Guptill, 1985.

A SELECTED BIBLIOGRAPHY OF PICTURE STORYBOOKS

The following picture storybooks are organized according to type of story—Folk Literature, Modern Fantasy, Realistic Story, or Anthropomorphic Story—as described in this chapter. This is only a very brief selection of the many wonderful picture-books available to young readers. Be sure to find other works by the writers and artists represented in this list. Unless otherwise indicated, the author is also the illustrator.

Folk Literature

Aardema, Verna. *Why Mosquitoes Buzz in People's Ears.* Illustrated by Leo and Diane Dillon. New York: Dial Press, 1975.

Andersen, Hans Christian. *The Nightingale.* Translated by Eva LeGallienne. Illustrated by Nancy Ekholm Burkert. New York: Harper, 1965.

Bishop, Claire Huchet. *The Five Chinese Brothers.* Illustrated by Kurt Wiese. New York: Coward, McCann & Geoghegan, 1938.

Brown, Marcia. *Cinderella.* New York: Scribner, 1954.

———. *Dick Whittington and His Cat.* New York: Scribner, 1950.

———. *Once a Mouse.* New York: Scribner, 1961.

Cendrars, Blaise. *Shadows.* Illustrated by Marcia Brown. New York: Scribner, 1982.

Climo, Shirley. *The Egyptian Cinderella.* Illustrated by Ruth Heller. New York: Crowell, 1989.

De Paola, Tomi. *Strega Nona.* New York: Prentice-Hall, 1975.

Domanska, Janina. *Little Red Hen.* New York: Macmillan, 1973.

Emberley, Barbara. *Drummer Hoff.* Illustrated by Ed Emberley. New York: Prentice-Hall, 1967.

Hodges, Margaret. *The Wave.* Illustrated by Blair Lent. Boston: Houghton Mifflin, 1964.

———. *Saint George and the Dragon.* Illustrated by Trina Schart Hyman. Boston: Little, Brown, 1984.

Hogrogian, Nonny. *One Fine Day.* New York: Macmillan, 1971.

Jarrell, Randall, reteller. *Snow White and the Seven Dwarfs.* Illustrated by Nancy Ekholm Burkert. New York: Farrar, Straus & Giroux, 1972.

Louie, Ai-Ling. *Yeh-Shen: A Cinderella Story from China.* Illustrated by Ed Young. New York: Philomel (Putnam), 1982.

McDermott, Gerald. *Anansi the Spider.* New York: Holt, Rinehart and Winston, 1972.

———. *Arrow to the Sun.* New York: Viking, 1974.

Mosel, Arlene. *The Funny Little Woman.* Illustrated by Blair Lent. New York: Dutton, 1972.

———. *Tikki Tikki Tembo.* Illustrated by Blair Lent. New York: Holt, Rinehart and Winston, 1968.

Ness, Evaline. *Tom Tit Tot.* New York: Scribner, 1965.

Nic Leodhas, Sorche (pseudonym of LeClaire G. Alger). *Always Room for One More.* Illustrated by Nonny Hogrogian. New York: Holt, Rinehart and Winston, 1965.

Ransome, Arthur. *The Fool of the World and the Flying Ship.* Illustrated by Uri Shulevitz. New York: Farrar, Straus & Giroux, 1968.

Robbins, Ruth. *Baboushka and the Three Kings.* Illustrated by Nicolas Sidjakov. Boston: Houghton Mifflin, 1960.

Sawyer, Ruth. *Journey Cake, Ho!* Illustrated by Robert McCloskey. New York: Viking, 1953.

Singer, Isaac Bashevis. *The Fearsome Inn.* Illustrated by Nonny Hogrogian. New York: Macmillan, 1984.

Slobodkina, Esphyr. *Caps for Sale.* Reading, MA: Addison-Wesley, 1940.

Zemach, Harve, reteller. *Duffy and the Devil.* Illustrated by Margot Zemach. New York: Farrar, Straus & Giroux, 1973.

Zemach, Margot, reteller. *The Little Red Hen.* New York: Farrar, Straus & Giroux, 1983.

———. *The Three Little Pigs.* New York: Farrar, Straus & Giroux, 1988.

Modern Fantasy

Aiken, Joan. *The Moon's Revenge.* Illustrated by Alan Lee. New York: Knopf, 1987.

Blos, Joan. *Lottie's Circus.* Illustrated by Irene Trivas. New York: Morrow, 1989.

Brown, Margaret Wise. *The Little Island.* Illustrated by Leonard Weisgard. New York: Doubleday, 1946.

———. *The Steamroller.* Illustrated by Evaline Ness. New York: Walker, 1974.

Burningham, John. *Mr. Gumpy's Motorcar.* New York: Crowell, 1976.

———. *Mr. Gumpy's Outing.* New York: Holt, Rinehart and Winston, 1971.

Conrad, Pam. *The Tub People.* Illustrated by Richard Egielski. New York: Harper, 1989.

Daugherty, James. *Andy and the Lion.* New York: Viking, 1938.

De Regniers, Beatrice Schenk. *May I Bring a Friend?* Illustrated by Beni Montresor. New York: Atheneum, 1964.

Gág, Wanda. *Millions of Cats.* New York: Coward, McCann & Geoghegan, 1928.

Gerstein, Mordicai. *Arnold of the Ducks.* New York: Harper, 1983.

Hale, Lucretia. *The Lady Who Put Salt in Her Coffee.* Illustrated and adapted by Amy Schwartz. New York: Harcourt Brace Jovanovich, 1989.

Johnson, Crockett. *Harold and the Purple Crayon.* New York: Harper, 1981.

———. *Harold's Circus.* New York: Scholastic, 1959.

Kellogg, Steven. *The Island of the Skog.* New York: Dial Press, 1973.

Lionni, Leo. *Alexander and the Wind-Up Mouse.* New York: Pantheon Books, 1969.

Pearce, Philippa. *Emily's Own Elephant.* Illustrated by John Lawrence. New York: Greenwillow (Morrow), 1988.

Sendak, Maurice. *In the Night Kitchen.* New York: Harper, 1970.

———. *Outside Over There.* New York: Harper, 1981.

———. *Where the Wild Things Are.* New York: Harper, 1963.

Seuss, Dr. (pseudonym of Theodore Geisel). *The Cat in the Hat.* New York: Random House, 1957.

———. *And To Think That I Saw It on Mulberry Street.* New York: Vanguard Press, 1973.

Steig, William. *Sylvester and the Magic Pebble.* New York: Windmill (Simon & Schuster), 1969.

Thurber, James. *Many Moons.* Illustrated by Louis Slobodkin. New York: Harcourt Brace Jovanovich, 1973.

Ungerer, Tomi. *The Beast of Monsieur Racine.* New York: Farrar, Straus & Giroux, 1971.

Van Allsburg, Chris. *The Garden of Abdul Gasazi.* Boston: Houghton Mifflin, 1979.

———. *Jumanji.* Boston: Houghton Mifflin, 1981.

———. *The Wreck of the Zephyr.* Boston: Houghton Mifflin, 1983.

Wells, Rosemary. *Morris' Disappearing Bag.* New York: Dial Press, 1978.

Willard, Nancy. *The Nightgoon of the Sullen Moon.* Illustrated by David McPhail. New York: Harcourt Brace Jovanovich, 1983.

———. *A Visit to William Blake's Inn.* Illustrated by Alice and Martin Provensen. New York: Harcourt Brace Jovanovich, 1981.

Willis, Val. *The Secret in the Matchbox.* Illustrated by John Shelley. New York: Farrar, Straus & Giroux, 1988.

Zolotow, Charlotte. *Mr. Rabbit and the Lovely Present.* Illustrated by Maurice Sendak. New York: Harper, 1962.

Realistic Stories

Ackerman, Karen. *Song and Dance Man.* New York: Knopf, 1988.

Alexander, Martha. *Nobody Asked Me If I Wanted a Baby Sister.* New York: Dial Press, 1971.

Aliki. *At Mary Bloom's.* New York: Greenwillow (Morrow), 1983.

Anno, Mitsumasa. *Anno's Britain.* New York: Philomel (Putnam), 1982.

———. *Anno's Journey.* New York: Philomel (Putnam), 1978.

Ardizzone, Edward. *Little Tim and the Brave Sea Captain.* 1936. New York: Penguin Books, 1983.

Asch, Frank. *Sand Cake.* New York: Crown, 1987.

Bemelmans, Ludwig. *Madeline.* New York: Viking, 1937.

———. *Madeline's Rescue.* New York: Penguin Books, 1953.

Beskow, Elsa. *Pelle's New Suit.* New York: Harper, 1929.

Clifton, Lucille. *Some of the Days of Everett Anderson.* Illustrated by Evaline Ness. New York: Holt, Rinehart and Winston, 1970.

Cooney, Barbara. *Island Boy.* New York: Viking, 1988.

Ets, Marie Hall. *Nine Days to Christmas.* New York: Penguin Books, 1959.

———. *Play with Me.* New York: Penguin Books, 1955.

de Angeli, Marguerite. *Thee Hannah!* New York: Doubleday, 1940.

De Paola, Tomi. *Nana Upstairs, Nana Downstairs.* New York: Putnam, 1973.

Flack, Marjorie. *The Story about Ping.* Illustrated by Kurt Weise. New York: Penguin Books, 1933.

Fleischman, Sid. *The Scarebird.* Illustrated by Peter Sis. New York: Greenwillow (Morrow), 1988.

Fox, Mem. *Night Noises.* Illustrated by Terry Denton. New York: Harcourt, 1989.

Goble, Paul. *The Girl Who Loved Wild Horses.* New York: Bradbury, 1978.

Godden, Rumer. *The Story of Holly and Ivy.* Illustrated by Barbara Cooney. New York: Penguin Books, 1987.

Greenfield, Eloise. *She Come Bringing Me That Little Baby Girl.* Illustrated by John Steptoe. Philadelphia: Lippincott, 1974.

Hader, Berta, and Elmer Hader. *The Big Snow.* New York: Macmillan, 1948.

Hall, Donald. *The Ox-Cart Man.* Illustrated by Barbara Cooney. New York: Penguin Books, 1983.

Handforth, Thomas. *Mei Lei.* New York: Doubleday, 1938.

Keats, Ezra Jack. *A Letter to Amy.* New York: Harper, 1984.

———. *Peter's Chair.* New York: Harper, 1967.

———. *The Snowy Day.* New York: Viking, 1962.

Keeping, Charles. *Joseph's Yard.* New York: Watts, 1969.

Lawson, Robert. *They Were Strong and Good.* New York: Penguin Books, 1940.

McCloskey, Robert. *Blueberries for Sal.* New York: Viking, 1948.

———. *Make Way for Ducklings.* New York: Viking, 1941.

———. *Time of Wonder.* New York: Viking, 1957.

Miles, Miska. *Annie and the Old One.* Boston: Little, Brown, 1971.

Milhous, Katherine. *The Egg Tree.* New York: Macmillan, 1971.

Ness, Evaline. *Sam, Bangs & Moonshine.* New York: Holt, Rinehart and Winston, 1966.

Politi, Leo. *Song of the Swallows.* New York: Macmillan, 1986.

Provensen, Alice, and Martin Provensen. *The Year at Maple Hill Farm*. New York: Atheneum, 1978.
Shulevitz, Uri. *Dawn*. New York: Farrar, Straus & Giroux, 1974.
———. *Rain, Rain, Rivers*. New York: Farrar, Straus & Giroux, 1969.
Tresselt, Alvin. *White Snow, Bright Snow*. Illustrated by Roger Duvoisin. New York: Lothrop, 1947.
Turkle, Brinton. *Thy Friend, Obadiah*. New York: Viking, 1967.
Udry, Janice M. *The Moon Jumpers*. Illustrated by Maurice Sendak. New York: Harper, 1959.
———. *A Tree Is Nice*. Illustrated by Marc Simont. New York: Harper, 1956.
Waber, Bernard. *Ira Sleeps Over*. Boston: Houghton Mifflin, 1972.
Ward, Lynd K. *The Biggest Bear*. Boston: Houghton Mifflin, 1952.
Yashima, Taro (pseudonym of Jun Iwamatsu). *The Crow Boy*. New York: Viking, 1955.

Anthropomorphic Stories

Brooke, L. Leslie. *Johnny Crow's Garden*. 1903. London: Warne, 1978.
———. *Johnny Crow's Party*. 1907. London: Warne, 1966.
Brown, Margaret Wise. *Goodnight Moon*. Illustrated by Clement Hurd. New York: Harper, 1947.
———. *The Runaway Bunny*. Illustrated by Clement Hurd. New York: Harper, 1962.
Burton, Virginia L. *The Little House*. Boston: Houghton Mifflin, 1942.
———. *Mike Mulligan and His Steam Shovel*. Boston: Houghton Mifflin, 1939.
Dana, Doris. *The Elephant and His Secret*. Illustrated by Antonio Frasconi. New York: Knopf, 1989.
de Brunhoff, Jean. *The Story of Babar, the Little Elephant*. 1933. New York: Knopf, 1989.
Duvoisin, Roger. *Petunia*. New York: Knopf, 1950.
Fatio, Louise. *The Happy Lion*. Illustrated by Roger Duvoisin. 1954. New York: Scholastic, 1986.
Freeman, Don. *Corduroy*. New York: Viking, 1968.
———. *Will's Quill*. New York: Penguin Books, 1977.
Gramatky, Hardie. *Hercules*. New York: Putnam, 1960.
———. *Little Toot*. Reprinted New York: Putnam, 1978.
Carle, Eric. *Do You Want to Be My Friend?* New York: Harper, 1987.
———. *The Very Hungry Caterpillar*. Cleveland: World, 1970.
Hutchins, Pat. *Good-Night Owl*. New York: Macmillan, 1972.
Kraus, Robert. *Leo the Late Bloomer*. Illustrated by Jose and Ariane Aruego. New York: Simon & Schuster, 1987.
Kuskin, Karla. *The Bear Who Saw the Spring*. New York: Harper, 1961.
Langstaff, John M. *A Frog Went A-Courtin'*. Illustrated by Feodor Rojankovsky. Reprinted New York: Scholastic, 1985.
Leaf, Munro. *The Story of Ferdinand*. Illustrated by Robert Lawson. New York: Viking, 1936.
Lionni, Leo. *Fish Is Fish*. Reprinted New York: Knopf, 1987.
———. *Frederick*. New York: Pantheon Books, 1967.
Lobel, Arnold. *Frog and Toad Are Friends*. New York: Harper, 1970.
———. *Frog and Toad Together*. New York: Harper, 1972.
Minarik, Else Holmelund. *Little Bear*. Illustrated by Maurice Sendak. New York: Harper, 1957.
———. *Little Bear's Visit*. Illustrated by Maurice Sendak. Reprinted New York: Harper, 1984.
Peet, Bill. *Encore for Eleanor*. Boston: Houghton Mifflin, 1985.
———
Piatti, Celestino. *The Happy Owls*. New York: Atheneum, 1964.
Potter, Beatrix. *The Tale of Peter Rabbit*. London: Warne, 1901.
Rey, A. H. *Curious George*. Boston: Houghton Mifflin, 1973.
Swift, Hildegarde. *The Little Red Lighthouse and the Great Gray Bridge*. Illustrated by Lynd Ward. New York: Harcourt Brace Jovanovich, 1974.

Waber, Bernard. *The House on East 88th Street*. Boston: Houghton Mifflin, 1975.
———. *Lyle, Lyle, Crocodile*. Reprinted Boston: Houghton Mifflin, 1987.
Wells, Rosemary. *Noisy Nora*. New York: Dial Press, 1980.
Zion, Gene. *Harry, the Dirty Dog*. Illustrated by Margaret Bloy Graham. New York: Harper, 1956.
———. *Harry and the Lady Next Door*. Illustrated by Margaret Bloy Graham. New York: Harper, 1960.

CHAPTER 4

Alphabet, Counting, and Concept Books

DEFINITION

Alphabet, counting, and concept books are first and foremost instructional books; they are intended to teach children certain facts or ideas. Since the intended audience for most of these books consists of children in the preschool or very early elementary years, these are also picture-books and demonstrate the same diverse qualities of art as do the picture storybooks discussed in the previous chapter. But since the texts are meant to teach as well as to entertain, these books operate by a somewhat different set of guidelines and require that we view them from a different perspective.

ALPHABET AND COUNTING BOOKS

Alphabet and counting books are similar in their purposes and approaches. Typically they follow three general organizational patterns, and these are based on the objects chosen to illustrate the concept. A *theme* book is one that provides a thematic or topical focus for the objects depicted—an animal alphabet book or an animal counting book, for example. Jan Garten's *The Alphabet Tale,* using wild animals to represent the letters of the alphabet, or Ezra Jack Keats's *Over in the Meadow,* using various animals in a meadow as the count-able objects, are examples of theme books, as is Muriel Feelings's *Moja Means One,* which uses references to Swahili culture as well as Swahili numbers from one to ten. A *potpourri* book disregards any unity in subject matter; virtually anything may go, but the book is usually given some sense of unity through the style of its illustrations or its overall tone. *Anno's Alphabet* by Mitsumasa Anno, uses sophisticated trompe l'oeil artwork, in which each picture plays tricks with us. *Dr. Seuss's ABC,* on the other hand, uses decidedly unsophisticated but thoroughly enjoyable cartoons. The potpourri book allows the artist the greatest freedom—but that, at the same time, is its limitation if an artist is a bit short of imagination. (The potpourri pattern is the reason we end up with a multitude of "A is for Apple" books.) The rarest is the *sequential-story book,* which illustrates the alphabet or numbers through a continuous story line. Wanda Gag's *ABC Bunny* or Miska Miles's *Apricot ABC* are examples, and they are also books that demonstrate the difficulties of teaching the alphabet through well-plotted stories. Usually, the challenge of learning to recognize letters and their sounds is difficult enough for small children, without further complicating matters for them by incorporating a plot line to follow as well.

Design and Content of Alphabet Books

Although, some alphabet books seem intended for older children who already know the alphabet (*Anno's Alphabet* and Chris Van Allsburg's *Z Was Zapped* seem almost adult-oriented), for the most part, we assume that alphabet books are meant to instruct young children who have limited experiences. Consequently, the letters and their sounds must be associated with objects that are not beyond the children's grasp. An effective alphabet book represents a happy combination of design and accessible content. The design and the illustrations are appropriate for the intended age level. It is important that the author/illustrator not introduce unnecessary confusion, or the purpose of teaching children the sounds of letters will be defeated.

Dr. Seuss's ABC comically reinforces the phonetic associations with such rollicking lines as "Y—A yawning, yellow yak and young Yolanda Yorgenson is yelling on his back." Three- or four-year-olds may not initially know what a yak is, but the illustration will quickly teach them. On the other hand, Joan Walsh Anglund's *A Is for Always* uses abstractions such as "C [for] Courteous," "D [for] Determined," "E [for] Exuberant," and so on. Such concepts are beyond the comprehension of preschoolers, but Miss Anglund, like many well-meaning parents and grandparents, might mistakenly have believed that young children can learn these virtues by simply reading them.

Additionally, we are usually dealing with phonetic sounds when teaching the alphabet. A very good alphabet book will recognize that C has two sounds—"K" and "S"—and that G also can be hard or soft. Most books rely on "Xylophone" for X—but the phonetic sound is closer to "Z." Dr. Seuss perhaps has a sensible compromise, by using such words as "Ax" and "Extra Fox." A peculiar mistake in alphabet books for the very young—but one that can all too often be found—is representing letters like K and G with "Knife" or "Gnat"! Children need challenges, but not unnecessary confusion.

Also, remember that the visual representation of the letter is important. If the letters are drawn too fancifully (*A, G, S,* for example), children may have a difficult time recognizing them in other contexts. There are, of course, common distinctions between the way some letters are printed in texts and the way we normally write them in handwriting (**a** and *a* or **s** and *s*, for instance). Surprisingly few books incorporate both upper- and lower-case letters, but children need to understand that letters appear in different forms. Ideally, children should be exposed to a wide variety of alphabet books that include a generous selection of typefaces. However, for beginners, simple block lettering is probably preferable. And nothing can improve on repetition and broad exposure.

Design and Content of Counting Books

Like alphabet books, counting books have an educational purpose, and that purpose is best served when the book effectively combines design and content. Among the things to look for in counting books is whether or not the objects to be counted stand out clearly on the page. Exactly what is being counted needs to be very obvious. And when a large number of items appear on a single page, the artist can avoid a cluttered appearance and possible confusion by grouping the objects. Also, children expect to find a clear and logical relationship among the objects to be counted.

Very young children require that the objects they are expected to count be nearly identical. In other words, small children will understand the counting of five apples before they will grasp the significance of counting five objects whose relationship is an abstract: an apple, an orange, a pear, a plum, and an apricot, for example. *Brian Wildsmith's 1, 2, 3's* contains some fascinating and imaginative illustrations, but at times he asks his child readers to count dissimilar shapes—a circle, a triangle, a square, a rectangle, and so on—and this could easily muddle them, since these objects are themselves made up of even more geometric designs. Learning to recognize the difference between shapes is a cognitive skill that requires special attention, and it probably ought not to be confused with the task of learning to count. As with the alphabet books, the simple approach is usually best for beginners. But even simple approaches can incorporate such concepts as the spelling of the number words (*one, two, three*) and the object words.

CONCEPT BOOKS

Because of the endless variety of subjects that may be covered in a concept book, there are equally endless variations in their possible layout. It is good to keep in mind that the concept book is intended to convey a certain body of knowledge and that an attractive and clear format can greatly aid in getting information across to the youthful audience. Concept books can be found dealing with almost any subject. (Of course, alphabet and counting books are concept books, too. They have been singled out for special consideration only because they represent such a large share of the children's book market and have their own distinctive features.) Some concept books deal with sensory experiences such as textures, colors, or spatial relationships. Bernice Kohn's *How High Is Up?* is a fine example of such a book, effectively helping a young child to associate such concepts as "high," "low," "rough," "smooth," "loud," and "quiet." Others deal with intellectual skills such as telling time, identifying the seasons, or naming the months of the year or the days of the week. Nancy Tafuri's stunningly illustrated *All Year Long* cleverly combines the recognition of seasonal changes, the months of the year, and the days of the week. *John Burningham's Opposites* effectively illustrates semantic meanings of common words—it serves, in fact, as a sort of predictionary. Still other books may focus on specific objects or classes of objects—boats, supermarkets, animals, and even professions. Donald Crews's *Truck* is a widely acclaimed example, as is his *Freight Trains*.

We expect concept books to be, above all, accurate in their information, omitting nothing that is essential for understanding. We also expect that they should be objective and avoid unfair distortion of the facts or issues. A clear and logical text, moving from the simple to the complex or from the logical beginning to the end, is necessary if children are to learn easily from a concept book. In illustrating a concept book, clarity and simplicity are the virtues. The illustrations should relate clearly to the text on the same or adjacent page. They too should be clear and logical. Highly imaginative illustrations that do not clearly explain or demonstrate the subject of a concept book will defeat its purpose. Finally, the most successful concept book is attractive. It is not enough that a book merely teach; it should delight as well. A good concept book invites the child into its world and makes learning a rewarding experience.

We never outgrow concept books; we simply demand more from them as we mature. When concept books contain advanced information, we generally refer to them as nonfiction books or informational books. These will be discussed in somewhat more detail in Chapter 12.

EDUCATIONAL PICTURE-BOOKS AND THE YOUNG READER

The various types of books we have been discussing in this chapter are didactic in nature, clearly intending to teach some lesson or intellectual concept. There comes a time in nearly every reading child's life when he or she will specifically request a book on "How to tell time" or "How to count money" or "How babies are made" or "Why the leaves fall off the trees in the fall." Fortunately, there are an increasing number of excellent concept books on the market. And the fact that many of these are winning awards (Molly Bang's *Ten, Nine, Eight* and Donald Crews's *Truck* are two examples) is evidence that adults are taking these books more seriously than they had in the past.

Modern alphabet, counting, and concept books have become more than vehicles of education and purveyors of fact; they have joined the ranks of the picture storybooks in becoming works of art and objects of pleasure.

BIBLIOGRAPHY OF CRITICAL STUDIES

Debes, John L., and Clarence M. Williams. "The Power of Visuals." *Instructor* (December 1974): 32–39.

Hall, Mary Anne, and Jane Mantango. "Children's Literature: A Source for Concept Enrichment." *Elementary English* (April 1975) : 487–494.

Kiefer, Barbara. "Critically Speaking: Literature for Children." *The Reading Teacher* (January 1985): 458–463.

Schoenfield, Madalynne. "Alphabet and Counting Books." *Day Care and Early Education* 10 (Winter 1982): 44.

Stewig, John Warren. "Alphabet Books: A Neglected Genre." In *Jump Over the Moon,* edited by Pamela Barron and Jennifer Q. Burley. 115–120. New York: Holt, Rinehart and Winston, 1984.

Thomas, Della. "Count Down on the 1-2-3's." *School Library Journal* (15 March 1971): 95–102.

A SELECTED BIBLIOGRAPHY OF ALPHABET, COUNTING, AND CONCEPT BOOKS

There are scores of alphabet books and only somewhat fewer counting and concept books. This selection only suggests the breadth and diverse range of books available.

Alphabet Books

Anno, Mitsumasa. *Anno's Alphabet.* New York: Harper, 1975.

Brown, Marcia. *Peter Piper's Alphabet.* New York: Scribner, 1959.

Burningham, John. *John Burningham's ABC's.* New York: Crown, 1985.

Duvoisin, Roger. *A for the Ark.* New York: Lee & Shepard, 1952.

Feelings, Muriel. *Jambo Means Hello: A Swahili Alphabet Book.* Illustrated by Tom Feelings. New York: Dial Press, 1974.

Fujikawa, Gyo. *A to Z Picture Book.* New York: Grosset & Dunlap, 1974.

Gág, Wanda. *The ABC Bunny.* New York: Coward, McCann & Geoghegan, 1933.

Garten, Jan. *The Alphabet Tale.* New York: Random House, 1964.

Isadora, Rachel. *City Seen from A to Z.* New York: Greenwillow (Morrow), 1983.

Kitchen, Bert. *Animal Alphabet.* New York: Dial Press, 1984.

Lionni, Leo. *The Alphabet Tree.* New York: Pantheon Books, 1968.

MacDonald, Suse. *Alphabatics.* New York: Bradbury, 1986.

Miles, Miska. *Apricot ABC.* Illustrated by Peter Parnall. Boston: Little, Brown, 1969.

Munari, Bruno. *Bruno Munari's ABC.* New York: Philomel (Putnam), 1960.

Musgrove, Margaret. *Ashanti to Zulu: African Traditions.* Illustrated by Leo and Diane Dillon. New York: Dial Press, 1976.

Oxenbury, Helen. *Helen Oxenbury's ABC.* New York: Dell (Delacorte Press), 1983.

Seuss, Dr. (pseudonym of Theodore Geisel). *Dr. Seuss's ABC.* New York: Random House, 1988.

Tudor, Tasha. *A Is for Annabelle.* New York: Walck, 1954.

Wildsmith, Brian. *ABC.* New York: Watts, 1962.

Counting Books

Anno, Mitsumasa. *Anno's Counting Book.* New York: Crowell, 1977.

Bang, Molly. *Ten, Nine, Eight.* New York: Greenwillow (Morrow), 1983.

Burningham, John. *John Burningham's 1,2,3's.* New York: Crown, 1985.

Carle, Eric. *1, 2, 3 to the Zoo.* Cleveland: World, 1968.

Feelings, Muriel. *Moja Means One: A Swahili Counting Book.* Illustrated by Tom Feelings. New York: Dutton, 1971.

Hoban, Russell. *Ten What? A Mystery Counting Book.* New York: Scribner, 1974.

Hoban, Tana. *Count and See.* New York: Macmillan, 1972.

Langstaff, John. *Over in the Meadow.* Illustrated by Feodor Rojankovsky. New York: Harcourt Brace Jovanovich, 1973.

McMillan, Bruce. *Here a Chick, There a Chick.* New York: Lothrop, 1983.

Reiss, John. *Numbers.* New York: Bradbury, 1971.

Wildsmith, Brian. *Brian Wildsmith's 1 2 3's.* New York: Watts, 1965.

Concept Books

Brown, Marcia. *Listen to a Shape.* New York: Watts, 1979.

Brown, Margaret Wise. *Country Noisy Book.* Illustrated by Leonard Weisgard. New York: Harper & Row, 1940.

Burningham, John. *John Burningham's Opposites.* New York: Crown, 1986.

Crews, Donald. *Freight Train.* New York: Greenwillow (Morrow), 1978.

———. *Truck.* New York: Greenwillow (Morrow), 1980.

Grifalconi, Ann. *The Village of Round and Square Houses.* Boston: Little, Brown, 1986.

Hoban, Tana. *Shapes and Things.* New York: Macmillan, 1970.

Kohn, Bernice. *How High Is Up?* Illustrated by Jan Pyk. New York: Putnam, 1971.

Maestro, Betsy, and Guilio Maestro. *Traffic: A Book of Opposites.* New York: Crown, 1981.

Pienkowski, Jan. *Shapes.* New York: Simon & Schuster, 1981.

Reiss, John. *Colors.* New York: Macmillan, 1987.

———. *Shapes.* New York: Macmillan, 1987.

Robbins, Ken. *Tools.* New York: Macmillan, 1983.

Rockwell, Anne, and Harlow Rockwell. *Machines.* New York: Macmillan, 1972.

———. *The Supermarket.* New York: Macmillan, 1979.

Rockwell, Harlow. *My Dentist.* New York: Greenwillow (Morrow), 1975.

———. *My Doctor.* New York: Harper, 1985.

Ruben, Patricia. *True or False?* New York: Harper, 1978.

Schwartz, David M. *If You Made a Million.* Illustrated by Steven Kellogg. Photos by George Ancona. New York: Lothrop, 1989.

Spier, Peter. *Fast-Slow, High-Low: A Book of Opposites.* New York: Doubleday, 1972.

Tafuri, Nancy. *All Year Long.* New York: Penguin Books, 1984.

Testa, Fulvia. *If You Look Around You.* New York: Dial Press, 1983.

CHAPTER 5

Folk Literature

DEFINITION

Folk literature consists of all those stories handed down from generation to generation, from elder, parent, or nurse to child, begun in the time before writing. The body of folk literature includes not only what we—somewhat inaccurately—refer to as fairy tales, but also the myths, legends, fables, tall tales, and other inventions associated with preliterate societies. Although now most of these stories have been committed to paper, for centuries they lived only in people's heads and survived only by word of mouth. Consequently, folktales were apt to change with each successive telling (much as complicated phrases get altered as they pass from person to person in that childhood game of Telephone). We may find hundreds of variations for a single tale, each variation containing elements peculiar to the society and culture that produced it. These tales form the roots of all literature, and their story lines still form the foundations for virtually every book we read or movie we watch. They speak to our most basic human emotions, to our deepest hopes and fears, and it is little wonder that even the youngest children feel a great affinity with these stories that have been with us for as long as civilization.

ORIGIN AND PURPOSES OF FOLK LITERATURE

Two principal theories attempt to explain the origins of folktales. *Monogenesis* is the theory that all tales were ultimately derived from a single source (such as Mesopotamian culture) and were disseminated throughout the world gradually. *Polygenesis,* on the other hand, is the theory that similar tales emerged independently in many different places throughout the world. Polygenesis attributes these marked similarities in form and content to the fundamental similarities in the human psyche—similar human hopes, fears, dreams, and psychological needs. Neither theory has yet produced sufficient evidence to prove that it alone is accurate, and the truth may lie somewhere in between—some tales emerging independently and others adapted from neighboring cultures.

Undoubtedly, folktales, myths, legends, and fables originally served a variety of purposes. Some stories may have served as educational tools for preliterate societies, passing on knowledge essential for survival. Others surely helped to reinforce cultural practices and social mores: the importance of certain virtues, the significance of marriage or of the established social or political order, the superiority of one's clan or tribe over its neighbors, and so on. Vital to nearly all peoples were creation myths—how the world, *their* world, came to be. And we should not forget what must have been one of the most driving forces behind the telling of these tales—entertainment. These tales served primitive societies in place of books, plays, movies, and television, and as such they embodied the popular attitudes, beliefs, and preferences of the culture. If many of them remain meaningful for us today, it is probably because, inside us all, we still share a great deal more with our ancestors than we like to think.

FOLKTALES

We shall first look at folktales and then at myths, legends, and fables, which have their own readily observable characteristics. Folktales can be classified according to several different features. Among the most common are the following.

Varieties of Folktales

Talking Beast Tales. Animals that can talk appear in virtually all folktales. A story is classified as a Talking Beast Tale only when *all* the principal characters are animals with human traits. In most Talking Beast Tales, the animals serve as symbols for humans, and in no way do they behave as real-life animals behave. These tales tend to be very appealing to young children, who enjoy a great affinity with most animals. "The Town Musicians of Bremen" is one of the most famous, and we also include such simple tales as "The Little Red Hen" (which includes elements of a Cumulative Tale as well). Virtually all fables, as will be noted later, are Talking Beast Tales.

Noodlehead Tales. Noodlehead Tales (also termed Droll or Simpleton Tales) have as their principal characters fools, albeit lovable fools. "Hans in Luck," in which the title character repeatedly trades one possession for another of lesser value until he is left with nothing (except happiness), is an excellent example of such a tale. "The Three Wishes," about a simple peasant couple who manage to waste three magical wishes on nonsense but are nonetheless content with their lot, is another well-known example. The appeal in these tales is sometimes the sense of superiority we enjoy over the fools, but often we enjoy the triumph of the good-hearted simpleton over craftier evil characters. And occasionally, the simpleton is indeed far wiser than anyone else, suggesting that it is the world at large that is foolish, unable to recognize true wisdom. Basically, the Noodlehead Tale is that of the underdog, always popular.

Märchen or Wonder Tales. The best-known of the traditional folktales are those Märchen or Wonder Tales. Focusing on magical wonders long ago in faraway lands, these tales typically depict the conflict between good and evil, usually enacted by characters of royal birth. Typically they conclude with the triumph of virtue and a happy marriage. "Cinderella," "Snow White and the Seven Dwarfs," and "Sleeping Beauty" are the classic examples. It is largely from these tales that the term "fairy tale"—however inaccurate, since very few actually do contain fairies—emerged.

Cumulative Tales. Most folktales include repetitious patterns—three wishes, seven brothers, twelve deeds to be accomplished, and so on. But certain tales rely entirely on repetition for their total effect. As each new detail is added to earlier ones, the entire list is repeated in order, so that the accumulation becomes a kind of chorus—and a challenge to the memory of the listener/reader. These Cumulative Tales are generally brief (otherwise they become tiresome), but their appeal lies in their musical quality and often in their flippant humor. That old rhyme, "This Is the House That Jack Built," is an example of repeated language patterns, and those familiar tales "The Gingerbread Boy" and "The Turnip," wherein additional characters are called in to help the protagonist, are examples of cumulative actions. Young children especially love these repeated patterns, which typically allow them to join in the telling.

Pourquoi Tales. Pourquoi Tales (the name derives from the French word for "why") seek to explain natural phenomena. Many familiar Native American folktales fall into this category, like the moving tale that explains the creation of the Sleeping Bear Dunes on the northwest coast of Michigan's lower peninsula. In the story, the massive dunes cover the body of a mother bear mourning the loss of her two cubs, who drowned in Lake Michigan, and North and South Manitou islands, just off the coast, represent the two cubs themselves. Many American Tall Tales, which are discussed below, often take on the qualities of Pourquoi Tales—Paul Bunyan is reportedly responsible for creating lakes, mountain passes, and even the Grand Canyon. Many Pourquoi Tales, such as stories of creation of the world, take on deep religious significance and are more properly considered myths.

Artistic Elements

It is possible to identify certain artistic elements that most tales have in common. (Since folktales are derived from the oral and not the literary or written tradition, we hesitate to term these literary elements, but they amount to the same thing.) As might be expected, these elements are all decidedly influenced by the oral nature of the tales.

Settings. The settings of most folktales are not sharply defined. Often brief conventional phrases ("Once upon a time in a kingdom far, far away") are typical. The time and place are usually vague and often distant. The purpose of most folktale settings would seem to be to remove the tale from the real world, taking the events to a world where magic can easily and unabashedly occur. Only occasionally do we find actual place names in tales, and even then we have the feeling that we could substitute the name of any other city or forest or country—which is undoubtedly what early storytellers did as they tailored their recitations to individual audiences.

Characters. The characters in folktales are usually flat (with only one side to their person-alities) and stereotyped. Stereotypical characters populate most tales: powerful, wicked stepmothers; weak-willed, ineffectual fathers; jealous siblings. A character is typically either all good or all evil, and it is usually not difficult for the audience to separate the good from the bad. Physical appearance often readily defines a character; wicked witches are ugly, good princesses are beautiful, noble princes are strong and handsome. Of course, magic occasionally does intervene. The Beast in "Beauty and the Beast" has been transformed from his handsome self into a monstrosity by a jealous witch. Another witch transforms a handsome prince into a frog. But once the character's true nature has been acknowledged by the appropriate person—usually some unsuspecting and strikingly beautiful maiden or prince charming—the deceptive guise vanishes. Only rarely do we find a truly beautiful character to be wicked. Snow White's stepmother is an example, and even her beauty is outshone by that of her virtuous stepdaughter, and she performs her most powerful magic when she assumes the disguise of an ugly hag. In folktales, truth cannot long remain hidden.

The main character—the hero or heroine—is often isolated and forced to act alone. More often than not, the hero/heroine is the youngest child (and thus pitted unfairly against older siblings) or is an only child and/or orphaned. (Not surprisingly, this feature of folktales makes them especially appealing to young children, who see themselves as equally helpless against the adult world and their older siblings.) The heroes or heroines are usually cast out into the open world or are apparently without any human friends. And, if that were not enough, the forces of evil seem unfairly stacked against them. Often the evil is represented by groups of characters—two wicked stepsisters and a stepmother, for example. Consequently, to offset the apparent imbalance, the hero/heroine must be aided by supernatural forces (such as magic devices or enchanted or talking animals). The hero/heroine is clearly blessed and not infrequently discovered to be of royal blood (most folktales place a great deal of importance on one's appropriate station in life).

In short, the folktale hero/heroine is someone very much like us, and as young children picture themselves—the helpless but well-meaning victims of overweaning evil forces (sometimes appearing in the form of our parents). And the evil characters are incredibly evil—symbolizing all of our fears and frustrations. Naturally, imbued with the hope of youth, we expect the evil characters to get what is coming to them and the good characters to triumph in the end.

Plots. The plots, or the sequence of events, are among the most identifiable features of folktales. Suspense and action are far more important to these tales than character development. Conflicts are quickly established, and events move swiftly to their conclusion, and although there may be subsidiary plots or the events may seem to get sidetracked, the action never slows down.

Because these tales were not originally written down, they are characterized by considerable repetition of both words and actions, the repetition serving as a memory aid. This repetition may also be suggestive of the ritual nature of many folktales. Rituals depend upon repetition—repetition of the same prayers and symbolic acts in church, of the same oaths of allegiance in government, of the same practices at weddings and funerals. Folktales frequently deal with rites of passage, especially that passage from childhood into adulthood, which is a familiar theme in folk literature. And finally, the great majority of folktales end happily, with poetic justice being meted out—the good rewarded and the wicked punished.

Themes. Folktale themes are usually quite simple, but always serious and powerful. They deal with such subjects as escaping mighty and evil enemies, earning a place in the world, accomplishing monumental tasks, and so on. Values are clearly defined, and folktale heroes and heroines do not wrestle with perplexing moral dilemmas; there is seldom a question about what is right or wrong. But if choices are clear, they are also very demanding.

If we had to make a general statement about themes in folktales, we might well turn to themes of Greek tragedy: *Wisdom comes through suffering.* The message rings loud and clear: for every benefit there is a condition; nothing in life comes without strings attached; responsibilities must be met and bargains kept. And folktale themes, especially in the Western tradition, espouse the virtues of compassion and humility over the vices of greed, selfishness, and excessive or overweening pride. (Pride, which has customarily been regarded in the Judaeo-Christian ethic as the worst sin, is not to be confused with self-respect. Self-respect means that we see ourselves as just as good as everybody else; pride means that we see ourselves as better than the rest.)

Style. The style in folktales is largely regulated by the oral nature of their origins. The language is typically economical, with a minimal amount of description and a heavy reliance on formulaic patterns—conventional openings and closings, for instance ("Once upon a time in a kingdom far, far away" and "They lived happily ever after"). Repetitious phrases are common; they supply a rhythmic quality desirable in oral tales and undoubtedly once served as mnemonic devices to make the tales easy to memorize. Dialogue is frequently used, and, in literary retelling of these tales, it captures the nature of the character speaking—a lowly peasant will use a folksy manner whereas the speech of a king or princess is more refined. (Joseph Jacobs wonderfully captures these differences in English speech patterns in his retellings of the old tales.)

Most folktales offer examples of simple *images*—simple but concrete and powerful—that leave us with indelible mental pictures: a glass slipper, a beanstalk and talking harp, golden eggs, a bloody handkerchief, a red riding hood, and so on. Related to images are *motifs*. A motif has been defined by folklorist Stith Thompson as "the smallest element in a tale having power to persist in tradition." In folk art, a motif is a repeated figure or element in a larger design—ducks and geese or hearts and flowers, and so on. In music, a motif is a repeated pattern of notes. In literature, a motif is a recognizable element that recurs in different tales; it often carries symbolic value and is useful for oral storytellers in their memorizing. Examples of popular motifs are magical transformations (an enchanted beast reverts to a handsome prince, usually after some expression of true love), the use of magical objects (a cloak of invisibility), the appearance of deceitful animals (or helpful ones), the making of foolish bargains, and the list continues.

Many folklore motifs are examples of magic—granted wishes, fairy godmothers, superhuman powers (extreme speed or the ability to see for miles), vanishings, and so on. One important stylistic feature of the folktale is that the magic, when it inevitably appears, is always greeted by the characters matter-of-factly. In folktales magic is an almost normal part of life. No one is ever amazed or disbelieving when a wolf speaks politely or an elf makes exotic promises. This accepting attitude toward magic further distances the folktale from reality, and it provides an important distinction between folk literature and much of literary fantasy. In many literary fantasies (heroic fantasy being one of the exceptions), magical occurrences are not necessarily taken for granted and may even be regarded with surprise, awe, and disbelief. (Both Alice and Dorothy, those most famous of child travelers in fantasy worlds, are in constant wonder at the characters and circumstances they encounter.)

A word must be said about violence in folktales. Foolish and irresponsible little pigs are devoured, wolves are cooked in boiling water, witches are pushed into hot ovens, characters are mutilated in any number of ways—folktales have their fair share of horror.

Certainly much of the violence is the product of earlier, less squeamish eras. But before we seek to exorcise such elements from stories for the young, we should remember that it is at least motivated. By contrast, much of the excessively gruesome violence on television—all too often found in children's Saturday morning cartoons—is gratuitous, without sense or purpose other than to arouse or amuse the audience. In folktales, violence perpetrated by the wicked always results in their downfall and deaths; violence perpetrated by the good is always a response to evil. It is interesting that, when given the choice, children usually prefer versions of "Little Red Riding Hood" in which Grandmother is devoured and the wolf is ultimately killed to those versions in which the ravenous wolf, after inexplicably tying up Grandmother and tossing her in the closet, is miraculously reformed and promises to be good henceforth.

Children demand justice in life: Good should be rewarded, and evil should be punished. They demand the same simplistic justice in their literature also. Who wants to see a wicked, cannibalistic witch set free at the story's end, even if she does promise to behave herself? Finally, there is simply no evidence that the reading of folktales, including their violent elements, will turn children to a life of cruelty. On the contrary, there is evidence (most notably that presented by the famed psychologist Bruno Bettelheim) that venting anxieties and hostilities through the vicarious experience of art and literature is a healthy and much-needed outlet.

OTHER VARIETIES OF FOLK LITERATURE

Myths

Myths are the stories of gods, goddesses, and heroes of a given culture, and these stories serve a variety of purposes, combining science, religion, and even sociology and psychology. Myths may explain the ultimate origin of the world and of human beings—virtually every culture from the most primitive to the most advanced has some creation myth, such as those wonderfully recounted in Virginia Hamilton's *In the Beginning: Creation Stories from Around the World*. Myths also help explain the origins of customs and societal beliefs. Ancient Greeks and Romans placed coins in the mouths of their dead that they might have the fare for Charon to ferry them over the River Styx to the Underworld. Myths also provide explanations for natural phenomena, the most familiar perhaps being the myth of Persephone; when she was carried off by Hades (Pluto in Roman mythology), the god of the Underworld, her mother Demeter, goddess of the grain and harvest, was plunged into deep sorrow and thus allowed winter to visit the world.

Myths also help to define the human relationships with the god (or gods and goddesses). In the Judaeo-Christian culture, God is a paternal figure demanding complete obedience in return for care and nurture; in classical Greece, the gods and goddesses were powerful figures who often struggled against one another for human favor and typically were pragmatic in their dealings with humans (I'll do that for you if you do this for me). In Norse mythology, the gods and goddesses were defenders of humanity against the mighty forces of evil. Myths may reinforce cultural values, drawing attention to what the culture sees as primary good and evil; ancient Norse myths are full of stories of valiant warriors, and physical strength and bravery were—not surprisingly—two of the most important values of that culture. Not least, myths help to resolve humanity's fear of the unknown, whether it was fear of thunder and lightning (explained as activities of the gods) or fear of death (typically explained as a passage from one world into another).

Classical Greek and Roman Mythology. To people of Western cultures, the most familiar mythology outside the Judaeo-Christian tradition is that of ancient Greece and Rome. Our daily lives are imbued with references to the extensive pantheon and the notable heroes of that civilization: the names of the planets (Venus, Jupiter), the stars (Boötes, Alpha Centauri), the constellations (Orion, Aries), and on a more mundane level, months of the year (January, March), body parts (Achilles tendon), cleaning agents (Ajax), synthetic fibers (Herculon), automobiles (Mercury), tires and mapbooks (Atlas), athletic games (Olympics), and so on. A knowledge of these myths is important if only to make us more culturally aware. But in addition to recognizing the multitude of references to Greek and Roman mythology in the modern world, we learn a great deal about human nature from these myths. The questions of humanity's obedience to a higher power, the relationships of men and women to one another, the power of love, and the strength of parental devotion are all addressed in this body of mythology. Perhaps more than any other world mythology, classical Greek and Roman mythology focuses on the significance of humanity in the world.

Norse Mythology. Second only to Greek and Roman mythology in its influence on the Western tradition, Norse mythology reflects the harsh way of life engendered by the severe, yet dramatically beautiful, Scandinavian lands. Like the Greek and Roman gods and goddesses, the Norse deities were anthropomorphic—that is, they took human form (a practice not common, considering the many monsters, demons, multiarmed deities, feathered serpents, and animal forms worshiped throughout the world). But compared to the Greek deities, the Norse gods and goddesses tend to be a much more serious lot, engaged in a perpetual struggle with the forces of evil, a struggle that they were destined to lose eventually. Individual codes of honor were highly esteemed in this war-conscious society, and the thunder god, Thor, with his mighty hammer is among the most familiar of images from Norse mythology. Thor is remembered weekly in our own culture, for Thursday was named for him, just as Tuesday, Wednesday, and Friday were named for other Norse deities, Tiw, Woden, and Fria. The tales of Norse mythology are both exciting and moving.

American, African, and Oriental Mythologies. The cultures of Native America (including North, Central, and South America), Mesopotamia, Africa, India, and the Far East all developed highly complex and sophisticated mythologies. Unlike Greek, Roman, and Norse mythologies, the deities of these cultures are frequently polymorphic, combining the forms of animals and/or humans. Sometimes, the gods and goddesses took extraordinary forms— humans having many arms, heads, eyes, and so on. The great majority of world mythologies are, of course, polytheistic—that is, they contain many gods and goddesses. In fact, animistic cultures tend to have hundreds, even thousands, of deities, for they believe that supernatural beings inhabit every tree, animal, and stream. Nevertheless, these disparate mythologies all have a common need to explain our relationship to the wondrous and mysterious forces that drive the universe. Thus, many myths are Pourquoi Tales, explaining the natural world.

Heroic Legends, Epics, and Fables

A word must be said of legends and epics, which are related to mythology in that they are stories of cultural interest, but they focus on the achievements of mortal heroes rather than on gods and goddesses. Among the most popular figures from Greek and Roman mythology are the great human heroes—Achilles, Odysseus (or Ulysses), Hector, Jason, Heracles (or Hercules), and Perseus. They were indeed the first superheroes, the prototypes of Superman, Batman, and Wonder Woman.

Medieval Europe saw the rise of *epic tales* deriving from Christian sources; King Arthur and the Knights of the Round Table and Charlemagne with his Paladins provided the sources of the most popular tales, Malory's *The Death of Arthur* and the French epic *The Song of Roland* being among the most famous. Also popular in the Middle Ages were the *saints' legends,* recounting often apocryphal tales of the lives and miracles of saints. In a similar fashion, *local legends* emerged, focusing on secular (as opposed to religious) heroes and typically departing from reality quite readily. Some such legends grow up around real people (George Washington's chopping down the cherry tree) and others around clearly fictional characters (Paul Bunyan). The numerous tales of Paul Bunyan's extraordinary exploits belong to the genre of American Tall Tale. Tall Tales—those comic stories of preposterous exaggeration—illustrate the American preference for broad humor and overstatement, and they are, in a sense, modern versions of the saints' legends.

Although epics and legends were probably never intended specifically for children, children have enjoyed them from time immemorial—and for many of the same reasons that children enjoy folktales. Epics and legends include dynamic and clearly defined characters, plenty of action, and popular themes. There are many modern retellings of these old stories that are wonderfully suited for children: Howard Pyle's *The Merry Adventures of Robin Hood,* Padraic Colum's moving *The Children's Homer* and *The Sons of Odin,* Rosemary Sutcliff's retelling of *Beowulf,* to name just a few.

Finally, we must mention *fables,* which are among the oldest and simplest of literary forms. Fables are brief tales, usually with animals as the characters portraying human virtues and vices. Most fables conclude with a blatantly stated moral, scolding some form of human behavior, and are therefore openly didactic. Aesop, a famed teacher of the ancient Greeks, is credited with the most famous of fables, and it is usually assumed that he used them in his teaching. Ironically, even though their outward form would suggest a strong appeal among young children, most fables demand abstract thinking and are more akin to parables than to folktales. Thus their attraction is more apt to be for adults.

THE APPEAL OF FOLK LITERATURE

Folktales appeal to children in a variety of ways. The theories of Piaget and Erikson (see Chapter 2) go a long way in helping us to understand much of this appeal. The simple fact is that children believe—or perhaps want to believe—that objects, actions, thoughts, and words can exert a magical influence over events. Also, they see no reason why inanimate objects should not be able to think and speak, and they freely accept a human consciousness in animals. In this way, folktales, myths, legends, and so on constitute a form of wish fulfillment.

This concept can be taken one step further when we consider that children—especially the very young—perceive themselves as the center of the world. Folktale heroes and heroines are often quite clearly the centers of their respective worlds. Consequently, it is easy for children to identify with these characters, who are beset by woes and yet overcome them through their own tenacity and will, with the aid of magical or divine intervention. Folktales, in this way, provide what some feel to be the most important element of all children's literature—hope.

FOLK LITERATURE AND EMOTIONAL/ INTELLECTUAL DEVELOPMENT

This brings us finally to what folk literature can do for children. The hope that they can provide is crucial, and psychologists such as Bruno Bettelheim have made great claims for the ability of folktales to help children cope with psychological tribulations encountered in the process of growing up. But, aside from this widely disputed theory, the various forms of folk literature can help children learn about human problems and show them that they are not alone in their troubles. Not incidentally, folktales can broaden their cultural experiences, showing them about new and fascinating cultures and teaching them that we share the world with many diverse peoples.

THE TELLERS OF THE TALES

Almost as soon as human beings invented the art of writing, they began to record their oral tales—on stone, on papyrus, and on paper. So far as Western culture is concerned, virtually the entire body of ancient Greek literature consists of renderings and retellings of their myths, legends, and fables. The ancient Romans followed this practice similarly. The ancient Jews recorded their stories with a rich mixture of history and legend. The Christian Middle Ages built up a body of literature on the legendary lives of the saints as well as on the glorified deeds of heroes. But by and large, the folktales remained only in oral form, except for a few recorded by such medieval writers as Chaucer in *The Canterbury Tales,* Boccaccio in *The Decameron,* and Giambattista Basile in *The Pentamerone.* Consequently, the folktales survived chiefly by word of mouth until the seventeenth and eighteenth centuries when writers began to collect them and put them down on paper.

Among the first and most famous of these writers was Charles Perrault, whose *Tales of Mother Goose* made such stories as "Cinderella," "Sleeping Beauty," and "Little Red Riding Hood" standard fare in children's literature. In the early nineteenth century, the famous Grimm brothers gathered together German folktales, which included, not surprisingly, versions of "Cinderella" ("Aschenputtel") and "Little Red Riding Hood" ("Little Red Cap"), as well as such familiar favorites as "Snow White and the Seven Dwarfs."

In fact, none of these early collectors recorded the tales specifically for children. Many people even thought folktales too harsh for children and sought to protect them from these stories. But children, of course, devoured the tales anyway. It was not until the last half of the nineteenth century that folktales were actually collected and retold for children. The most noted retellers were the English collector Joseph Jacobs, famed for his *English Fairy Tales,* and Andrew Lang, who brought children fairy tales from all over the world in a celebrated series: *The Blue Fairy Book, The Red Fairy Book, The Green Fairy Book,* and so on through twelve colors. Since that time, folktales have been virtually the exclusive property of children. The twentieth century has seen an explosion in the interest in folklore, and hundreds, even thousands, of collections of tales have come out all over the world. Moe and Abjörnson's *East o' the Sun, West o' the Moon* is a popular collection of Scandinavian folktales; the poet Padraic Colum has given us beautiful versions of the classical Greek myths as well as the Norse myths, and more recently storytellers such as Virginia Hamilton and Julius Lester have supplied versions of African-American tales and myths for children.

All the collectors we have mentioned may have revised and polished the stories they presented, but they did not invent them. That is the hallmark of folk literature: It remains the property of the people, not of an individual narrator. There are, of course, some writers who, following folktale patterns, create their own original tales. Hans Christian Andersen did some of this (although many of his tales have clear sources in Scandinavian folklore). Critic John Ruskin and humorist James Thurber have tried their hands at this art too. These original tales are technically not "folktales." Some people prefer to call these tales literary fairy tales, because original works of a known author are not the same things as folktales. True folktales have lasted for centuries and have undergone (and are still undergoing) dramatic changes in form and content. But it is interesting to note that, even when we are reading literary fairy tales, the qualities we look for are the freshness and spontaneity of the old tales.

The old tales have been told and retold, updated and embellished, distorted and expurgated, yet still survive—an indication of their tough endurance. With each retelling, the tales are changed to suit the teller's individual tastes and purposes. Their adaptability is perhaps the source of their vitality. It is right that each succeeding generation retell the tales to suit the changing times.

BIBLIOGRAPHY OF CRITICAL STUDIES

Bettelheim, Bruno. *The Uses of Enchantment: The Meaning and Importance of Fairy Tales.* New York: Knopf, 1976.

Campbell, Joseph. *The Hero with a Thousand Faces.* 2d ed. Princeton, NJ: Princeton University Press, 1968.

Cook, Elizabeth. *The Ordinary and the Fabulous.* Cambridge, U.K.: Cambridge University Press, 1969.

Luthi, Max. *Once Upon a Time: On the Nature of Fairy Tales.* Bloomington, IN: Indiana University Press, 1976.

Sawyer, Ruth. *The Way of the Storyteller.* New York: Viking, 1962.

Shedlock, Marie L. *The Art of the Storyteller.* New York: Dover, 1951.

Storr, Catherine. "Folk and Fairy Tales." *Children's Literature in Education* 17 (Spring 1986): 63–70.

Thompson, Stith. *The Folktale.* New York: Holt, Rinehart and Winston, 1951.

Walker, Virginia, and Mary E. Lunz. "Symbols, Fairy Tales and School-Age Children." *The Elementary School Journal* (November 1976): 94–100.

Yolen, Jane. *Touch Magic.* New York: Philomel (Putnam), 1981.

FOLKTALE COLLECTIONS

Scores of individual folktales can be found in the form of children's picture-books. Below is a brief selection from the vast number of collected folktales, fables, and legends that are available for older children. Also included are some notable editions of national epics. Check the booklist following Chapter 2 for picture-book versions of individual tales.

Aesop's Fables. Illustrated by Fritz Kredel. New York: Grosset & Dunlap, 1947.

Asbjörnsen, Peter, and Jorgen Moe. *East o' the Sun and West o' the Moon.* New York: Dover, 1970. Scandinavian folktales.

Bloch, Marie Halun. *Ukrainian Folk Tales.* New York: Coward, McCann & Geoghegan, 1964.

Briggs, Katharine. *British Folk Tales.* New York: Pantheon Books, 1977.

Bryson, Bernarda, reteller. *Gilgamesh.* New York: Holt, Rinehart and Winston, 1967.

Bushnaq, Inea, tr. *Arab Folktales*. New York: Pantheon Books, 1986.

Chandler, Robert, tr. *Russian Folk Tales*. New York: Shambhala/Random House, 1980.

Chase, Richard. *The Jack Tales*. Boston: Houghton Mifflin, 1971. American tall tales.

Cole, Joanna, selector. *Best-Loved Folktales of the World*. Garden City, NY: Doubleday, 1982.

Colum, Padraic. *The Children's Homer*. New York: Macmillan, 1982. Classical Greek mythology.

———. *The Children of Odin*. New York: Macmillan, 1984. Norse mythology.

Coolidge, Olivia. *Greek Myths*. Boston: Houghton Mifflin, 1949.

de Wit, Dorothy. *The Talking Stone: An Anthology of Native American Tales and Legends*. New York: Greenwillow (Morrow), 1979.

Finger, Charles. *Tales from Silver Lands*. New York: Doubleday, 1924. Native Central American folktales.

Gág, Wanda. *Tales from Grimm*. New York: Coward, McCann & Geoghegan, 1981.

Glassie, Henry. *Irish Folk Tales*. New York: Pantheon Books, 1985.

Goldston, Robert, reteller. *The Legend of the Cid*. Indianapolis: Bobbs-Merrill, 1963.

Green, Roger Lancelyn. *Heroes of Greece and Troy: Retold from the Ancient Authors*. Illustrated by Heather Copley and Christopher Chamberlain. New York: Walck, 1961.

Grimm, Jakob, and Wilhelm Grimm. *Household Stories*. Translated by Lucy Crane. New York: Dover, 1963.

Hamilton, Virginia. *In the Beginning: Creation Stories from Around the World*. New York: Harcourt Brace Jovanovich, 1988.

———. *The People Could Fly*. New York: Knopf, 1985. African-American folktales.

Haviland, Virginia. *Favorite Tales Told in India*. Boston: Little, Brown, 1973.

Hieatt, Constance, reteller. *Sir Gawain and the Green Knight*. Illustrated by Walter Lorraine. New York: Crowell, 1967.

Hoogasian-Villa, Susie. *One Hundred Armenian Tales*. Detroit: Wayne State University Press, 1966.

Jacobs, Joseph. *Celtic Fairy Tales*. New York: Dover, 1968.

———. *English Fairy Tales*. New York: Dover, 1967.

Kingsley, Charles. *The Heroes*. New York: Dutton, 1963.

Lang, Andrew. *The Blue Fairy Book*. New York: Dover, 1965.

———. *The Green Fairy Book*. New York: Dover, 1965.

———. *The Red Fairy Book*. New York: Dover, 1966.

Lester, Julius. *Black Folktales*. New York: Baron, 1969.

MacLeod, Mary. *The Book of King Arthur and His Noble Knights*. Philadelphia: Lippincott, 1949.

Malcolmson, Anne, ed. *The Song of Robin Hood*. Boston: Houghton Mifflin, 1947.

Nic Leodhas, Sorche. *Thistle and Thyme: Tales and Legends from Scotland*. New York: Holt, Rinehart and Winston, 1962.

Opie, Iona, and Peter Opie. *The Classic Fairy Tales*. New York: Oxford University Press, 1974.

Phelps, Ethel Johnson. *The Maid of the North: Feminist Folk Tales from Around the World*. New York: Holt, Rinehart and Winston, 1981.

Pyle, Howard. *Some Merry Adventures of Robin Hood*. New York: Scribner, 1954.

———. *The Story of King Arthur and His Knights*. New York: Scribner, 1954.

Sherwood, Merriam, tr. *The Song of Roland*. New York: McKay, 1938.

Singer, Isaac Bashevis. *Zlateh the Goat and Other Stories*. New York: Harper, 1966. Yiddish folktales.

Thompson, Vivian L. *Hawaiian Tales of Heroes and Champions*. New York: Holiday House, 1971.

Westwood, Jennifer, reteller. *Gilgamesh and Other Babylonian Tales*. New York: Coward, McCann & Geoghegan, 1970.

Wolkstein, Diane. *The Magic Orange and Other Haitian Folktales*. New York: Knopf, 1978.

Yeats, W. B., and Lady Gregory. *A Treasury of Irish Myth, Legend, and Folklore*. New York: Avenel, 1986.

Yolen, Jane, ed. *Favorite Folktales from Around the World*. New York: Pantheon Books, 1986.

CHAPTER 6

Mother Goose Rhymes

DEFINITION

A great deal of time has been devoted to speculations on the origin of the term "Mother Goose." Suffice it to say that the seventeenth-century French reteller of folktales, Charles Perrault, named his book *Tales from Mother Goose,* and that by the end of the eighteenth century "Mother Goose" was clearly associated with a teller of nursery rhymes for young children—at least in the United States. Mother Goose rhymes (in England they are called nursery rhymes) are typically a child's first introduction to literature, beginning with the parents' singing of lullabies, such as "Rock-a-bye, Baby," or counting out tiny toes with "This little pig went to market."

THE ORIGINS OF MOTHER GOOSE RHYMES

Most Mother Goose rhymes are folk literature and as such were passed down by word of mouth long before they were written down. While some nursery rhymes are exceedingly old (the counting-out rhyme "Eena, meena, mona, my" and its variations seem to harken back to the sounds of ancient names for the numerals), most date from the sixteenth, seventeenth, and eighteenth centuries. "The Three Blind Mice" was set to music as early as 1609; "Jack Sprat" may have ridiculed a certain Archdeacon Spratt in the midseventeenth century, and some identify "Jack Horner" with Thomas Horner of Mells whose "plum" was much valuable land he acquired through Henry VIII's dissolution of the monasteries in 1536. Nursery rhymes are derived from a number of sources: war songs, romantic lyrics, proverbs, riddles, political jingles and lampoons, street cries (the early counterparts of today's television commercials), and unknown. But one thing can be said for certain: Few or none were initially intended for children.

Nursery rhymes are often delightfully irreverent (a feature that distinguishes them from most folktales, which extoll the virtues of compassion, generosity, and humility), and their heroes come typically from the lower walks of life: Simple Simon, Tom the Piper's Son, Mother Hubbard, the Old Woman in the Shoe, and so on. Those that do include kings and queens frequently have a satirical bite to them.

It has often been pointed out that the nursery rhymes contain their share of violence. Some of this realism could be shocking if we take it literally: babes dropping from treetops, cradle and all; a farmer's wife cutting off the tails (some say "heads") of three blind mice; a beleaguered old woman giving her children broth without bread and soundly whipping them; a man imprisoning his troublesome wife in a pumpkin shell; and so on. One assiduous critic, Geoffrey Handley-Taylor, noted that in a single collection of 200 familiar nursery rhymes, he discovered clearly 100 rhymes with "unsavoury elements," including eight allusions to murder, two cases of choking to death, one case of decapitation, seven cases of severing of limbs, one case of body snatching, four cases of breaking of limbs, and the list goes on (cited in Baring-Gould 1962, 20). The important thing to realize is that this "violence" is not sensationalized and the context of the violence is not only fictional but absurd. (Who puts wives in pumpkin shells? Who really lives in a shoe?) The violence is never presented realistically or seriously, and it may effectively serve to help children vent those hostilities and pent-up anxieties to which all human beings are subject.

THE IMPORTANCE OF MOTHER GOOSE RHYMES

Perhaps the only defense that Mother Goose rhymes need is that they are purely fun; their delightful nonsense and wonderful characters remain with us long beyond childhood. We should never underestimate the value of the sheer pleasure that literature can offer, but these rhymes, in fact, provide much more than an enjoyable pastime. Mother Goose rhymes may actually contribute significantly to a child's development in a surprising variety of ways.

Cognitive Development

With such rhymes as "One, two, buckle your shoe/Three, four, shut the door," and "One, two, three, four, five/Once I caught a fish alive," young children are encouraged to learn numbers and counting. The letters of the alphabet are the subjects of such rhymes as "A—apple pie." Nursery rhymes—perhaps because many of them were originally intended for adults—often include challenging words. "Mary, Mary, quite *contrary*" or "Jack be *nimble*" or "Peter Piper picked a *peck of pickled peppers*" all provide opportunities for young children to expand their vocabularies painlessly. And we must not forget that because the nursery rhymes are easily memorized, young children frequently are able to "pretend" to read them and soon, almost without knowing it, actually begin to read the words. In this way, Mother Goose can be a tremendous stimulant to reading.

We must not forget too that the appreciation of nonsense, such as that in most nursery rhymes, requires a firm grasp of reality, for nonsense is only amusing if we see its absurdity, its incongruity, when we place it next to what we know to be real. Therefore, it might be argued that Mother Goose rhymes help to develop a child's sense of humor in that they force intellectual comparisons of fantasy with reality.

Aesthetic Development

By aesthetic development, we mean the forming of an appreciation for beautiful things; in the case of literature, we are referring specifically to an appreciation of the beauty of language. Mother Goose rhymes appeal to a child's natural sense of rhythm—perhaps learned in the womb from the steady rhythm of the mother's heartbeat. The repeated refrains also provide children with the pleasures of anticipating something familiar. The playful use of sounds, including those wonderful nonsense words, appeals to the natural delight and curiosity that very young children find in language. The rhymes also encourage children to experiment in the making of sounds—a necessary process. Children learn to speak through much experimentation, aided by the encouraging responses of adults. In Japan, for example, when toddlers say "Dada" (as they surely do) no one gets excited, for that sound carries no semantic meaning in Japanese. But in English "Dada" means something important, as the child discovers when his parents react to his babbling with delight.

In addition to providing children with a wonderful introduction to linguistic sounds, the nature of rhyming, and the joy of rhythm, nursery rhymes also develop a child's sensitivity to *pattern*. The idea of pattern forms the basis of much of art, for pattern imposes form, order, and logic on life. "A little girl was sitting on the ground eating and was scared away by a spider" is an event in life. But notice how much more memorable the scene is when a pattern is imposed on the content as follows:

> Little Miss Muffet sat on a tuffet
> Eating her curds and whey;
> > Along came a spider
> > And sat down beside her
> And frightened Miss Muffet away.

Naturally, we hope that, with maturity, readers come to appreciate more sophisticated poetry than this, but without this foundation—verse forms and the repetition of sound that we call rhyme—a deeper appreciation is not very likely to develop.

Mother Goose rhymes may also help children recognize the distinction between fact and fiction—that is, understanding when something is a "story" and when it is "real life." This is not to suggest that fiction may not reveal deep truths about life. That is part of the miracle of literature. But being able to draw a line between the events of a story and the events of their real lives is a distinction that is absolutely essential if children are to lead psychologically healthy lives. In addition to recognizing a fictional work, children may also begin to comprehend rudimentary plot structures. The above example of Miss Muffet contains the basic elements of a simple plot structure: a conflict between a protagonist and antagonist, a climax with the confrontation, and a denouement or conclusion. Nursery rhymes are children's first introduction to fictional characters and fictional events, and these rudimentary experiences can prepare them for the somewhat more complex fictional experiences awaiting them in the folktales. And finally, the rhymes, with their vivid imagery and precise mental pictures, provide an important stimulus to children's imaginations.

Emotional Development

Children return again and again to favorite nursery rhymes, which become like old friends, providing a measure of security. This is important for very young children, to whom every day presents a host of new and unusual experiences. The frank realism of many of the rhymes may help children in coping with aggressive behavior. Some psychologists believe that children who are able to vent aggressive feelings through literature and art are less likely to vent those feelings by throwing tantrums or popping their siblings and friends in the noses. That Mother Goose rhymes can provide similar assistance in emotional growth has been suggested (see Bremner, "The World According to Mother Goose," and, for a related discussion but one focusing on folktales, see Bettelheim, *The Uses of Enchantment,* cited in Chapter 5).

Social and Physical Development

Many nursery rhymes are based on cooperative play—"Pat-a-cake, pat-a-cake" requires physical coordination and interpersonal contact, for example. Other rhymes, such as "Ring-a-ring o' roses" or "London Bridge is falling down," require the interaction of several children and thus encourage games and cooperative play. Jump-rope rhymes are simply nursery rhymes gone to the playground, and they have been shown to exhibit a considerable amount of aggression, and even hostility. Take this popular jump-rope jingle, for instance:

> Fudge, fudge, tell the judge
> Mother has a newborn baby;
> It isn't a girl and it isn't a boy;
> It's just a fair young lady.
> Wrap it up in tissue paper
> And send it up the elevator:
> First floor, miss;
> Second floor, miss;
> Third floor, miss;
> Fourth floor,
> Kick it out the elevator door.

In one playful action, the skipping children are developing large motor coordination skills, engaging in a cooperative social activity, and rather harmlessly verbalizing some of the hostility that is an inevitable part of every sibling relationship. It is more socially acceptable than punching out one's kid brother—and almost as efficacious.

CHOOSING MOTHER GOOSE BOOKS

A good Mother Goose book is typically a picture-book and may be evaluated along standards similar to those applied to picture-books. However, it is also desirable that there be a balance between both the familiar rhymes and the more unfamiliar ones. The inclusion of rhymes from other cultures—African, Asian, Native American—is also the sign of a healthy Mother Goose collection. Additionally, the format of the book is important. Uncluttered page layouts with the illustrations right next to the rhymes they depict are the most appealing. Because prices of children's books can run high, most people will prefer a Mother Goose book containing a generous number of rhymes to one with only a handful. The large collections (such as those of de Angeli, Briggs, Wright, and Smith noted in the bibliography) contain hundreds of ryhmes, not all of which are illustrated. But a few unillustrated rhymes may be a small sacrifice for the sake of a richer variety of verses. And, for the adult reader, an index, table of contents, or other reference aids may be very helpful. Every household with children deserves to have a good collection of Mother Goose rhymes—and if they select a book with a good verse collection, it will, before all is said and done, be a well-worn, perhaps even tattered, book.

Illustrators of Mother Goose

Jack Sprat. "Jack Sprat" has been especially popular among illustrators of Mother Goose rhymes and has inspired a wide variety of individual interpretations. The appeal of this nursery rhyme for illustrators has undoubtedly been the opportunity afforded by its two distinctive characters, each with a clearly defined character trait. The accompanying illustrations suggest the range of artistic styles one might find available in Mother Goose books.

JACK SPRAT

Jack Sprat could eat no fat,

His wife could eat no lean,

And so between them both, you see,

They licked the platter clean.

Figure 6.1. Raymond Briggs's little drawing captures the Sprats in their most bizarre behavior—that of licking the platter clean. Appropriate to the subject, Briggs's style is cartoon, which heightens the effect of the absurd.

Figure 6.2. Blanche Fisher Wright depicts an eighteenth-century husband and his solicitous mate. Typical of her illustrations for the popular collection, *The Real Mother Goose*, the lines are clean and sharp and her characters well-defined.

Figure 6.3. Marguerite de Angeli's lush painting of the Sprats from her *Book of Nursery and Mother Goose Rhymes* is a feast for the eye. Her illustration contrasts interestingly with Wright's, for although both these artists have chosen virtually the same pose (even to the pet before the table), de Angeli's use of line makes her version much more animated. De Angeli's style comes closer to Expressionism, although she is still seeking that pictorial quality of representational art.

J ACK SPRAT could eat no fat,
   His wife could eat no lean:

And so, betwixt them both, you see,
   They lick'd the platter clean.

Figure 6.4. L. Leslie Brooke depicts a decidedly older couple and from an earlier time—the costumes are fifteenth century. As always with Brooke, a close examination of his illustration reveals his wry humor: Notice the Sprats' coat-of-arms, displaying a bovine fattened for market. Like many Victorian children's artists, Brooke imbued his representational drawings with rich, subtle details.

Little Miss Muffet. "Little Miss Muffet" is one of the great dramas of the nursery. It is a wonderfully constructed tale, complete with setting, characters, conflict, climax, and resolution. With its clearly defined beginning, middle, and end, and its distinct characterization, this rhyme has been among the most popular of all Mother Goose verses. Most illustrators understandably choose to depict the moment just prior to the verse's climax: It provides the most drama and the greatest possibilities for interpretation. The accompanying illustrations indicate the extent of these interpretations.

Little Miss Muffet,
Sat on a tuffet,
Eating some curds and whey ;
There came a great spider,
And sat down beside her,
And frightened Miss Muffet away.

Figure 6.5. Kate Greenaway could not bring herself to include unsavory elements in her illustrations; consequently she detracts from the drama by focusing all attention on the prim and proper Miss Muffet. The spider is barely noticeable off to the left. The colors are subdued and contribute to the air of quietness belying the circumstances.

Little Miss Muffett

Figure 6.6. Arthur Rackham, on the other hand, portrays a truly monstrous-looking, but not ungentlemanly, spider. The spider's appearance completely overwhelms the picture, and there is a wonderful contrast between the sedate Miss Muffet (somewhat more mature than Greenaway's), her lip daintily pursed, and the grotesque creature about to interrupt her. Rackham's Surrealistic, frequently nightmarish, quality is tempered here by a bit of wry humor as the spider gallantly doffs his hat.

LITTLE MISS MUFFET

Little Miss Muffet
Sat on a tuffet,
Eating her curds and whey;
There came a big spider,
Who sat down beside her
And frightened Miss Muffet away.

Figure 6.7. Raymond Briggs likewise portrays a looming creature, but his Miss Muffet looks more like a nineteenth-century school marm. The fact that Briggs's spider does not have the anatomically correct number of legs need not bother us, since the illustration is in a cartoon style and exaggerations and distortions are to be expected.

Little Miss Muffet
Sat on a tuffet,
Eating her curds and whey;
Along came a spider,
Who sat down beside her
And frightened Miss Muffet away.

Figure 6.8. Alice and Martin Provensen depict the real moment of drama in the rhyme—Miss Muffet actually encountering the spider and her spilling of the curds and whey. The old-fashioned flavor of the illustration, reminiscent of eighteenth-century New England Folk Art, helps to distance the viewer from the action, and Miss Muffet's horror is therefore not necessarily shared by the audience.

BIBILOGRAPHY OF CRITICAL STUDIES

Baring-Gould, William S., and Ceil Baring-Gould. *The Annotated Mother Goose*. New York: Potter, 1962.

Bodger, Joan. "Mother Goose: Is the Old Girl Relevant?" *Wilson Library Bulletin* (December 1969): 402–408.

Bremner, Moyra. "The World According to Mother Goose." *Parents Magazine* (December 1983):61–67.

Butler, Francelia. "Skip-Rope Rhymes as a Reflection of American Culture." In *Sharing Literature with Children*, edited by Francelia Butler. 8–14. New York: Longman, 1977.

Chisolm, Margaret. "Mother Goose—Elucidated." *Elementary School English* (December 1972): 1141–1144.

Eckenstein, Lina. *Comparative Studies in Nursery Rhymes*. 1906. Detroit: Singing Tree, 1968.

Green, Percy B. *A History of Nursery Rhymes*. Detroit: Singing Tree, 1968.

Nadasan, Ardell. "Mother Goose Sexist?" *Elementary English* (March 1974): 375–378.

Opie, Iona, and Peter Opie. *The Oxford Dictionary of Nursery Rhymes*. Oxford: Oxford University Press, (Clarendon Press), 1951.

Thomas, Katherine Lewis. *The Real Personages of Mother Goose*. New York: Lothrop, 1930.

MOTHER GOOSE COLLECTIONS

The following list is only a brief selection of the many Mother Goose and Nursery Rhyme collections available.

Alderson, Brian, comp. *The Helen Oxenbury Nursery Rhyme Book*. Illustrated by Helen Oxenbury. New York: Morrow, 1986.

Baring-Gould, William S., and Ceil Baring-Gould, eds. *The Annotated Mother Goose*. New York: New American Library, 1967.

Briggs, Raymond, illus. *The Mother Goose Treasury*. New York: Coward, McCann & Geoghegan, 1966.

de Angeli, Marguerite, illus. *Book of Nursery and Mother Goose Rhymes*. Garden City, NY: Doubleday, 1953.

Hader, Berta, and Elmer Hader. *Picture Book of Mother Goose*. 1930. New York: Crown, 1987.

Lang, Andrew, ed. *The Nursery Rhyme Book*. Illustrated by L. Leslie Brooke. New York: Dover, 1972.

Lines, Kathleen, ed. *Lavender's Blue*. Illustrated by Harold Jones. New York: Watts, 1973.

Lobel, Arnold, illus. *The Random House Book of Mother Goose*. New York: Random House, 1986.

Opie, Iona, and Peter Opie, eds. *The Oxford Nursery Rhyme Book*. New York: Oxford University Press (Clarendon Press), 1955.

Petersham, Maud, and Miska Petersham, illus. *The Rooster Crows: A Book of American Rhymes and Jingles*. New York: Macmillan, 1945.

Provensen, Alice, and Martin Provensen, illus. *The Mother Goose Book*. New York: Random House, 1976.

Rackham, Arthur, illus. *Mother Goose*. New York: Marathon. 1978.

Reed, Philip, illus. *Mother Goose and Nursery Rhymes*. New York: Atheneum, 1963.

Scarry, Richard, illus. *Richard Scarry's Mother Goose*. New York: Western, 1983.

Smith, Jessie Willcox, illus. *The Jessie Willcox Smith Mother Goose*. New York: Derrydale, 1986.

Tripp, Wallace, illus. *Granfa' Grig Had a Pig and Other Rhymes Without Reason from Mother Goose*. Boston: Little, Brown, 1976.

Tudor, Tasha, illus. *Mother Goose*. New York: Walck, 1944.

Wildsmith, Brian, illus. *Brian Wildsmith's Mother Goose*. New York: Watts, 1965.

Wright, Blanche Fisher, illus. *The Real Mother Goose*. New York: Rand McNally, 1916.

CHAPTER 7

Poetry

DEFINITION

Perhaps one of the loveliest descriptions of poetry comes from the poet Paul Roche, who remarked that poetry is like a stained-glass window: It lets the light shine through but exists for its own beauty. The "light" is a metaphor for knowledge, wisdom, or truth. The "beauty" refers to both the sounds of the language and the poet's imaginative use of the language, creating fresh and stimulating imagery. Good poetry is the effective combination of sound and sense. As adults we typically have little use for beautiful sounding words if they make no sense. Nevertheless, most nonsense verse—such as that of Edward Lear or Lewis Carroll—possesses its own internal logic (even if it is a logical contradiction of logic). Conversely, a profound thought expressed in a clumsy, inarticulate fashion would hardly be labeled poetic.

Poetry is the most personal of all literary forms, and as such is the most misunderstood. We often labor under the misconception that poetry is obscure (a puzzle to be unraveled by English teachers), "pretty" (without any particular meaning), and not about anything especially important (mostly flowers, birds, and brooks). These are the very misconceptions that are passed on to children—the very children who could not get enough of Mother Goose rhymes or the delightful verses of Jack Prelutsky, Shel Silverstein, and others. And many of these children may have dabbled in poetry writing themselves in early elementary school. Unfortunately, the approach to poetry in many classrooms actually encourages a fear and even a dislike of poetry among most children. But it does not have to be that way. Poetry—good poetry at least—is not intended to be obscure and to "muddy" things up, but is supposed to enlighten us, to make us see something we have not seen before, feel something we have never felt. The best poetry is a union of beauty and truth, but we must not forget that the best poets speak to us with *beauty that we can appreciate* and in *truths that we can understand*.

POETRY FOR THE VERY YOUNG

Toddlers and preschoolers, as we might expect, respond first to the beauty of poetry and not its truth. Infants and preschoolers are captivated by the sounds of "Pat-a-cake, pat-a-cake," or "Hickory dickory dock"—the fact that these are largely nonsense sounds is decidedly secondary to the enjoyment. And Lewis Carroll's "Jabberwocky" remains a pleasure to listen to and to read, however obscure its meaning. All poetry is musical, and rhythm is a fundamental quality of poetry. Babies respond to rhythmical patterns almost from birth, whether it be swaying or rocking or a simple caressing of the back. And who is to say that our first sensory experience is not, in fact, prenatal—that steady, rhythmical pulsation of our mother's body and the gentle undulations of the embryonic fluids sweeping about us? And, of course, rhythm is everpresent in nature, the orbiting of the planets and the cyclical birth, flourishing, death, and rebirth revealed to us through the changing seasons. Rhythm—be it in nursery rhymes or Shakespeare—is inseparable from poetry, although the more sophisticated the poem, the less obvious the rhythm. The point is that poetry and music spring from the same impulse, and we may even suggest that the love of poetry is a natural impulse, and that music, dancing, and poetry are all parts of our earliest artistic expression.

But poetry is as much an appeal to the mind's eye as it is to the ear. Once children begin to comprehend meaning through language, they begin to demand vivid mental images in their stories and poems. (Hence, we have one of the reasons that the folktales are so successful with the very young, for those tales rely heavily on sharp, concrete images to convey their messages.) Imagery in literature is simply the quality that allows language to paint pictures with words. The Mother Goose rhymes are filled with memorable mental pictures: Miss Muffet on her tuffet, Jack and Jill tumbling down the hill, another Jack suspended in midair over a candlestick, and the miserable Old Woman attempting to corral her unruly children into an oversized shoe. It is no accident that nursery rhymes are among the most-often illustrated of children's literature. The vivid pictures conveyed by the words so readily lend themselves to the artist's brush and pen.

TOOLS OF THE TRADE: THE FORMS OF POETRY

When we talk about poetry, it is easy to get bogged down with complex terminology and obscure references, and it is certainly not necessary for children to be able to recognize and label poetic techniques. But in order for us, as adults, to appreciate fully the craft of the poet, it is helpful to have at least a passing acquaintance with the poet's "tools." There are two sets of tools: the poem's *external form* (usually identified as a stanza) and the poem's *internal sound and imagery.* Let us start by considering the external forms of poetry, for the first decision a poet must make concerns the choice of poetic form. Which one will best suit the particular message he or she wishes to convey?

Narrative Poetry

Narrative poems tell (or narrate) a story. The most accessible narrative poems for children are ballads. Ballads are typically straightforward and easy to understand; like a story, they include a setting, characters, and events with a climax. (Many readers find ballads less intimidating than the shorter, more compact lyric poems.) Most ballads follow a four-line scheme with the second and fourth lines rhyming, such as in this stanza from the anonymous ballad called "The Dying Cowboy" or "The Streets of Laredo":

> Let sixteen gamblers come handle my coffin,
> Let sixteen young cowboys come sing me a song,
> Take me to the green valley and lay the sod o'er me,
> For I'm a poor cowboy and I know I've done wrong.*

Occasionally, ballads (like the above) are set to music, and the perennial favorite "Wreck of the Edmund Fitzgerald" by Gordon Lightfoot is an interesting example of a modern-day disaster supplying the inspiration for a modern-day ballad.

A hundred years ago, lengthy narrative poems enjoyed some popularity, but today few readers, young and old alike, have the patience required to read them. Nevertheless, Robert Browning's *The Pied Piper of Hamelin* and Henry Wadsworth Longfellow's *The Song of Hiawatha* are examples of nineteenth-century narrative verse that are still found in print. Longfellow's famous lines from *Hiawatha*—work based on a famous Native American legends of the Great Lakes—demonstrate the twin talents of the storyteller and the lyricist, which are commonly found in narrative poetry:

> By the shores of Gitche Gumee,
> By the shining Big-Sea-Water,
> Stood the wigwam of Nokomis,
> Daughter of the Moon, Nokomis,
> Dark behind it rose the forest,
> Rose the black and gloomy pine-trees,
> Rose the firs with cones upon them;
> Bright before it beat the water,
> Beat the clear and sunny water,
> Beat the shining Big-Sea-Water.

The early twentieth-century poet Alfred Noyes wrote narrative poems imbued with drama on subjects that appeal to readers in the upper elementary years, such as "The Highwayman" and "A Song of Sherwood."

Lyric Poetry

By far the most popular poetry enjoyed by children is *lyric poetry*. Lyric poetry expresses a poet's emotional or intellectual response to a subject. Unlike a narrative poem, a lyric does not tell a story, but describes the feeling of a moment. Lyrics tend to focus on a single experience and are brief, which undoubtedly accounts for much of their popularity. In the absence of exciting narrative action, the lyric must depend heavily on musical and rhythmical qualities. There seems to be an endless variety of stanza forms in lyric poetry, and new ones are still being created. Some forms have proved very popular with children, and we shall look at just a few.

---

* There are many versions of this popular folksong, so don't be surprised if the words you know differ from this version.

Haiku. The Japanese *haiku* consists typically of seventeen syllables divided into three lines and usually on the subject of nature and our relationship to nature, such as this by Ruby Lytle:

> The moon is a week old—
> A dandelion to blow
> Scattering star seed.

The strength of haiku lies in its suggestive quality. In this haiku, the imagery of the stars seen as tiny seeds blown from the moon, a whispery soft dandelion puff gone to seed, brings us at once closer to the starry night sky and reminds us of that curious interrelationship of all nature. Successful haiku uses metaphor (which will be further explained below) to give us a fresh and imaginative look at something we view as quite ordinary.

Cinquain. The *cinquain* generally consists of five lines containing two, four, six, eight, and two syllables, respectively. Teachers of young children, however, might employ a modified cinquain consisting of five lines containing one, two, three, four, and one words, respectively. The first word, always a noun, serves as the title and subject. The second line contains two adjectives describing the noun; the third line contains three present participles also describing the noun; the fourth line contains a four-word statement about the noun; and the last line is a single noun that is a synonym for the subject. The following cinquain was written by a group of fourth graders working together:

> Nature
> Beautiful, quiet,
> Blowing, glowing, sparkling,
> Running happily in Spring—
> Living.

Concrete Poetry. When the words of a poem are so arranged that they form a pictorial representation of the subject of the poem, we have what is called a *concrete poem*. These are really not new, for the English Metaphysical poets were practicing this sort of poetry in the seventeenth century. George Herbert, for example, wrote "The Altar" so that the lines formed the shape of an altar; also popular were poems in shapes of crosses and pyramids, and Herbert's "Easter Wings" was designed to suggest angel wings. In the twentieth century, much more liberty has been taken with this sort of thing, and sometimes the poem will consist of only letters or perhaps a single word repeated to create a visual pattern. Such works can only loosely be considered poetry, perhaps, but they do invite imitation by young children and can generate enthusiasm for poetry.

Limerick. Among the most popular forms for children is the *limerick,* a five-line humorous poem, the first, second, and fifth rhyming, and the third and fourth rhyming. The following limerick has been attributed to President Woodrow Wilson:

> I sat next to the Duchess at tea;
> It was just as I thought it would be;
>   Her rumblings abdominal
>   Were simply phenomenal,
> And everyone thought it was me.

The limerick's form is easily imitated, and young children can have a great deal of fun creating their own.

Free Verse. The twentieth century has popularized *free verse,* which adheres to no set of predetermined rules, but nevertheless good free verse establishes its own criteria for rhyming and rhythmical patterns. Free verse is much more demanding on the poet than most readers suppose, and it requires the same thoughtful choice of words and sentence patterns as the more rigid stanza forms. The following example, "The Drum," was written by Nikki Giovanni while working with a group of young children. Notice how it focuses on a single concrete image:

> daddy says the world is
> a drum tight and hard
> and i told him
> i'm gonna beat
> out my own rhythm

There are potentially as many stanza forms as there are poets. For example, we have omitted here a discussion of the *sonnet* (a sophisticated 14-line stanza with an intricate rhyme scheme) as well as other widely used forms that are primarily restricted to poetry for adults. Perhaps the best we can do for children is to make them aware of the vast array of choices open to them as both readers and writers of poetry, and in this way try to prevent some of the misconceptions that arise about what a poem is.

TOOLS OF THE TRADE: THE ELEMENTS OF POETRY

Poetry—like all literature—depends upon the effective union of form and content, but poetry is at once more compact than most literature and more reliant upon certain literary devices for its effect. These devices constitute the second set of tools that the poet uses to create interesting and stimulating poetry. The skilled poet knows when and how to use these tools to the greatest advantage.

Sound Patterns

Most poems are written expressly for oral delivery, and consequently how they sound is extremely important. *Rhythm,* one of the most important features of all poetry, is simply the pattern of stressed and unstressed syllables in a poem. Nursery rhymes tend to have very regular rhythms, which result in a singsong quality. More sophisticated poetry, in an attempt to avoid monotony, may exhibit subtly varied rhythms for a musical quality.

Rhyme, as we all know, is achieved through the similarity of sound that exists between two or more words. *Alliteration* is the repetition of initial sounds in two words, such as the *b* and *l* sounds in these lines by A. E. Housman:

> **By b**rooks too **b**road for **l**eaping,
> The **l**ightfoot **b**oys are **l**aid.

Assonance is the repetition of identical vowel sounds, such as the long *a,* long *u,* and long *i* sounds in these lines by Carl Sandburg: "Let me be the great nail holding a skyscraper through blue nights into white stars."

Consonance is the repetition of consonant sounds within words, often with a variation in adjoining vowels, such as the **f** and **d** sounds in these lines by William Jay Smith:

> Butterflies . . .
> Gliding over field and stream—
> Like fans unfolding in a dream.

Obviously, too much of any repetitive sound pattern becomes noticeable and begins to detract from the content. The good poet knows just how much to include to make music, and just when to stop before the result is tongue-tying racket.

Imagery Devices

Imagery refers simply to mental pictures created by words. Since words are the poem's medium, their selection is the most crucial aspect of their creation.

Direct Images. Imagery may be direct, using a word or words to describe a sensory response to a subject. Images may be *visual,* referring to things we can see (shapes, sizes, colors). Images may be *tactile,* appealing to our sense of touch (slippery, rough, soft). *Auditory* images suggest the sounds of things (squeals, rumbles, thuds). *Olfactory* images suggest the smells of things (redolent, rank, sweet). *Kinesthetic* images refer to actions or motions (swift, slow, ambling). And *gustatory* images suggest the taste of things (rich, pungent, bitter, salty).

Indirect Images. Images may also be *indirect,* describing something by comparing it to something else with which we are more familiar. The three common methods of comparing are through similes, metaphors, and personification.

A *simile* is a stated comparison, employing a connective such as "like" or "as"; take Robert Burns' famous line: "My luve is like a red, red rose." The unknown is "My luve" (presumably the poet's girlfriend) and the known is the "red, red rose" (a flower, the poet assumes, that is familiar to his listeners). As readers/listeners we may have somewhat different attitudes toward the "red, red rose" (those who have violent allergies to roses are apt to have a quite different conception of roses from most readers), but most people think of them as examples of extraordinary delicacy and beauty. We would certainly have a very different conception of the lover if the poet had written, "My love is like a mighty oak." The poet's objective was not to confuse us, but to help us share in his good feelings about his lover.

A *metaphor* is an implied comparison, and is consequently often more subtle to grasp. In this brief poem "City," Langston Hughes implies a comparison of the city in morning with a songbird:

> In the morning the city
> Spreads its wings
> Making a song
> In stone that sings.

Or let us consider Carl Sandburg's familiar "Fog":

> The fog comes
> on little cat feet.
> It sits looking
> over harbor and city
> on silent haunches
> and then moves on.

The metaphor compares the fog (the unknown, since the poet is describing both a particular fog and his feelings about that fog) with a cat (the known). It is a poem of clear, sharp images; we clearly see a cat creeping stealthily into view, pausing, looking, and then stealing quietly away. The poem's form is significant also. The short lines may suggest delicate, catlike movements and carefully measured steps. The deliberately planted vowel sounds—particularly the *O*'s—contribute to the subtle, irregular rhythm, much as we might expect from a cat stepping over obstacles. It is an example of the form and the meaning successfully interweaving to create a satisfying whole that is greater than the individual parts.

One might also argue that both Sandburg and Hughes are using the third form of comparison, *personification,* the application of human or animate characteristics to an inanimate object, an abstract idea, or a force of nature. Personification is by its nature metaphorical, although all metaphors do not necessarily involve personification.

PRESENTING POETRY TO OLDER CHILDREN

As children mature and lay aside the nursery rhymes and Prelutsky and Silverstein, they require poetry equally vivid, but more intellectually challenging. Unfortunately, as has been suggested, poetry education in the schools most often results in children's stereotyping of poetry as something that is supposed to be "pretty," but not especially meaningful and certainly not useful. The best way to dispel these misconceptions is to make poetry a regular part of a child's reading program (rather than an intensive two-week unit to be forgotten as quickly as it was begun or a marathon week-long poetry drill once a year). And it is important to eliminate those tedious academic exercises (memorizing irrelevant poems, counting meters, scanning lines, and so on) that can form the academic study of poetry.

Most poetry is best read aloud and—in the classroom, at least—it is best read frequently. There are wonderful poems suitable for special occasions (or even ordinary occasions—poems for a partly cloudy day, for instance). Too often children are asked to read poems that were clearly intended for adults. And then we wonder why the children are confused or bored. The truth is that much of the poetry of our most revered poets speaks about adult emotions and adult perceptions of the world. How can we expect even teenagers to identify with these subjects? And we need not expect them to do so; there are plenty of very good poems for young readers. Every classroom and home should include a generous supply of poetry books, both anthologies and books by individual poets. With all the thousands of good poems available, every child is bound to find some favorites. The key is, of course, to supply a wide and varied sampling—poems on all subjects, poems representing a myriad of stanza and rhyme schemes and rhythms.

Children should be encouraged (but not required) to write poetry—but perhaps only after they have read a great deal and realized the possibilities open to them. It is also helpful to encourage children to form collections of their own favorite poems (and every adult presenting poetry to children should do the same). By all means, teachers should not presume to "grade" a student's poem—that's a surefire way of putting a damper on the fun. Artistic children may wish to illustrate poems. Young thespians may wish to deliver dramatic readings. Endless possibilities are offered by poetry—a well-presented poem can fill a relatively small time slot in a day and provide some welcome, joyous relief. If we begin to think of poetry in this fashion, we may begin to dispel some of the notions of drudgery and perplexity that currently surround poetry.

In many ways, a poet is a visionary, one who sees the world in fresh and unusual ways, and one who has the gift of making us see it too. The success of a poem depends upon this ability of the poet to make us share this vision. Adults have been notoriously unsuccessful in conveying this aspect of poetry to young people, partly because of their own distaste for so subtle a subject or fear of not understanding it. But the more we understand poetry, the better we come to know it, the richer our experience will be. And few literary forms offer such a wealth of pleasure and knowledge as poetry. Lovers of poetry are not born but made through patient and careful nurturing.

BIBLIOGRAPHY OF CRITICAL STUDIES

Baskin, Barbara Holland, Karen H. Harris, and Coleen C. Salley. "Making the Poetry Connection." *The Reading Teacher* 30 (December 1976): 259–265.

Ciardi, John, and Miller Williams. *How Does a Poem Mean?* 2d ed. Boston: Houghton Mifflin, 1975.

Fisher, Carol J., and Margaret A. Natarella. "Of Cabbages and Kings: Or What Kinds of Poetry Children Like." *Language Arts* 56: 4 (April 1979): 380–385.

Higginson, William J., with Penny Harter. *The Haiku Handbook: How to Write, Share and Teach Haiku.* New York: McGraw-Hill, 1985.

Hopkins, Lee Bennett. *Pass the Poetry Please.* New York: Citation Press, 1972.

Hurst, Carol. "What to Do with a Poem." *Early Years* 11 (February 1980): 28–29, 68.

Kennedy, X. J. "'Go and Get Your Candle Lit!' An Approach to Poetry." *Horn Book Magazine* 57: 3 (June 1981): 273–279.

Krogness, Mary Mercer. "Imagery and Image Making." *Elementary English* 51: 4 (April 1974): 488–490.

Larrick, Nancy, ed. *Somebody Turned on a Tap in These Kids.* New York: Dell (Delacorte Press), 1971.

Lewis, Marjorie. "Why Is a Poem a Four-Letter Word?" *School Library Journal* 23: 9 (May 1977): 38–39.

Shapiro, Jon E. *Using Literature and Poetry Affectively.* Newark, DE: International Reading Association, 1979.

Steiner, Barbara. "Writing Poetry for Children." *Writer's Digest* (February 1986): 34–35.

A BRIEF SELECTION OF POETRY ANTHOLOGIES
FOR YOUNG PEOPLE

The advantage of an anthology is that it provides a taste of the works of many different poets, and consequently anthologies are often a good place to get acquainted with poetry. This list provides a sampling of the many anthologies of poetry that have been compiled with young readers in mind.

Abdul, Raoul, ed. *The Magic of Black Poetry.* Illustrated by Dane Burr. New York: Dodd, Mead, 1972.

Adoff, Arnold, ed. *Celebrations: A New Anthology of Black American Poetry.* Chicago: Follett, 1977.

——. *The Poetry of Black America: An Anthology of the 20th Century.* New York: Harper, 1973.

Arbuthnot, May Hill, and Shelton L. Root, eds. *Time for Poetry.* Illustrated by Arthur Paul. Glenview, IL: Scott, Foresman, 1968.

Blishen, Edward, comp. *Oxford Book of Poetry for Children.* Illustrated by Brian Wildsmith. New York: Watts, 1963.

Cole, William, comp. *Poems of Magic and Spells.* Illustrated by Peggy Bacon. Cleveland: World, 1960.

De La Mare, Walter, ed. *Come Hither.* 3d ed. Illustrated by Warren Chappell. New York: Knopf, 1957.

——. *Tom Tiddler's Ground.* Illustrated by Margery Gill. New York: Knopf, 1962.

Dunning, Stephen, Edward Lueders, and Hugh Smith, comps. *Reflections on a Gift of Watermelon Pickle.* Glenview, IL: Scott, Foresman, 1967.

——. *Some Haystacks Don't Even Have Any Needle.* Glenview, IL: Scott, Foresman, 1969.

Houston, James, ed. *Songs of the Dream People.* New York: Atheneum, 1972. Eskimo and other Native American poems.

Jones, Hettie, sel. *The Trees Stand Shining: Poetry of the North American Indians.* Illustrated by Robert Andrew Parker. New York: Dial Press, 1971.

Larrick, Nancy, ed. *Piping Down the Valleys Wild.* Illustrated by Ellen Raskin. 1968. New York: Dell, 1982.

Livingston, Myra Cohn, comp. *Dilly Dilly Piccalilli: Poems for the Very Young.* New York: McElderry, 1989. Nonsense verse.

Moore, Lilian, ed. *Go with the Poem.* New York: McGraw-Hill, 1979.

Moore, Lilian, and Judith Thurman, comps. *To See the World Afresh.* New York: Atheneum, 1974.

Opie, Iona, and Peter Opie, eds. *The Oxford Book of Children's Verse.* New York: Oxford University Press, 1973.

Sullivan, Charles, ed. *Imaginary Gardens: American Poetry and Art for Young People.* New York: Abrams, 1989.

Townsend, John Rowe, comp. *Modern Poetry.* Philadelphia: Lippincott, 1974.

Whipple, Laura, comp. *Animals Animals.* Illustrated by Eric Carle. New York: Philomel (Putnam), 1989.

A BRIEF SELECTION OF POETRY BOOKS BY INDIVIDUAL POETS

Also look for other books by these popular poets.

Adoff, Arnold. *All the Colors of the Race.* Illustrated by John Steptoe. New York: Lothrop, 1982.

Armour, Richard. *A Dozen Dinosaurs.* Illustrated by Paul Galdone. New York: McGraw-Hill, 1970.

Blake, William. *Songs of Innocence and Experience.* Illustrated by Harold Jones. New York: Barnes, 1961.

Cawthorne, William Alexander. *Who Killed Cockatoo?* Illustrated by Rodney McRea. New York: Farrar, Straus & Giroux, 1989. Australian adaptation of "Who Killed Cock Robin?"

Ciardi, John. *The Man Who Sang the Sillies.* Illustrated by Edward Gorey. Philadelphia: Lippincott, 1961.

——. *The Reason for the Pelican.* Illustrated by Madeleine Gekiere. Philadelphia: Lippincott, 1959.

Coatsworth, Elizabeth. *Under the Green Willow.* Illustrated by Janina Domanska. New York: Macmillan, 1971.

Cummings, E. E. *Hist Whist.* Illustrated by Deborah Kogan Ray. New York: Crown, 1989.

De La Mare, Walter. *Peacock Pie.* Illustrated by Barbara Cooney. New York: Knopf, 1961.

Dickinson, Emily. *Letter to the World.* Edited by Rumer Godden. Illustrated by Prudence Seward. New York: Macmillan, 1969.

Eliot, T. S. *Old Possum's Book of Practical Cats*. Illustrated by Edward Gorey. New York: Harcourt Brace Jovanovich, 1982.

Farjeon, Eleanor. *Then There Were Three*. Illustrated by Isobel and John Morton-Sale. Philadelphia: Lippincott, 1965.

Field, Rachel. *Poems*. New York: Macmillan, 1957.

Fisher, Aileen. *Cricket in a Thicket*. Illustrated by Feodor Rojankovsky. New York: Scribner, 1963.

———. *Feathered Ones and Furry*. Illustrated by Eric Carle. New York: Crowell, 1971.

Fleischman, Paul. *Graven Images*. Illustrated by Andrew Glass. New York: Harper, 1982.

———. *A Joyful Noise*. New York: Harper, 1988.

Froman, Robert. *Seeing Things: A Book of Poems*. New York: Crowell, 1974.

Frost, Robert. *Birches*. Illustrated by Ed Young. New York: Holt, 1988.

Giovanni, Nikki. *Spin a Soft Black Song*. Illustrated by George Martins. New York: Hill & Wang, 1985.

Hughes, Langston. *Selected Poems*. New York: Knopf, 1959.

Hughes, Ted. *Moon-Whales and Other Moon Poems*. Illustrated by Leonard Baskin. New York: Viking, 1976.

———. *Season Songs*. Illustrated by Leonard Baskin. New York: Viking, 1975.

Issa. *A Few Flies and I: Haiku by Issa*. Translated by R. H. Blyth and Nobuyaki Yuasa. Edited by Jean Merrill and Ronni Solbert. New York: Pantheon Books, 1969.

Kennedy, X. J. *Chastlies, Goops & Pincushions: Nonsense Verse*. Illustrated by Ron Barrett. New York: McElderry, 1989.

Kuskin, Karla. *Near the Window Tree*. New York: Harper, 1975.

Lear, Edward. *The Complete Nonsense Book*. Edited by Lady Strachey. New York: Dodd, Mead, 1942.

———. *The Quangle-Wangle's Hat*. Illustrated by Helen Oxenbury. New York: Watts, 1969.

Livingston, Myra Cohn. *The Way Things Are and Other Poems*. Illustrated by Jenni Oliver. New York: Atheneum, 1974.

———. *Whispers and Other Poems*. Illustrated by Jacqueline Chwast. New York: Harcourt Brace Jovanovich, 1958.

McCord, David. *One at a Time: His Collected Poems for the Young*. Illustrated by Henry Kane. Boston: Little, Brown, 1977.

Mahy, Margaret. *Nonstop Nonsense*. Illustrated by Quentin Blake. New York: McElderry, 1989.

Merriam, Eve. *Catch a Little Rhyme*. Illustrated by Imero Gobbato. New York: Atheneum, 1966.

———. *Chortles: New and Selected Wordplay Poems*. Illustrated by Sheila Hamanaka. New York: Morrow, 1989.

———. *There Is No Rhyme for Silver*. Illustrated by Joseph Schindelman. New York: Atheneum, 1962.

Milne, A. A. *The World of Christopher Robin*. Illustrated by Ernest Shephard. New York: Dutton, 1958.

Moore, Lilian. *I Feel the Same Way*. Illustrated by Robert Quackenbush. New York: Atheneum, 1967.

Nash, Ogden. *Custard and Company: Poems by Ogden Nash*. Compiled and illustrated by Quentin Blake. Boston: Little, Brown, 1980.

O'Neill, Mary. *Hailstones and Halibut Bones*. Illustrated by John Wallner. New York: Doubleday, 1989.

Prelutsky, Jack. *Nightmares: Poems to Trouble Your Sleep*. Illustrated by Arnold Lobel. New York: Greenwillow (Morrow), 1976.

———. *Ride a Purple Pelican*. New York: Greenwillow (Morrow), 1986.

———. *The Sheriff of Rottenshot*. Illustrated by Victoria Chess. New York: Greenwillow (Morrow), 1982.

Richards, Laura. *Tirra Lirra: Rhymes Old and New*. Illustrated by Marguerite Davis. Boston: Little, Brown, 1955.

Roethke, Theodore. *Dirty Dinky and Other Creatures*. Selected by Beatrice Roethke and Stephen Lushington. New York: Doubleday, 1973.

Service, Robert W. *The Shooting of Dan McGrew*. Illustrated by Ted Harrison. Boston: Godine, 1988.

Silverstein, Shel. *A Light in the Attic*. New York: Harper, 1981.

———. *Where the Sidewalk Ends*. New York: Harper, 1974.

Starbird, Kaye. *The Covered Bridge House.* Illustrated by Jim Arnosky. New York: Four Winds, 1979.

Stevenson, Robert Louis. *A Child's Garden of Verses.* Illustrated by Jessie Willcox Smith. 1905. New York: Scribner, 1969.

Viorst, Judith. *If I Were in Charge of the World and Other Worries.* Illustrated by Lyn Cherry. New York: Atheneum, 1969.

Whitman, Walt. *Voyages: Poems by Walt Whitman.* Selected by Lee Bennett Hopkins. Illustrated by Charles Mikolaycak. New York: Harcourt Brace Jovanovich, 1988.

Wilbur, Richard. *Opposites.* New York: Harcourt Brace Jovanovich, 1973.

Willard, Nancy. *Household Tales of Moon and Water.* New York: Harcourt Brace Jovanovich, 1982.

———. *A Visit to William Blake's Inn.* Illustrated by Alice and Martin Provensen. New York: Harcourt Brace Jovanovich, 1981.

CHAPTER 8

The Nature of Fiction

DEFINITION

By the term "fiction" we mean any prose story, whether realistic or fanciful, about make-believe characters engaged in a series of actions aimed at a specific end. Fiction is primarily a literary product—that is, it is written down and not usually meant for oral delivery.

However, not surprisingly, the child who has been avidly read to as a preschooler already has a solid foundation in understanding the *art* of fiction. Fiction is an art form and, like all art forms, observes certain conventions or implied rules. In this chapter, we will examine the conventions common to all fiction and, in the two following chapters, the two great divisions of fiction, fantasy and realism.

THE ELEMENTS OF FICTION

Point of View

Before there is a story, there has to be someone who will tell it. Every story is told from someone's point of view, and that someone is called the narrator. The narrator is decidedly *not* the author, but rather a *persona* (sort of like a mask) assumed by the author for storytelling purposes. It is important for us as readers to be aware of who is telling the story and how that narrator affects the story itself. Almost invariably, regardless of the point of view, the protagonists in children's books are roughly the same age as the intended readers. Eight-year-olds want to read about eight-year-olds. Consequently, narrators in children's books either are children themselves, or tell the story as children would see it. There are essentially three kinds of narrator.

First-Person Narrator. If a character in the story narrates the events, we call him or her a first-person narrator. He or she is involved in the action (sometimes more, sometimes less) and refers to himself or herself as "I." The first-person narrator may be either a major or a minor character, but *must* be one of the characters, and the vocabulary and narration must be limited by his or her age, position, and attitudes. For example, Robert Lawson's fanciful biography of Benjamin Franklin, *Ben and Me,* is told by the irrepressible mouse who inhabits the great man's fur hat. Although the usual practice is for one character to relate the entire story, Robert Louis Stevenson's *Treasure Island* provides an interesting variation, for it includes two first-person narrators. The beginning and the ending of the story are told by the young hero, Jim Hawkins. Dr. Livesay, Jim's adult friend, takes over and narrates a middle section of the tale.

First-person narration enjoys several advantages. It is easy to empathize with a first-person narrator who takes us into confidence and quickly embroils us in the action. On the other hand, there are drawbacks. We are able to experience only one side of the story, only one point of view, and the narrator's personal biases and attitudes become ours. (For example, Amos, the mouse narrator in *Ben and Me,* is an incredible egotist and takes credit for nearly every notable accomplishment of Franklin's life. Or the narrator may be bad-tempered and unpopular, so the reader must empathize with that, too.)

Omniscient Narrator. An omniscient narrator is used when the author freely exercises the power to see all events, know all motives, and reveal all actions. The word "omniscient" means literally "all-knowing." In E. B. White's fantasy, *Charlotte's Web,* the author chooses to show us the thoughts and actions of Wilbur the pig at one time, and then, at another time, shows us Mrs. Arable, a human, in a conversation with the family physician. The omniscient narrator is not confined to a single character's point of view but may move about among the innermost thoughts of any character in the story. Effective omniscient narration requires the writer to identify with different character types at different times and to maintain a certain degree of detachment and objectivity. It thus imposes more limitations on an author than we may at first realize.

Limited Narrator. A limited narrator (also called a subjective consciousness) tells the story from an outsider's point of view and is not a character in the tale. But unlike the omniscient narrator, the limited narrator only describes what a single character sees, knows, and feels. That single character is virtually always the main character, and this makes the limited narrative different from the first-person narrative in which the narrator may be a relatively minor character (like Dr. Livesay), or the narrator may share the limelight equally with another character (as Amos the mouse does with Franklin). Laura Ingalls Wilder's popular *Little House in the Big Woods* and its sequels are told from a limited narrator's point of view. We experience everything as Laura sees and understands things although she does not tell the story—it is merely *about* her. In this way, we may readily identify with the character, but the author is not confined to the vocabulary and personal peculiarities of that character. Had Wilder written *Little House in the Big Woods* in the first person, she would either have had to have an older Laura reflecting back on her childhood, or she would have had to use the vocabulary and grammar of an eight-year-old.

The important thing is to realize as we read who is telling the story and why. We should never confuse the narrator with the author, for most authors of fiction actually pretend to be someone else when they write—that is, they assume the persona. It is also important that the point of view be consistent—for example, a narrator should not reveal material he or she could not have logically known at the time. We must be able to *believe in* the narrator and to accept the narrator's story as true (as least so far as the narrator sees it).

Setting

The setting consists of two features: place and time. Everything must happen somewhere and sometime. In all fiction, whether realistic or fanciful, readers usually expect the setting to be believable. An interesting contrast is provided with folktales in which the setting is given only cursory treatment: "Once upon a time, long, long ago." Folktales are built on familiar storytelling patterns and make heavy use of recognizable conventions, so that much is comfortably predictable. Fantasy and realistic fiction, however, are less formulaic, each work having its own peculiar setting that must be made familiar to the reader. As a result, in novels more energy is devoted to description of time and place.

Place. The place may be either vague (a big city, a small farm) or very specific (the streets of New York, a cay in the Caribbean, even a make-believe world). Further, the place may be relatively insignificant to the story. For example, it really does not matter that Shakespeare's *Romeo and Juliet* is set in Verona, Italy. The setting is only a backdrop like scenery, and it is so insignificant that the story has been readily adapted to modern dress and circumstances in *West Side Story.* On the other hand, the setting may be crucial to a story's meaning. The principal events in Stevenson's *Treasure Island,* for example, could only happen on a deserted tropical island, and the novel is appropriately named for its setting. Fantasy fiction may include rather detailed place descriptions if the author is describing a mythical world and this setting is important to the story. Ursula Le Guin's *Earthsea* tetralogy provides a thoroughly detailed study of Earthsea's geography. Lloyd Alexander's description of Prydain is another example.

A believable well-described setting can help to establish the proper mood (such as the mystical enchantment in Philippa Pearce's *Tom's Midnight Garden*), and it can give veracity to the events of a story. Even something simple, such as the inclusion of the railroad track behind the house in Bette Greene's *The Summer of My German Soldier,* may be a crucial element; in this case, it provides a logical means for a German soldier to find his way into this American setting.

Time. The time described in a novel may be past, present, or even future. *Contemporary fiction* focuses on the present, which means that the author may assume that the readers have a great deal of familiarity with such things as social customs, everyday gadgetry, trade names, and so on. *Historical fiction* focuses on a specific period in history, and occasionally even includes fictional accounts of historic personages. Jean Fritz's *The Cabin Faced West* describes a visit by George Washington, and Esther Forbes's *Johnny Tremain* virtually brims with renowned Revolutionary War heroes. For the setting, this generally means that some habits, customs, and paraphernalia peculiar to the historical period may need to be explained as part of the narrative. However, readers usually insist that this be done subtly so it will not impede the pace of the story or make it seem as if they are being lectured to. Many fantasies take place in the present or near present (*Charlotte's Web,* for instance, or Astrid Lindgren's *Pippi Longstocking,* or Norton Juster's *The Phantom Tollbooth*). Heroic fantasy, on the other hand, usually takes place in an undefined time, although there is often the sense that it is the distant past (Ursula Le Guin's *A Wizard of Earthsea* carries a distinctively medieval flavor, but since it takes place in an entirely other world, it operates on its own time scheme). *Science fiction*—like other fantasy—usually requires detailed place descriptions, since the time is set in a fantasized future, and the author must make this believable. Madeleine L'Engle's *A Wrinkle in Time* is set fairly close to the present, but it focuses on certain top-secret scientific discoveries to which the general population is supposedly not yet privy. The cloak of government secrecy enables the novelist to enhance the credibility of the story. Eventually the protagonists are transported to a distant planet, and to make that a realistic place L'Engle must provide a reasonably detailed description.

Characters

Regardless of the type of fiction, readers demand believable and memorable characters. Believable characters use convincing and natural speech patterns or speech patterns that suit their peculiar characteristics. We expect them to speak and act according to their respective ages, social and intellectual backgrounds, and so on. The principal characters include the *protagonist,* the hero or heroine, the main character with whom we empathize. There is also the *antagonist,* the villain or character who works against the protagonist. We also insist that characters be properly motivated, that there are good and believable reasons for doing what they do. We usually expect the story's action to develop out of character and not the other way around—that is, the characters behave as they do because they are the kind of people they are.

Static and Dynamic Characters. All characters may be identified as either static or dynamic, and all good fiction will include both types. A *static character* remains esentially the same throughout the story and has no noticeable development. Most characters are of this type. Charlotte the spider in *Charlotte's Web* is a wise, generous, and thoughtful creature from beginning to end; her character does not change. However, a *dynamic character* is one who undergoes some significant personality adjustment during the course of the story. Wilbur, the pig in *Charlotte's Web,* is a rather immature, self-centered, and insecure character at the outset, but by the end of the story he has matured into a caring and confident creature. The dynamic characters in any story—and there are seldom more than one or two in a story—are typically the focal characters.

Flat and Round Characters. All characters may also be identified as either flat or round. A *flat* character—who is also necessarily a static character—is one who exhibits only one side of his or her personality. Usually these characters are functionaries, needed to advance the plot, such as servants, police, store clerks, and so on. Many times in children's literature parents (such as Fern's in *Charlotte's Web*) and siblings are flat characters. Virtually all stories include flat characters, often many of them. But we do not want a story that contains *only* flat characters. Our ultimate interest is in the rounded, fully developed personalities—in the Wilburs and Charlottes, in the Huck Finns, and even the Long John Silvers (we are not interested only in the good guys).

Stereotype Characters. Many times a flat character will also be a *stereotype* or a *stock character,* possessing the traits considered to be typical of a group (such as disagreeable mothers-in-law, haughty English butlers, giddy schoolgirls, impish schoolboys, and so on). Whereas we guard against stereotyping real-life people, stereotypes are useful to an author. They help expedite the plot, avoid sidetracking the reader's attention, and save words. But the stereotype must be used with discretion. A good author will never employ stereotypes to advance his or her opinion. We might regard Templeton the rat as a stereotype, because he behaves selfishly and greedily as we expect from a rat. The wise and kindly family physician in *Charlotte's Web* is another example of a stereotyped character, this time a good one. Regrettably we do find offensive stereotypes from time to time—racial stereotypes, gender stereotypes (girls depicted as weak and helpless homebodies, boys as strong and bold adventurers), age stereotypes (crotchety and feeble old people)—but mostly in books written before 1930. Nothing should excuse such treatments in modern literature.

Foil Characters. A *foil character* is one who possesses personality traits opposite to those of another character, often the main character. One meaning of *foil* is a jeweler's term for the setting for a gem, and just as the proper setting can show off a diamond to great advantage, making it appear large and brilliant, so can certain character traits be highlighted when compared to the opposite traits in others. Hence, Templeton serves as a foil to Charlotte; his selfishness makes her own ultimate sacrifice that much more impressive and moving. Likewise, Captain Hook is a foil to Peter Pan and Long John Silver to Jim Hawkins (foils often pit good character traits against evil).

Character Development. We learn about characters in a variety of ways. The narrator may explain them to us, although this is usually the least memorable way. We may hear about them through what other characters say of them, although we must be wary of possible ulterior motives or prejudices in these other characters. We may learn about characters through what they say themselves, although we must remember that people do not always mean what they say. And, of course, we may learn about characters through observing their actions. The author drops many clues to character in a story, and we must not forget that all the clues may not be reliable—as in real-life experiences of people.

Plot

The novelist E. M. Forster provides us with the following definition of a plot:

> "The King died and then the queen died" is a story. "The king died, and then the queen died of grief" is a plot. (1954, 86)

The point is that a plot is more than simply a sequence of events; it is a sequence of interrelated events *linked by causality.* (The king's death *caused* the queen's death.)

The most important feature of a plot is the conflict—something must be at stake; some difficulty must be overcome; some goal achieved. This usually takes one of four methods: (1) person-against-person, such as we find in *Treasure Island* with Jim Hawkins and Dr. Livesay pitted against Long John Silver and the pirates; (2) person-against-society, such as we find in the struggles of Cassie Logan and her family with the dominant and bigoted white society in the American South of the 1930s, in Mildred Taylor's *Roll of Thunder, Hear My Cry;* (3) person-against-nature, such as the plight of Karana, stranded for eighteen years on a deserted island in Scott O'Dell's *Island of the Blue Dolphins;* (4) person-against-self, such as we see in the internal conflict of Leigh Botts as he adjusts to his parents' divorce and to his own growing up in Beverly Cleary's *Dear Mr. Henshaw.*

The plot of a good work of fiction grows logically out of the characterization and is both credible and interesting. By credible, we do not necessarily mean realistic, but rather believable according to the standards established by the work itself. A work of fantasy, although not realistic by normal standards, may still be convincing. Readers generally have low tolerance for unnecessary contrivance and coincidence (unless they are intentionally used for comic effect). In fact, although we hear of strange coincidences occurring all the time in real life and usually marvel at them, we normally do not like them in our fiction, and we regard them as crutches used by unimaginative writers.

In fact, one of the principal differences between art and life is that life is random, whereas art is meticulously planned. In real life, we may receive a telephone call, during dinner or late at night, that turns out to be a wrong number, and that event may have no effect whatever on the course of events. In a novel or a play, however, should such a telephone call be recorded, we fully expect it to have some bearing on the action. Writers may want the events of their stories to seem lifelike and random, but they seldom are. Everything that happens has a specific purpose. Whenever a character enters a room or whenever a change in the weather is noted or whenever a cup of coffee is spilled, we may expect that that event will have some significance. It may be to establish the atmosphere or to help us evaluate a character or a situation or to reinforce the theme—but it must always advance the plot in one way or another. Everything must happen for a good reason. Plots may be structured according to one of three general patterns.

Dramatic Plot Structure. A dramatic plot structure first establishes the setting and conflict, then follows the action through to a *climax* (the peak of the action and turning), and concludes with a *denouement* (a wrapping up of loose ends). This structure is probably the most familiar; it is the structure of most folktales, and it is adopted by most television drama. It is also the plot structure of such familiar works as *Charlotte's Web* and *Treasure Island.*

Episodic Plot Structure. An episodic plot structure consists of a series of loosely related incidents tied together by a common theme and a character or group of characters. Eleanor Estes' popular *The Moffats* is a series of independent episodes organized around the activities of a poor family in Connecticut over the course of a year. The unity is provided by the predominant theme of love and family togetherness overcoming hardship and the children's growing up and accepting responsibility. Laura Ingalls Wilder's *Little House in the Big Woods* is another example of an episodic novel. Since there is no single overriding conflict or complication in these books, there is no central climax or denouement. Episodic plots work best when the writer wishes to explore the personalities of the characters, the nature of their existence, and the flavor of an era.

Parallel Plot Structure. A parallel plot structure is one that links two plots, often with similar or contrasting themes, into an intertwining story line. If one of the plots is decidedly secondary, it is referred to as a subplot. Although parallel plot structure is typically found in books for older children, Robert McCloskey's delightful picture-book for young children, *Blueberries for Sal,* is actually built around two parallel plots, both with the same theme and same general design: Sal and her mother go blueberry picking on the same hill with a mother bear and her cub; both Sal and the cub are separated from their respective mothers and inadvertently end up with the wrong mother; following a double climax, in which the mix-up is discovered by each mother, things are set right once more. Lawson's *Ben and Me* provides us with another example: Amos begins telling the story of Franklin's Revolutionary War activities, but also tells us of a parallel struggle among the mouse population; the episodes occurring on the human level are thus reenacted in the mouse world. It is typical of parallel plots that one is more elevated or seemingly more important than the other—of course, Amos the mouse would have us believe that the more significant plot in his story is the one focusing on the mice.

Plot and the Intended Audience. For young readers, simple, direct plots, following a *chronological pattern* (arranged according to time, from beginning to end), are the most suitable. Young readers prefer a well-paced plot with plenty of *action* and a minimum of *exposition.* (Exposition is simply the narrator's explanation of necessary information.) Appropriate *humor,* suited to the age of the audience, is also a desirable (although not absolutely necessary) element.

Older readers (approximately fifth and sixth graders and older) may find enjoyment in more complex plot structures. *Flashbacks* (the movement of the narrative back in time to provide necessary background information) are more suited to this older age group, whereas they may be quite confusing to younger readers, who have not yet fully grasped the notion of time moving forward, let alone moving backward. Older readers, who are still enthralled by action, nevertheless begin to prefer more emphasis on characters and the exploration of ideas.

Theme

The theme is the principal *idea* behind a story. In a good work of fiction, the theme is substantial, not trivial—although this does not imply that the work must be heavy-handed. (Adolescent problem novels always flirt with subverting the plot and chacterization to the message.) As readers, we prefer a good, solid theme, but we generally do not like to be beaten over the head with it. Instead, we like the themes woven subtly into the fabric of the story.

When the theme is presented in a blatant and preachy fashion and is clearly intended to rap us over the knuckles with a good lesson, the work is *didactic.* As suggested in Chapter 2, overtly didactic works seldom appeal to children. They don't like being preached to, and, besides, didactic works usually consist of stiff characters and contrived plots (in didactic works, only the lesson is important). In works for younger children, the faddish "Care Bear" publications provide us with examples of heavy-handed didacticism. These works do have appeal, deriving chiefly from the exploitation of that favorite childhood companion, the teddy bear, and the fact that the characters originated as animated cartoons. But such gimmicks are examples of the commercial exploitation of children and should not be confused with literature.

The theme of a good work of fiction is made apparent through the actions of the characters and the consequences of those actions. Readers are therefore able to discover the theme themselves. A good work of fiction for young people avoids lectures by all-knowing adults and allows the youthful protagonists to learn by their own experiences (which, as is proved over and over again in real life, is the most effective learning method). Themes of most books for young people are positive and uplifting; the one feature that most adolescent books have in common with those for preschoolers is that, in the end, they give their readers hope. There are exceptions, of course, and Robert Cormier's controversial books, such as *The Chocolate War* and *I Am the Cheese,* focus on negative and even dismal themes; these books are popular, however, which suggests that many adolescents are quite capable of handling harsh realism.

Books for young readers offer many important themes, and a single book often includes several minor themes in addition to the major one. The problems of growing up and maturation are probably the most frequently found thematic issues. We see treatments of the individual's adjustment to society (Mildred Taylor's *Roll of Thunder, Hear My Cry*), the importance of love and friendship (E. B. White's *Charlotte's Web*), the acceptance of a stepparent (Patricia MacLachlan's *Sarah, Plain and Tall*), survival (Scott O'Dell's *Island of the Blue Dolphins*), sibling rivalry (Katherine Paterson's *Jacob Have I Loved*), the clash of cultures (Jean Craighead George's *Julie of the Wolves*), the death of a parent (Mollie Hunter's *The Sound of Chariots*), achieving one's identity (Virginia Hamilton's *M. C. Higgins the Great*), finding one's place in the world (Ursula Le Guin's *A Wizard of Earthsea*). The list is seemingly endless. Whatever the specific variation may be, the great number of these themes can be seen as encompassing the discovery of one's personal identity and the acceptance of one's place in the social order.

Style

The style of a good work of fiction is suited to the subject and to the audience. Prose consists of exposition (the narrator's comments and explanations) or of dialogue (the characters' words). The style refers to the selection and arrangement of the writer's words (diction) and sentences (syntax), and writers must be sensitive to the following considerations.

Exposition. Exposition is the information imparted to us by the narrator, usually descriptive and background information necessary for us to understand the events. Exposition must be both pertinent and interesting. It may be used to introduce a character: "Dorothy lived in the midst of the great Kansas prairies, with Uncle Henry, who was a farmer, and Aunt Em, who was the farmer's wife" (Baum, *The Wizard of Oz,* 1). Sometimes exposition is used to move the action along:

> When Laura and Mary said their prayers and were tucked snugly under the trundle bed's covers, Pa was sitting in the firelight with the fiddle. Ma had blown out the lamp because she did not need its light. On the other side of the hearth she was swaying gently in her rocking chair and her knitting needles flashed in and out above the sock she was knitting. (Wilder, *Little House in the Big Woods,* 236)

Other times exposition is used to summarize and focus ideas presented in a scene, and to suggest future directions:

> Wilbur was merely suffering the doubts and fears that often go with finding a new friend. In good time he was to discover that he was mistaken about Charlotte. Underneath her rather bold and cruel exterior, she had a kind heart, and she was to prove loyal and true to the very end. (White, *Charlotte's Web,* 41)

Dialogue. This refers to the words spoken by the characters, as opposed to *exposition,* the words of the narrator to the reader. All good works of fiction must rely on both dialogue and exposition. Young readers, especially, enjoy dialogue as a realistic and convincing way of defining character. Dialogue allows the author to convey individual peculiarities, such as the goose's stuttering in *Charlotte's Web* when she replies to Wilbur's inquiry about the time: "Probably-obably-obably about half-past eleven . . . Why aren't you asleep, Wilbur?" (33) Charlotte's intellectual superiority over the other barnyard animals is clearly demonstrated by her greeting to Wilbur: " 'Salutations!' said [Charlotte]. Wilbur jumped to his feet. 'Salu-*what*?' he cried" (35). Dialogue must above all be suited to the character who speaks it, otherwise it appears stilted and unnatural.

Diction.   The choice of words (diction) should be suited to the characters and to the theme. Naturally we would not expect to find sophisticated, multisyllabic, and bombastic orations in a work intended for preschoolers. On the other hand, if the vocabulary of a piece of fiction never challenges the reader, boredom may set in, or worse, the reader is never given a chance to expand his or her vocabulary. Reading is one of the most effective methods of language acquisition.

Beatrix Potter is famous for not using condescending language with her young readers. In *The Tale of Peter Rabbit,* in addition to "camomile tea," we find "exert" and "fortnight." These difficult words have not discouraged children from loving this enduring story for close to a century now. Young children, just as we do, discern the meanings of unfamiliar words from the context in which they appear. Of course, too many new and unfamiliar terms will be discouraging. But if we all stopped reading the moment we came upon a difficult word, few books would ever get read. An occasional challenging word should not dissuade us from sharing a good book with a child.

Even those words we know may carry more meaning than we first suspect. Words may be used denotatively—that is, according to their literal definitions. When we refer to "heart" as the biological organ that pumps blood throughout the body, we are using the word denotatively. However, when Elizabeth Coatsworth says, "The warm of heart shall never lack a fire/However far he roam," she is using the word "heart" *connotatively,* evoking in us all the associations we generally make when anyone (other than a physician) refers to "heart." The connotations of heart are many: Sometimes the word evokes a positive quality— "She has a kind heart" —or it can indicate weakness—"He has been blinded by his heart." It can mean generosity— "You're all heart" —or resolution— "I have the heart and stomach of a king." All these are connotations.

Finally, a word must be said about profanity. In books for adolescents, profanity is bound to appear if the dialogue is to be realistic, and this is bound to upset some parents. Yet it is disastrous for adults to attempt to censor the reading of upper elementary children and adolescents; a campaign against the book that contains foul language will simply spread the word and increase its popularity. The less said about profanity the better.

The best writers will use all language with discretion, remembering that an excess of anything dulls the senses. Moreover, the character who swears a lot sounds oafish and immature, and some of this impression overflows onto the author.

Syntax.   This refers to the placement of words in sentences. Short sentences convey suspense, tension, and swift action. Longer sentences work best when explanations and descriptions are needed. It is a myth that long sentences are necessarily complicated and confusing. A well-written long sentence can be just as easy to comprehend as a short sentence. What counts is placing thoughts in a clear and graceful sequence. Notice how E. B. White, in the following paragraph from *Charlotte's Web,* effectively combines short and long sentences as he moves from describing action to thought and back to action:

> Wilbur looked everywhere. He searched his pen thoroughly. He examined the window ledge, stared up at the ceiling. But he saw nothing new. Finally he decided he would have to speak up. He hated to break the lovely stillness of dawn by using his voice, but he couldn't think of any other way to locate the mysterious new friend who was nowhere to be seen. So Wilbur cleared his throat. (34)

Prose has its rhythm as well as poetry. The best writers can make a paragraph read as beautifully as a well-crafted poem. The right juxtaposition of sounds, the right measure of repetition, the right variety of patterns, the right choice of images, and the author produces a lyrical passage such as this, the final paragraph from Patricia MacLachlan's *Sarah, Plain and Tall:*

> Autumn will come, then winter, cold with a wind that blows like a wind off the sea in Maine. There will be nests of curls to looks for, and dried flowers all winter long. When there are storms, Papa will stretch a rope from the door to the barn so we will not be lost when we feed the sheep and the cows and Jack and Old Bess. And Sarah's chickens, if they aren't living in the house. There will be Sarah's sea, blue and gray and green, hanging on the wall. And songs, old ones and new. And Seal with yellow eyes. And there will be Sarah, plain and tall. (58)

A FINAL WORD

When all is said and done, good fiction, whether fantasy, romance, or realism, is both *entertaining* and *challenging.* If a book is not entertaining, the reader may soon lay it aside; if it is not challenging, the reader may soon stop thinking (and probably soon after that stop reading). The elements discussed above are the tools a writer uses to make a work of fiction interesting and challenging. Young children may lack the critical vocabulary to discuss fiction along these terms, but their open and honest responses to literature are often very wise and insightful. The books for young people that achieve the status of classics do so not because a handful of stuffy critics dubbed them so, but because reading children everywhere have loved them passionately.

WORKS CITED

Baum, L. Frank. *The Wizard of Oz*. 1900. Illustrated by Michael Hague. New York: Holt, Rinehart and Winston, 1982.

MacLachlan, Patricia. *Sarah, Plain and Tall*. New York, Harper, 1985.

White, E. B. *Charlotte's Web*. Illustrated by Garth Williams. New York: Harper, 1952.

Wilder, Laura Ingalls. *Little House in the Big Woods*. 1932. Illustrated by Garth Williams. New York: Harper, 1953.

BIBLIOGRAPHY OF CRITICAL STUDIES

Carlson, Ruth Kearney. *Emerging Humanity: Multi-Ethnic Literature for Children and Adolescents*. Dubuque, IA: Brown, 1972.

Cullinan, Bernice, and Carolyn Carmichael, eds. *Literature and Young Children*. Urbana, IL: National Council of Teachers of English, 1977.

Forster, E. M. *Aspects of the Novel*. New York: Harcourt Brace Jovanovich, 1954.

Hilkick, Wallace. *Children and Fiction*. Cleveland: World, 1971.

Lukens, Rebecca J. *A Critical Handbook of Children's Literature*. 2d ed. Glenview, IL: Scott, Foresman, 1981.

Otten, Charlotte F., and Gary D. Schmidt, eds. *The Voice of the Narrator in Children's Literature: Insights from Writers and Critics*. Westport, CT: Greenwood, 1989.

Purves, Alan. C., and Dianne L. Monson. *Experiencing Children's Literature.* Glenview, IL: Scott, Foresman, 1984.

Shapiro, Jon, ed. *Using Literature & Poetry Affectively.* Chicago: International Reading Association, 1979.

Smith, James Steel. *A Critical Approach to Children's Literature.* New York: McGraw-Hill, 1967.

Smith, Lillian. *The Unreluctant Years.* Chicago: American Library Association, 1953 (reprinted by Viking, 1967).

Stewig, John Warren, and Sam L. Sebesta, eds. *Using Literature in the Elementary Classroom.* Urbana, IL: National Council of Teachers of English, 1978.

CHAPTER 9

Fantasy

DEFINITION

Fantasy may be defined as any story of the impossible; it is to be distinguished from folk literature in that fantasy belongs to the literary and not to the oral tradition. Certainly the roots of all fantasies are the folktales, legends, and myths that rose out of early, preliterate societies, but today the term "fantasy" is used to designate an original story written by a specific author or authors. Consequently, it is not possible to speak of variants in fantasies, the text being established by the author.

Many fantasies draw heavily on traditional folktales for their inspiration and even structure, since no work of literature is created in a vacuum, oblivious to what has preceded it. The first important fantasies for children appear in the nineteenth century. Hans Christian Andersen, in addition to retelling traditional tales, wrote original fairy stories heavily influenced by the folk tradition. Lewis Carroll's *Alice in Wonderland* significantly departs from the folk tradition and is one of the pioneers in book-length fantasy for children. (It is also considered one of the first children's books written primarily for the pleasure of children without heavy underlying didacticism.) Since that time modern fantasy has prospered, producing some of the most memorable works of children's literature.

Zilpha Snyder suggests that there are two things children demand from fantasy—that it contain no nonsense and that it contain no treachery (1986, 230). These, at first, may appear to be curious requirements, but they are quite important. Even though fantasy presents situations that we know to be impossible, we do expect them to be presented as if they *were* possible. Consequently, children insist that writers of fantasy establish certain rules that operate within the fantasy world of the story itself and that the writers abide by those rules. Also, children insist that the fantasy not be unfairly taken away at the book's end— such as pretending that it never happened, that it was all a dream, and so on. Such a betrayal on the writer's behalf usually generates a groan from readers. After all, part of the readers' delight in fantasy is that of being completely absorbed into the fantasy, and, once having made that commitment, readers do not like to find out that it has all been a trick or an elaborate deception. For example, the MGM movie *The Wizard of Oz* ends with the implication that the entire adventure was just a dream, but Baum played no such trick on his readers. According to the original book, Dorothy *really* went to Oz and returned to Kansas. Baum wants us to believe in that magical land, and so do we want to believe.

TYPES OF FANTASY

Fantasy comes in a wide variety of types, all with differing degrees of fantastic elements. There are many ways of classifying fantasy, and each classification method has its drawbacks. But, since fantasies, virtually by definition, contain some form of enchantment, some unreality, it makes a great deal of sense to classify fantasies according to the predominant type of enchantment. We will briefly consider some of the more common of these.

The Literary Fairy Tale

The traditional folktales have inspired modern counterparts—original tales by modern writers that have all the flavor of an old tale. Sometimes, unless we know the origin, it is difficult to distinguish between the Literary Fairy Tale (the product of a specific author) and the oral folktale—and perhaps the writers of the Literary Fairy Tale would take that as a sign of their success. Hans Christian Andersen, a Danish writer, was one of the earliest creators of the Literary Fairy Tale, and he has proved one of the most enduring. His popularity inspired others, and by the last half of the nineteenth century many writers were experimenting with this form. George MacDonald's *The Light Princess, The Princess and Curdie,* and *The Princess and the Goblin* are all book-length works that we can label literary fairy tales. The Literary Fairy Tale exhibits many of the same features as its oral counterparts: conventional settings in a distant "generic" kingdom, an accepted magical element, and, of course, an inevitable happy ending. A modern variation on the Literary Fairy Tale is a spoof or satire on the form, such as James Thurber's delightful *Many Moons,* which takes a comic twist. Satire results when writers feel a literary form has been exhausted and that it offers no other serious possibilities; consequently they begin to poke fun at it, and, in doing so, give the form a new lease on life.

Animal Fantasy

Animal Fantasies focus on animals imbued with human traits. Young children are particularly fascinated by animals, and, in fact, see them as possessing human characteristics: having familial relationships similar to humans, enjoying pleasures similar to humans, and going to some animal heaven when they die. So it is only natural that among the favorite fantasies of children are those using animals as the main characters.

There are essentially two ways that an author may present animal characters in a fantasy. Kenneth Grahame, in his classic, *The Wind in the Willows,* creates animals who talk and behave almost entirely as humans. The animals live in houses (Mr. Toad inhabits Toad Hall, a sprawling English manor house), use furniture and human modes of transportation, wear clothes, and even eat human food. So realistically does Grahame portray his characters that readers usually do not question the incongruity of a water rat and a mole eating cold chicken for a picnic lunch. Part of the success for this type of Animal Fantasy results from the author's creating an almost entirely animal world. However, Grahame does include enough of the animals' natural traits to separate them from the humans, who play a small role in the story and are generally treated satirically.

E. B. White, in his classic *Charlotte's Web,* depicts animals living in a predominantly human world. Hence, Wilbur the pig, lives like a pig in a barnyard, eats like a pig and generally has all the habits of a pig. The only differences between Wilbur and any other pig we might expect to find on a farm is that Wilbur (along with the other barnyard animals) is imbued with the power of speech, and he exhibits rather deep emotions. But Wilbur's power of speech is even restricted: Wilbur may speak to and be understood by his child friend Fern, but the animals never speak to adult humans. Charlotte, likewise, lives the life of a spider; we see her entrap a fly and suck its blood, for example. But, as is customary in animal fantasy, Wilbur and his friends exhibit human personality traits: Charlotte is kind and wise, Templeton is greedy and selfish, Wilbur is lovable, and so on. Nevertheless, White is bound more closely to the laws of nature than is Grahame, and we would be disturbed if Wilbur should suddenly take to wearing a spiffy jacket and top hat.

In all cases of Animal Fantasy, the premise is that the animals have human feelings, and the animals are, in many respects, simply humans in animal guise. Consequently, it is possible for us to draw significant conclusions about human behavior from reading either *The Wind in the Willows* or *Charlotte's Web.* In other words, Animal Fantasy constitutes a form of literary symbolism, the animal characters symbolizing human counterparts, and these fantasies are often vehicles for exploring human emotions, values, and relationships.

Toy Fantasy

Similar to the Animal Fantasy, but with some distinct differences, is the Toy Fantasy, in which talking toys—usually dolls or stuffed animals—are the major characters. A frequent theme in the Toy Fantasy is the desire of toys to become living creatures. Collodi's *Pinocchio* is the classic of this type, in which the wooden puppet comes to life and wants nothing more than to become a real, live boy—a fact accomplished only after a series of harrowing experiences that presumably make him worthy of the gift of life. Margery Nicholson's *The Velveteen Rabbit* is another perennial favorite, and Leo Lionni's *Alexander and the Wind-Up Mouse* is a popular picture-book fantasy on a similar theme. The implication is, of course, that it is much better to be a living, breathing creature than an inanimate object, although, curiously enough, the toys generally exhibit human traits before their magical transformations.

Other Toy Fantasies depict toys who are apparently contented with their lot, happy to interact with each other or with a loving child caretaker. A. A. Milne's *Winnie-the-Pooh* is a delightful example of this type of fantasy. Each of the toys, all stuffed animals, has his or her own peculiar personality, and the prospect of becoming human is not a possibility (nor does it seem desirable). Don Freeman's beloved picture-book *Corduroy* is about a lovable stuffed bear who wants nothing more than to be enjoyed by a human child.

As with Animal Fantasies, Toy Fantasies imbue the characters with human traits; usually, but not always, the toys have the ability to move around. However, unlike the characters in Animal Fantasy, the toys are seldom perceived as symbolic humans. Their existence and its meaning usually depends upon humans, and, of course, the toys are not bound by mortal struggles. Rachel Field's *Hitty, Her First Hundred Years,* the first-person memoirs of a doll, illustrate some of the peculiar advantages of a toy protagonist, who can enjoy virtual immortality (barring wear and tear or natural disintegration, of course) and thereby witness the parade of history.

Eccentric Characters/Extraordinary Beings

Some fantasies have as their focus an Eccentric Character or an Extraordinary Being who may possess some strange powers. P. L. Travers' *Mary Poppins* and Astrid Lindgren's *Pippi Longstocking* are examples of such fantasies. (The fact that the books are named for their protagonists illustrates the preeminence given these characters.) In these stories some magical or, at least extraordinary, power is granted the protagonist, and our interest is in all the wondrous variations that can result from one possessing such a power. Occasionally we find a fantasy that relies not on magical elements but rather on wildly exaggerated peculiarities. An early example is Lucretia Hale's *The Peterkin Papers*. These stories, written in the nineteenth century, are about the extraordinarily inept and foolish Peterkin family who must be extricated from their nonsensical predicaments by the conventional wisdom of the lady from Philadelphia. Peggy Parrish's *Amelia Bedelia* and Harry Allard's stories of the Stupids are modern examples. These stories are closely related to the tall tale, a peculiarly American form of folklore deriving its strength from wildly fantastical exaggerations. Sid Fleischman is a master of the modern tall tale, and he has successfully developed the form into full-length books. His *The Ghost in the Noonday Sun* and *By the Great Horn Spoon!* are just two of his comical farces that skirt the border between fantasy and reality. Fleischman's Newbery Award-winning *The Whipping Boy* has the flavor of a mock-heroic fantasy, complete with a quasi-fairy tale setting, but its strength is in its depiction of a series of bizarre characters encountered by the heroes. Another charming twist on the extraordinary character motif is the miniaturized character. Jonathan Swift is usually singled out as the prototype for this form, with his description of the journey to Lilliput in the first book of *Gulliver's Travels;* however, the adventures of the folktale hero, Tom Thumb, predate Swift. Modern examples include Mary Norton's *The Borrowers,* a tale of a family of miniature people living in the walls of a house (they are the ones responsible for all those items that inexplicably disappear), and Carol Kendall's *The Gammage Cup,* about a revolt in a civilization of little people, the Minnipins. For the most part, the fantasies of Eccentric Characters are humorous stories meant to evoke laughter.

The Enchanted Journey

The journey motif is one of the oldest in literature, going back to Homer's *Odyssey* and beyond. The great advantage to sending fictional characters on a journey is that the possibilities for plot variation are virtually endless. Everyone is familiar with those fantasies that take a character—almost always a child—from the Real World into an Other World, a sort of never-never land where all manner of wondrous things can occur. These fantasies are especially popular with younger readers, and some of these tales include the most famous books of childhood. Lewis Carroll's *Alice in Wonderland,* Frank Baum's *The Wizard of Oz,* Charles Kingsley's *Water Babies,* and James Barrie's *Peter Pan* come immediately to mind. The fantasy of the Enchanted Journey typically opens in the real world (also called the Primary World) and then, through some means or device—such as a cyclone or a rabbit hole—the principal character is allowed to enter the enchanted realm (which is called the Secondary World).

The journey must have some purpose (Dorothy wants to find a way back home; Alice wants to find the Queen's Garden), but the purpose is usually overshadowed by the thrill and delight offered by the extraordinary events that can happen in the Secondary World. The credibility of these stories is typically aided by the fact that the fanciful events can only happen in the Secondary World and not in the Primary World—the Wicked Witch has no authority in Kansas. The plots of these tales are frequently quite loose—sometimes episodic—and we rely on the central character (the child human) to be our touchstone with reality. Alice and Dorothy judge everything they see in Wonderland and Oz, respectively, by the standards they knew at home.

Some books, such as William Pène Du Bois' *Twenty-One Balloons,* adhere more closely to reality—in fact, the island of Krakatoa, which constitutes the Secondary World for duBois' tale, did actually exist and was the site of one of history's greatest volcanic eruptions. Roald Dahl's *Charlie and the Chocolate Factory* and *James and the Giant Peach* combine elements of the Enchanted Journey and the Eccentric Character fantasy—James is treated to a hero's parade in New York City after his remarkable transatlantic crossing in the giant peach. In these Enchanted Journeys, as with Du Bois', the fantasy intrudes on the Primary World—no clear dividing line exists between the real and the fantasy worlds.

Heroic Fantasy

Alice and Dorothy, although they perform several acts that might be interpreted as heroic, remain clearly grounded in the primary world, and the primary world is the touchstone by which the wonders of the fantasy world are measured. However, in the Heroic Fantasy (sometimes referred to as High Fantasy—although that can be a troublesome term), we share the heroic exploits of a hero or heroine engaged in a monumental struggle against a seemingly all-powerful evil, and the fate of an entire civilization depends on the outcome of the struggle. Whereas the Enchanted Journey may be quite episodic, the Heroic Fantasy is typically more tightly woven, with all the action directed toward a single end—the triumph of good over evil.

The presentation of the fantasy world may occur in one of three ways. Occasionally, Heroic Fantasies, such as Susan Cooper's *The Dark Is Rising* series, are set in the real (Primary) world, which is threatened by dark forces. In Cooper's series, most of the fantasy, although it takes place technically in the Primary World, occurs on a psychological level understood only by certain "chosen" humans in the stories. In other Heroic Fantasies, the story begins in the Primary World and contains a passage to the Secondary World. C. S. Lewis's *The Lion, the Witch and the Wardrobe* is one of the best known examples, the children getting to the Secondary World of Narnia through the back of an old wardrobe in a country house. (Passages to Secondary Worlds are not restricted to Heroic Fantasies, however. Alice's rabbit hole and looking glass and Dorothy's cyclone are three of the most famous in literature.) And finally, many Heroic Fantasies, such as Ursula Le Guin's *Earthsea* tetralogy or Tolkien's *Lord of the Rings* trilogy, take place entirely in imaginary worlds inhabited by imaginary creatures (sometimes humanlike, sometimes not), in no way connected to the world as we know it. These works contain no passage between our world and the fantasy world, but focus on self-contained fictional worlds.

Heroic Fantasies are most often structured around the hero's or heroine's quest; this frequently turns out to be a quest for identity, although the hero or heroine usually does not realize that at first. The fate of a nation or a people is often dependent upon the success or failure of the quest, and the hero or heroine becomes a figure of adulation and may even by rewarded with a crown by the story's end. The important thing is that the central character acts decisively, is altruistic, and eventually becomes the savior of a people. The plot typically consists of a series of remarkable adventures—usually impediments which the central character must overcome in order to achieve the quest. Because of the seriousness of the themes—the necessity for good to overcome evil, the importance of one's achieving one's full potential, and so on—humor is either absent or a decidedly secondary element in Heroic Fantasy. (But not always; Lloyd Alexander's *Prydain* cycle, based on Welsh legend, is a good example of Heroic Fantasy employing comic elements, usually with the use of comic characters. The hero is always quite serious.) Most Heroic Fantasies do not shy away from tragedy, and the message is frequently that good is not accomplished without some significant sacrifice. It is undoubtedly quite obvious that Heroic Fantasy owes a great deal to the traditional folktale, from which are derived themes, plot structures, even characters and settings. If we understand the folktales, we are more likely to understand Heroic Fantasy.

Supernatural Fantasy

In the category of Supernatural Fantasy we place ghost stories, which are perennial favorites with many young people. (Even very young children are fascinated by ghosts; Robert Bright's *Georgie and the Robbers* is a picture-book about a shy ghost, and the cartoon figure of Casper the Friendly Ghost has a long history.) For older children, in fact, the more gruesome the story is, the better they seem to like it. Many people have deep within them something of the ambulance chaser. Nevertheless, the best tales of the supernatural are not those that dramatize and glamorize the blood and horror. Perhaps the most thrilling tales are those that leave something for our imagination to do. The best tales of the supernatural do not capitalize on the horror, but explore the possibilities offered by the presence of the supernatural. Penelope Lively's *The Ghost of Thomas Kempe* is a popular and well-told example of a modern ghost story.

Related to the supernatural tales are those stories that involve playing tricks with time—a ghost, after all, is usually depicted as simply a human presence operating in a time other than that in which it lived. Philippa Pearce's *Tom's Midnight Garden* and Natalie Babbitt's *Tuck Everlasting* both explore movement in and out of time, and both books deal sensitively with human relationships. Babbitt's additionally considers the advantages and disadvantages of immortality. These books are good examples of the ways in which fantasy can be both entertaining and provocative. In a similar vein are Lucy Boston's *Green Knowe* books and Alan Garner's *Owl Service,* the latter of which is a somewhat sophisticated tale of the occult, drawing on mysterious ancient powers.

Science Fiction

Mary Shelley's *Frankenstein* (1818) is usually credited with being the first true work of Science Fiction, followed by the works of Jules Verne (*Twenty Thousand Leagues Under the Sea* and *From Earth to the Moon Direct*), which achieved great popularity in the mid-nineteenth century. Today Science Fiction has a following among young readers, who make up in enthusiasm what they may lack in actual numbers. Science Fiction is speculative writing, usually focusing on life in the future, either on Earth or on some other planet. (When the setting is the present, the plot depends upon some presumably advanced, and often secret, science or technology.) In Science Fiction, magic is replaced by technological wonders. Much of Science Fiction is devoted to dramatizing the wonders of technology (although Science Fiction is usually not especially scientific). Science Fiction, in fact, closely resembles Heroic Fantasy, often unfolding mighty struggles between the forces of good and evil and with the fate of civilization hanging in the balance. As one critic notes, "How different, after all, is a wizard with a magic wand from a scientist with a microminiaturized matter-transformer? The reader does not know how either gadget works" (Roberts 1973, 90).

There is perhaps even less humor in science fiction than there is in Heroic Fantasy because the Science Fiction writer often wants to create the illusion that the world depicted is a world of possibility. There is no room for flippancy or lightheartedness. The exception may be Science Fiction written for the younger reader (six to eight years old); these works are largely space travel adventures (Ruthven Todd's *Space Cat*) or perhaps robot stories (Lester Del Rey's *The Runaway Robot*).

Some works we categorize as Science Fiction may be better termed "Space Fiction." This is the term preferred by Sylvia Engdahl, whose *Enchantress from the Stars, The Far Side of Evil,* and other works are set in the future and on distant planets, but otherwise are little concerned with scientific technological achievements. Engdahl's works, despite their futuristic setting, are usually preferred by readers who are not Science Fiction buffs. Engdahl treats her futuristic setting as simply the framework through which she conveys her sense of the development of human civilization, socially and psychologically rather than scientifically and technologically.

There is, in fact, a strong didactic strain in Science Fiction, and many works deal with ethical problems facing humanity as science and technology progress, but human values do not. Consequently, the question as to whether technological discoveries will be used for humanity's benefit or its destruction frequently becomes a theme of Science Fiction. Madeleine L'Engle, best known for *A Wrinkle in Time,* addresses such issues in her Science Fiction. Adolescent readers of Science Fiction often reach for adult representatives of this subgenre, such as Ray Bradbury's thought-provoking *The Martian Chronicles.* Ursula Le Guin, although best-known in children's literature for her Heroic Fantasies, is a highly regarded writer of Science Fiction for adults, *The Dark Side of the Moon* being among her most celebrated works.

JUDGING FANTASY

In addition to the general characteristics that we expect of all fiction, we expect good fantasy to meet some special requirements. Perhaps above all, we expect fantasy to be *original.* From a stylistic point of view, neither *The Wizard of Oz* nor *Peter Pan* are particularly well-written, but the ideas in these works are so imaginative and so original that the stories remain with us throughout our lives. The characters of good fantasy—Alice, Mr. Toad of Toad Hall, Winnie-the-Pooh, the Scarecrow and the Tin Woodsman—remain indelibly marked in our minds, and we inevitably measure every new character against these mainstays.

Secondly, we expect good fantasy to be *believable.* This may sound contradictory, but, in fact, fantasy often has to seem more believable than a realistic work. Readers want to believe in the fantasy, and we often resent it when an incompetent writer includes something that we immediately recognize as silly. ("Silly" is, of course, a relative term. We tolerate certain behavior in a story such as *Winnie-the-Pooh* that we would not tolerate in *The Lion, the Witch and the Wardrobe.* It is the writer who, in the creation of the fantasy, sets the limits of silliness, and those limits must not be overstepped.) A good writer achieves a level of believability in fantasy by several means. When a writer provides us with detailed descriptions of things seen and heard, we are more apt to believe that these do indeed exist. We expect the writer to maintain *consistency*—the writer must abide by the rules he or she has established. The wizards in Le Guin's *Earthsea* tetralogy possess magical powers, but we only believe in those powers because they have limitations, and Le Guin, once creating limitations, makes sure her characters do not exceed these bounds.

Finally, good fantasy is rooted in *reality* and in *human nature*. Even if the characters are not human or not of this world, the good fantasist realizes that readers are human and that if the readers are to identify with the characters and the situations these must be, disguised or otherwise, human characters and situations. Mr. Toad of Toad Hall may look like a toad, but he acts like a human and has human weaknesses. Winnie-the-Pooh, toy though he is, is capable of human adventures and even human responses to those adventures (despite his protest that he is only a bear of little brain). Most fantasy, despite its wondrous dress, is imbued with a strong sense of reality and a deep seriousness. The imaginary world captures us; the underlying reality of it all moves us.

Fantasy writer Joan Aiken (1984) has summarized what she sees to be the practical value of a developed imagination. In addition to amusing us, our imagination, she points out, keeps us hopeful, enabling us to see the myriad possibilities that life offers. It helps us to solve problems by allowing us to see things from different and fresh perspectives. It helps us see the points of view of others, thus serving as a check to fanaticism. Aiken goes further to suggest that the imagination is a bit like a muscle—if we do not exercise it, it becomes weak and ineffectual. Reading is the best way of exercising our imaginations. Although Aiken does not suggest that reading fantasy is a better exercise of the imagination than reading realism or nonfiction, we can safely say that fantasy does require a bit *more* exercise. Fantasy creates not only its own characters and plots, but also its own peculiar set of laws with which we as readers must become acquainted. Fantasy deliberately challenges our perceptions of reality and forces us to explore new, uncharted realms of thought. Not all readers are willing to accept the challenge. But for those who do, the rewards can be manifold.

BIBLIOGRAPHY OF CRITICAL STUDIES

Aiken, Joan. "On Imagination." *Horn Book Magazine* (November/December 1984): 735–741.

Alexander, Lloyd. "High Fantasy and Heroic Romance." *Horn Book Magazine* December 1971, 577–584.

Attebery, Brian. *The Fantasy Tradition in American Literature: From Irving to Le Guin*. Bloomington, IN: Indiana University Press, 1980.

Babbitt, Natalie. "Fantasy and the Classic Hero." *School Library Journal* (October 1987): 25–29.

Cameron, Eleanor. *The Green and Burning Tree*. Boston: Little, Brown, 1969.

Dickinson, Peter. "Fantasy: The Need for Realism." *Children's Literature in Education* 17:1 (1986): 39–51.

Egoff, Sheila. *Worlds Within: Children's Fantasy from the Middle Ages to Today*. Chicago: American Library Association, 1988.

Engdahl, Sylvia. "The Changing Role of Science Fiction in Children's Literature." *Horn Book Magazine* 47: 5 (October 1971): 449–455.

Hume, Kathryn. *Fantasy and Mimesis*. New York and London: Methuen, 1984.

Le Guin, Ursula. *The Language of the Night*. Edited by Susan Wood. New York: Putnam, 1979.

Lewis, C. S. "Three Ways of Writing for Children." *Horn Book Magazine* 39:5 (October 1963): 459–469.

Raynor, Mary. "Some Thoughts on Animals in Children's Books" *Signal* 29 (May 1979): 81–87.

Roberts, Thomas J. "Science Fiction and the Adolescent." *Children's Literature: The Great Excluded*. 2 (1973): 87–91.

Sale, Roger. *Fairy Tales and After: From Snow White to E. B. White*. Cambridge, MA: Harvard University Press, 1978.

Singer, Jerome. "Fantasy: The Foundation of Serenity." *Psychology Today,* July 1976, 33–37.

Snyder, Zylpha Keatley. "Afterword." *Tom's Midnight Garden* by Philippa Pearce, 230–232. New York: Dell, 1986.

Tolkien, J. R. R. *Tree and Leaf.* Boston: Houghton Mifflin, 1965.

Waggoner, Diana. *The Hills of Faraway: A Guide to Fantasy.* New York: Atheneum, 1978.

Wood, Michael. "Coffee Break for Sisyphus: The Point of Science Fiction." *New York Review of Books,* 2 October 1975, 3–4, 6–7.

A SELECTED BIBLIOGRAPHY OF FANTASY FICTION

The following list is only suggestive of the rich selection of fantasy works available for young readers. These are organized according to the classifications discussed in the chapter, but it is important to realize that not all fantasies are easily pigeonholed. These classifications are only to be considered as aids. Picture-book fantasies have been largely omitted, having been covered in Chapter 2, and the majority of these works are suitable for readers of fourth grade and older.

Literary Fairy Tales

Andersen, Hans Christian. *The Emperor and the Nightingale.* Translated by Eva LeGallienne. Illustrated by Nancy Burckert. New York: Harper, 1965.

———. *The Steadfast Tin Soldier.* Illustrated by David Jorgensen. New York: Knopf, 1986.

———. *Thumbelina.* Translated by R. P. Keigwin. Illustrated by Adrienne Adams. New York: Scribner, 1961.

———. *The Wild Swans.* Illustrated by Marcia Brown. New York: Scribner, 1963.

Babbitt, Natalie. *The Search for Delicious.* New York: Farrar, Straus & Giroux, 1969.

Bishop, Claire. *The Five Chinese Brothers.* Illustrated by Kurt Wiese. New York: Coward, McCann & Geoghegan, 1938.

Gardner, John. *Dragon, Dragon and Other Tales.* New York: Knopf, 1975.

Grahame, Kenneth. *The Reluctant Dragon.* Illustrated by Ernest Shepard. New York: Holiday House, 1923.

MacDonald, George. *The Light Princess.* Illustrated by Maurice Sendak. New York: Farrar, Straus & Giroux, 1969.

———. *The Princess and Curdie.* New York: Penguin Books, 1973.

Thurber, James. *Many Moons.* Illustrated by Louis Slobodkin. New York: Harcourt Brace Jovanovich, 1943.

Yolen, Jane. *The Emperor and the Kite.* Illustrated by Ed Young. Cleveland: World, 1967.

Animal Fantasies

Adams, Richard. *Watership Down.* New York: Macmillan, 1974.

Ets, Marie Hall. *Mister Penny.* New York: Viking, 1935.

Grahame, Kenneth. *The Wind in the Willows.* 1908. Several modern editions.

Jarrell, Randall. *The Animal Family.* Illustrated by Maurice Sendak. New York: Pantheon Books, 1965.

Lawson, Robert. *Rabbit Hill.* New York: Viking, 1944.

———. *The Tough Winter.* New York: Viking, 1970.

O'Brien, Robert. *Mrs. Frisby and the Rats of NIMH.* New York: Atheneum, 1971.

Rey, Hans A. *Curious George.* Boston: Houghton Mifflin, 1941.

Selden, George. *The Cricket in Times Square.* Illustrated by Garth Williams. New York: Farrar, Straus & Giroux, 1960.

Sharp, Margery. *The Rescuers.* Boston: Little, Brown, 1959.

Steig, William. *Abel's Island.* New York: Farrar, Straus & Giroux, 1976.

Titus, Eve. *Basil in Mexico.* Illustrated by Paul Galdone. New York: McGraw-Hill, 1976.

White, E. B. *Charlotte's Web.* New York: Harper, 1952.

———. *Stuart Little.* New York: Harper, 1945.

———. *The Trumpet of the Swan.* New York: Harper, 1970.

Toy Fantasies

Bailey, Caroline Sherwin. *Miss Hickory.* New York: Viking, 1968.

Clarke, Pauline. *The Return of the Twelves* (British title: *The Twelve and the Genii*). New York: Coward, McCann & Geoghegan, 1964.

Collodi, Carlo [pseudonym for Carlo Lorenzini]. *The Adventures of Pinocchio.* 1883. Several modern editions.

Field, Rachel. *Hitty, Her First Hundred Years.* New York: Macmillan, 1929.

Godden, Rumer. *The Dolls' House.* New York: Viking, 1962.

———. *Impunity Jane.* New York: Viking, 1964.

Hoban, Russell. *The Mouse and His Child.* New York: Harper, 1967.

Lionni, Leo. *Alexander and the Wind-Up Mouse.* New York: Pantheon Books, 1969.

Milne, A. A. *The House at Pooh Corner.* 1928. Illustrated by Ernest Shepard. New York: Dutton, 1961.

———. *Winnie-the-Pooh.* (1926) Illustrated by Ernest Shepard. New York: Dutton, 1961.

Nicholson, Margery. *The Velveteen Rabbit.* Illustrated by Michael Hague. New York: Holt, Rinehart and Winston, 1983.

Eccentric Characters/Extraordinary Beings

Aiken, Joan. *Black Hearts in Battersea.* New York: Doubleday, 1964.

———. *The Wolves of Willoughby Chase.* New York: Doubleday, 1963.

Allard, Harry. *The Stupids Step Out.* Boston: Houghton Mifflin, 1974.

Atwater, Richard, and Florence Atwater. *Mr. Popper's Penguins.* Illustrated by Robert Lawson. Boston: Little, Brown, 1938.

Fleischman, Sid. *By the Great Horn Spoon!* Boston: Little, Brown, 1963.

———. *The Whipping Boy.* New York: Morrow, 1986.

Hale, Lucretia. *The Peterkin Papers.* 1880. Boston: Houghton Mifflin, 1960.

Kastner, Erich. *The Little Man.* Translated by James Kirkup. Illustrated by Rick Schreiter. New York: Knopf, 1966.

Lindgren, Astrid. *Pippi Longstocking.* New York: Viking, 1950.

Lofting, Hugh. *The Adventures of Dr. Dolittle.* Philadelphia: Lippincott, 1920.

Merrill, Jean. *The Pushcart War.* Reading, MA: Scott/Addison-Wesley, 1964.

Norton, Mary. *The Borrowers.* New York: Harcourt Brace Jovanovich, 1953.

Travers, P. L. *Mary Poppins.* New York: Harcourt Brace Jovanovich, 1934.

The Enchanted Journey

Barrie, Sir James. *Peter Pan.* New York: Scribner, 1950.

Baum, L. Frank. *The Wizard of Oz.* 1900. Several modern editions.

Carroll, Lewis. *Alice's Adventures in Wonderland.* Illustrated by John Tenniel. London: Macmillan, 1984.

Dahl, Roald. *Charlie and the Chocolate Factory.* New York: Knopf, 1964.
———. *James and the Giant Peach.* New York: Knopf, 1961.
Du Bois, William Pène. *Twenty-One Balloons.* New York: Viking, 1947.
Juster, Norton. *The Phantom Tollbooth.* New York: Random House, 1961.
Kingsley, Charles. *The Water Babies.* New York: Watts, 1961.
Lagerlof, Selma. *The Wonderful Adventures of Nils.* 1906. New York: Doubleday, 1907.
Steele, Mary Q. *Journey Outside.* New York: Viking, 1969.

Heroic Fantasies

Alexander, Lloyd. *The High King.* New York: Holt, Rinehart and Winston, 1968. Last of five books in the *Prydain* Chronicles.
Cooper, Susan. *The Grey King.* New York: Atheneum, 1975. Third of a trilogy.
Kendall, Carol. *The Gammage Cup.* New York: Harcourt Brace Jovanovich, 1959.
Le Guin, Ursula. *A Wizard of Earthsea.* New York: Parnassus, 1968. First of a tetralogy.
Lewis, C. S. *The Lion, the Witch and the Wardrobe.* New York: Macmillan, 1950. First of seven books in the *Narnia* series.
McCaffrey, Anne. *Dragonsong.* New York: Atheneum, 1976. First of a trilogy.
Tolkien, J. R. R. *The Hobbit.* Boston: Houghton Mifflin, 1938. Followed by the *Lord of the Rings* trilogy.
Yolen, Jane. *Dragon's Blood.* New York: Dell (Delacorte), 1982.

Supernatural Fantasies

Babbitt, Natalie. *Tuck Everlasting.* New York: Farrar, Straus & Giroux, 1975.
Boston, Lucy. *The Children of Greene Knowe.* New York: Harcourt Brace Jovanovich, 1964.
Cameron, Eleanor. *The Court of the Stone Children.* New York: Dutton, 1973.
Coatsworth, Elizabeth. *The Cat Who Went To Heaven.* Illustrated by Lynd Ward. New York: Macmillan, 1930.
Cobalt, Martin [pseudonym for William Mayne]. *Pool of Swallows.* New York: Nelson, 1974.
Dunlop, Eileen. *Elizabeth, Elizabeth.* New York: Holt, Rinehart and Winston, 1977.
Farmer, Penelope. *A Castle of Bone.* New York: Philomel (Putnam), 1982.
———. *Charlotte Sometimes.* New York: Harcourt Brace Jovanovich, 1969.
Garfield, Leon. *Mister Corbett's Ghost.* New York: Pantheon Books, 1968.
———. *The Restless Ghost: Three Stories.* New York: Pantheon Books, 1969.
Garner, Alan. *The Owl Service.* New York: Walck, 1968.
Hamilton, Virginia. *Sweet Whispers, Brother Rush.* New York: Philomel (Putnam), 1982.
Lively, Penelope. *The Ghost of Thomas Kempe.* Illustrated by Antony Maitland. New York: Dutton, 1973.
Mayne, William. *Earthfasts.* New York: Dutton, 1967.
———. *A Game of Dark.* New York: Dutton, 1971.
Nesbit, E. *The Enchanted Castle.* Harmondsworth, U.K.: Penguin Books, 1979.
Norton, Mary. *Bed-Knob and Broomstick.* Illustrated by Erik Blegvad. New York: Harcourt Brace Jovanovich, 1957.
Pearce, Philippa. *Tom's Midnight Garden.* New York: Dell, 1986.
Westall, Robert. *The Devil on the Road.* New York: Greenwillow (Morrow), 1979.

Science Fiction

Cameron, Eleanor. *Wonderful Flight to the Mushroom Planet.* Illustrated by Robert Henneberger. Boston: Little, Brown, 1954.
Christopher, John. *The White Mountains.* New York: Macmillan, 1967.

Clarke, Arthur C. *Dolphin Island*. New York: Holt, Rinehart and Winston, 1963.

Del Rey, Lester. *The Runaway Robot*. Philadelphia: Westminster, 1965.

Engdahl, Sylvia. *Beyond the Tomorrow Mountains*. New York: Atheneum, 1973.

———. *Enchantress from the Stars*. New York: Macmillan, 1970.

———. *The Far Side of Evil*. New York: Atheneum, 1971.

Hamilton, Virginia. *Justice and Her Brothers*. New York: Greenwillow (Morrow), 1978.

Heinlein, Robert. *Have Space Suit—Will Travel*. New York: Scribner, 1958.

Lawrence, Louise. *Moonwind*. New York: Harper, 1986.

L'Engle, Madeleine. *A Wrinkle in Time*. New York: Farrar, Straus & Giroux, 1962.

Norton, Andre. *Moon of Three Rings*. New York: Viking, 1966.

Todd, Ruthven. *Space Cat*. Illustrated by Paul Galdone. New York: Scribner, 1952.

Verne, Jules. *Twenty Thousand Leagues Under the Sea*. 1864. New York: Penguin Books, 1987.

Wells, H. G. *The Time Machine*. New York: Bantam Books, 1982.

———. *War of the Worlds*. New York: Putnam, 1978.

CHAPTER 10

Realistic Fiction

DEFINITION

Realistic Fiction consists of those stories set in the world as we know it, governed by the laws of the natural world as we understand them, and intended to provide a believable verisimilitude to life as we experience it. This is in contrast to fantasy, which ignores the natural laws and establishes its own set of rules. The appeal of realistic fiction resides in its ability to re-create artistically a vision of the human condition and to enable the readers either to identify or empathize with the characters and their predicaments.

Although realistic fiction by definition is a story that is *possible,* it need not always be especially *probable.* A work of realistic fiction may, in fact, treat material that may seem remote from ordinary life. An example is Robert Louis Stevenson's classic *Treasure Island,* which includes technically realistic, albeit highly improbable adventures, complete with pirates, secret maps, and buried treasure. Realistic fiction containing predominantly extravagant and improbable story lines might be more properly labeled Romantic Realism, and it does seem to represent a transitional literary type between pure fantasy and hard realism. The general rule is, nevertheless, that Realistic Fiction may contain very ordinary or quite exaggerated characters and mundane or preposterous plots, but it does not violate the essential rules of nature. Reality is its touchstone. Consequently, Realistic Fiction presents us with an artist's vision of the world we live in.

VARIETIES OF REALISTIC FICTION

Realism, like fantasy, comes in a wide variety of forms, and it is possible to find realistic books on virtually every imaginable subject. We can identify some broad classes of realism, but, the lines are not easily drawn, and we often find a work that, because of the writer's inventiveness and ingenuity, refuses to fit neatly into a single category. The following classification will suggest the wealth of realistic fiction available to young readers between the ages of about eight and sixteen.

Domestic Realism

It is probably only natural that young readers should be interested in reading stories about home and family—or, stories of Domestic Realism. The British author Charlotte Yonge is usually credited with writing the first domestic novel for young people—*The Daisy Chain* (1862). But the American writers were the ones who ultimately became most comfortable with this type, beginning with Louisa May Alcott's *Little Women* (1867). Alcott, drawing on her own girlhood experiences, presents us with a realistic portrayal of midnineteenth-century American family life, with all its ups and downs. For Alcott, the family is a constant source of strength and stability, the parents are idealized role models, the troubles of the outside world are kept at bay by the family's industry and good humor.

Alcott's successors (and there were many) include Margaret Sidney, author of the once enormously popular *The Five Little Peppers and How They Grew.* Unlike Alcott, Sidney was not able to restrain the sentimental, and her story of the destitute but virtuous Pepper family is saccharine. The children are all self-sacrificing and dutiful, always doing more than their fair share for the family's well-being. The mother seems to draw strength from her poverty, and no one ever complains. Their patience and goodness are rewarded in the end with the almost miraculous bestowal of good fortune. Sidney responded to public demand by producing numerous sequels.

Other books for young readers along these lines include Johanna Spyri's *Heidi,* Eleanor Porter's *Pollyanna,* and Kate Douglas Wiggin's *Rebecca of Sunnybrook Farm,* all of which are highly sentimentalized portraits of young girls (rarely boys) of incredible goodness, who bring much needed happiness to the adult world. That these were all the subjects of romantic movies of the 1930s, when the world was in the throes of the Great Depression, suggests their escapist qualities. Frances Hodgson Burnett's *The Secret Garden* is a refreshing change from the overly sweet domestic romance, for her heroine, Mary, is initially a rather unpleasant child placed in an even more unpleasant home—that of her wealthy, but very mysterious, uncle. It is the story of Mary's "humanization," something she learns, not surprisingly, from the example of a large, and ecstatically happy, peasant family who live nearby. *The Secret Garden* contains mystery and suspense, as well as engaging characters, making it one of the most enduring of childhood stories, and difficult to pigeonhole. It celebrates the virtues of family life, but is certainly not a domestic tale in any traditional sense.

Almost an archetype of the family story, Laura Ingalls Wilder's *Little House* books, published in the 1930s and 40s, drew on her own childhood experiences from the latter half of the nineteenth century. Combining the features of survival fiction with the family story and using the theme of familial love and the interdependence of humanity, Wilder created one of the most popular of all series. Her tales are episodic and not really novels, and she does not hesitate to expose the grim side of that hard life. Nevertheless, the pervasive mood is highly romantic; there is always the underlying feeling that life in those simpler pioneer days was somehow better than it is today. The frontier was full of honest, hard-working, and independent people—but not so independent that they did not realize the importance of mutual assistance and cooperation when circumstances demanded. It is difficult not to detect the sense of nostalgia that lies just beneath the surface of Wilder's work.

Two notable writers, Eleanor Estes (of the *Moffat* series) and Elizabeth Enright (of the *Melendy* series), produced successful domestic fiction in the midtwentieth century. Both take a romantic view of the family and present us with households that, even though on the brink of poverty, are filled with warmth and caring. Both writers adopt the episodic plot, with the individual chapters loosely connected by some overriding theme. Estes's works might almost be considered historical fiction, for she sets them in the 1910s, whereas Enright's stories are set in the period of their writing, the 1940s. Beverly Cleary's delightful *Ramona* tales (*Ramona the Pest, Ramona the Brave,* and others) focus on a spirited young girl and the traumas of growing up. Because of their episodic structure and comic nature, they have much in common with the works of Estes and Enright. For somewhat older readers, Madeleine L'Engle's stories of the Austin family (*Meet the Austins* and others) have continued the tradition of the domestic story.

With the dramatic change in the family structure in the latter half of the twentieth century, the romantic family scenes described by Estes, Enright, Cleary, and L'Engle are becoming rare—particularly in literature for older readers. Today we more commonly find, in place of the happy family unit once exemplified by such television programs as "Father Knows Best," "The Donna Reed Show," and "Leave It to Beaver," stories of emotionally charged situations, broken homes, and nontraditional domestic arrangements. Bill and Vera Cleaver's *Where the Lilies Bloom* describes the trials of an Appalachian family of poor, orphaned children, who survive and are held together chiefly through the valiant efforts of the thirteen-year-old middle sister. Virginia Hamilton's *M. C. Higgins, the Great,* also about a mountain family—this one African-American—likewise addresses the issues of family survival and family pride in the face of an increasingly insensitive technological world. Robert Newton Peck's *A Day No Pigs Would Die,* an account of a Shaker boyhood in New England of the late 1920s, reveals the clash of cultures as the simple Shaker life is challenged by the rapidly advancing world around it. Katherine Paterson's *Jacob Have I Loved* is the story of the tenuous relationship between twin sisters, focusing primarily on the emotional growth of one, Louise, who must come to terms with herself as well as with the rest of her family. The trend of the domestic novel in the twentieth century has been toward greater realism and less sentimentality. This change has been inevitably necessitated by the changing nature of the family—a perfect example of the response of art to life.

Social Realism

Social Realism in fiction for young people is a phenomenon of the latter half of the twentieth century. Decidedly unromantic, these works openly examine the important issues facing the world today. Some of the domestic novels we noted above actually transcend the distinction between domestic fiction and social realism. *Where the Lilies Bloom* can be read as a treatise on the plight of the rural poor. And a work such as Mildred Taylor's *Roll of Thunder, Hear My Cry,* a moving account of the struggles of an African-American family in rural Mississippi in the 1930s, combines the features of a domestic novel (focusing on the family unit) and the novel of Social Realism. The issue of racism provides the most dramatic material, although Taylor makes it clear that the characters' ability to endure comes from the close familial ties they enjoy. In some sense, novels dealing with social issues take on the appearance of survival fiction. In an age when technology threatens the individual's sense of identity and, at times, even the nature of society and civilization as we know it, we may well feel that growing up in a city slum or an Appalachian hovel is as much a challenge as being abandoned on a desert island or in the frozen Arctic reaches. The plight of the inner-city poor—whether African-American, Hispanic, or white—is the subject of numerous books, including S. E. Hinton's *The Outsiders,* Frank Bonham's *Durango Street,* Kristin Hunter's *The Soul Brothers and Sister Lou.*

Typically, the novels of Social Realism offer hope amid the struggle, although the message is usually that, if hardship is to be overcome, it will be through perseverance and determination and not through some fortuitous event showering rich blessings upon the protagonist. However, Robert Cormier's novels (including *I Am the Cheese, The Chocolate War, Beyond the Chocolate War,* and *Bumblebees Fly Anyway*) take a much bleaker look at society than most books for young people. In his works, adults and children alike may be depicted in the worst possible light—self-serving, vicious, unscrupulous, even downright evil. Society as Cormier paints it takes on an Orwellian flavor—Big Brother is watching every move, spies lurk around every corner, and even infiltrate the sanctity of the home. Adults criticize Cormier's unhappy—even grimly depressing—endings, but he has remained a consistently popular novelist with adolescents, proving once again that adults have under-estimated the capacity of the young to face serious issues.

The Problem Novel and the Psychological Novel

An important body of fiction for young people addresses individual personal issues, as distinguished from societal issues. To be sure, psychological issues are often intermingled with societal issues—the rising divorce rate (a social phenomenon) has resulted in the need for emotional adjustment on the part of children from broken homes (a psychological issue). Nevertheless, it is possible to identify books whose primary focus is on the individual's response to specific personal crises or other problems, whereas the novel of Social Realism is more universal in its treatment. Almost an invention of the 1960s, the Problem Novel typically focuses on a single issue of immediate concern to young people—parents' divorce, the first date, the onset of puberty, adjusting to a new home, teenage pregnancy, drugs, homosexuality, and so on. The traditional domestic story depicts a family (usually the parent or parents) that assists the protagonist in resolving personal difficulties. In the Problem Novel the family is depicted as either helpless or, just as likely, part of the problem. The solutions, therefore, come from outside the home, perhaps from a sympathetic adult or even a peer.

The Problem Novel is a reflection of the perceived breakdown of the modern family structure (we should note that the breakdown of the American family has been predicted since at least the Civil War). But the Problem Novel also represents an acknowledgment of the abilities of young people to face up to serious troubles and cope with them effectively. Charlotte Zolotow has written dozens of books for early readers that explore a wide variety of personal issues facing children. *William's Doll,* to name one, deals with the very natural desire for a young boy to have a doll, and his conventional father's worry that the desire may be unnatural. For readers in the middle and upper grades, such books as Judy Blume's *Are You There, God? It's Me, Margaret* (focusing in part on a girl's coming to terms with menstruation and the psychological confusion surrounding it), Betsy Byars's *The Summer of the Swans* (about mental retardation), Robert Lipsyte's *One Fat Summer* (about obesity), and Norma Klein's *Mom, the Wolf Man and Me* (about an illegitimate child's adjusting to her mother's marriage) are just a few examples of some of the popular titles in this category and of the range of topics Problem Novels explore.

The Problem Novel is extremely popular with many adolescents. They find in these fictional works characters with whom they can identify. Problem Novels have been used as part of bibliotherapy, a process by which young people are assisted in coping with personal problems through directed reading. There is evidence that bibliotherapy can be an effective means of coping. On the other hand, there is the notion that Problem Novels themselves often encourage a rather self-indulgent attitude (see, especially, Nodelman (1981), "How Typical Children Read Typical Books"). Teenagers, according to this theory, read only about other teenagers just like themselves, suffering from the same traumas as they are, and they soon get a distorted sense of the magnitude of their problems. In other words, instead of giving them a fresh outlook on their problems, the books allow them to wallow in self-pity, which eventually narrows their world instead of widening it. Perhaps a truly effective bibliotherapy is that which expands the reader's experiences, broadens the mind, and thus multiplies the possible responses to problems. At its worst, the Problem Novel becomes formulaic, predictable, and even sensationalized, with mechanical characters in plastic settings. And the Problem Novel is always at risk of seeming to imply that problems have simple solutions.

At its best, the Problem Novel explores significant psychological and sociological issues with sensitivity, and it gives us vivid characters with depth of emotion. Since their purpose is the exploration of a personality and not merely the solution of a problem, we may find the term Psychological Novel more accurate for some of these works. They tend to be for older readers and are written on a somewhat more sophisticated plane. They contain not so much a social message (as we come to expect from the novels of Social Realism) or the implication that every problem has a solution (as we come to believe from many Problem Novels). Instead, they reveal life in all its fascinating complexity. Writers such as Irene Hunt (in *Up a Road Slowly*), Katherine Paterson (in *Great Gilly Hopkins* and *A Bridge to Terabithia*), and Zibby Oneal (in *The Language of Goldfish* and *Summer's Light*) sensitively explore the personal difficulties facing young people in the process of maturing, but more importantly, there is the implicit faith in the resilience and ultimate good sense of young people. Most, if not all, fiction for young readers ultimately is about the rites of passage, the initiation into adulthood (or into advancing stages of adolescence). But this initiation is the special focus of the Psychological Novel, the goal of which is to present an honest account of that passage as the writer sees it.

Adventure and Survival Stories

The Adventure Story is characterized by exciting, fast-moving plots, unusual, often bizarre, characters, and frequently exotic settings. Stevenson's *Treasure Island,* and Mark Twain's *Huckleberry Finn* and *Tom Sawyer* are classic adventure stories, although the nineteenth century was rife with hack writers who cranked out formulaic adventure books primarily for boys. Edgar Rice Burroughs' popular *Tarzan* series includes all the necessary ingredients of adventure romance—inventiveness, suspense, exotic setting, clearly defined good and evil characters, and happy endings. (The recent movies of the exploits of the adventurer/archeologist/professor Indiana Jones, although satiric in their excesses, outdo the Tarzan tales in their hair-raising escapades, giving the viewers barely time to catch their breaths from thrill to thrill.)

The mystery has long been a favorite kind of adventure story for young readers, and such serial detectives as Nancy Drew, the Hardy Boys, the Bobbsey Twins, and Donald Sobol's *Encyclopedia Brown* series are enormously popular. The mystery always involves the solving of a puzzle—typically, but not necessarily, a crime—and consequently depends heavily upon plot intricacy and clever twists. The success of a mystery depends upon the clever planting of clues and the ingenuity of the crime and its solution. Although most of the characters in mystery tend to be stereotypes—the principal interest is, after all, in the plot—some writers enrich their tales by creating memorable detectives, usually with exaggerated personalities (such as Agatha Christie's Miss Marple or Hercule Poirot). There are examples of exceptionally fine mysteries for young people. E. L. Konigsburg's *From the Mixed-Up Files of Mrs. Basil E. Frankweiler* recounts the exploits of a young brother and sister detective as they follow clues to the unraveling of a mystery, largely set in the Metropolitan Museum of Art. And Ellen Raskin's *The Westing Game* likewise depicts a young detective searching out the word clues of a cleverly devised mystery, containing numerous surprising twists. Both of these works won the coveted Newbery Medal for the best American literary work for young people in their respective years of publication. Virginia Hamilton's *The House of Dies Drear* may be regarded as a mystery of sorts, weaving suspense into a tale of the discovery of African-American heritage. Hamilton has the uncanny ability to take seemingly ordinary people and places and weave an almost magical story. Her characters are so richly developed that we come to believe in even the most bizarre of them.

The Survival Story is an adventure that focuses on an individual or individuals pitted usually against the forces of nature, which they must either outwit or (more likely) unite with in order to survive. Daniel Defoe's *Robinson Crusoe* is often regarded as the granddaddy of the survival story. But whereas Defoe has his hero taming the wild tropical paradise in which he found himself (and his story has much of the flavor of romance), twentieth-century survival stories depict their heroes or heroines humbled before the forces of nature. The native girls, Karana in Scott O'Dell's *Island of the Blue Dolphins* (set on an island off the California coast) and Julie in Jean Craighead George's *Julie of the Wolves* (set in the Arctic wilds), even adopt the ways of the wild animals inhabiting their environment. Instead of controlling nature, these brave protagonists learn to live with it—and, of course, the implication is that civilized man can well learn from these experiences. Theodore Taylor's *The Cay* and Harry Mazer's *Snowbound* and *The Island Keeper* are other examples of this popular form of fiction, with Mazer's works representing a combination of the Adventure Story with the Problem Novel.

Whitley Strieber's *Wolf of Shadows* relates the grim experiences of a pack of wolves and a human mother and her young daughter trying to survive together in the aftermath of a nuclear war. One might argue that this work is fantasy, although in fact the author has taken no liberties with natural laws and has attempted to provide us with a starkly realistic account of a nuclear winter. This story is speculative fiction, realistic in every detail—so far as specualitive fiction can be—and it combines the elements of survival fiction and, with its admonitive message, Social Realism.

Realistic Animal Fiction

Strieber's *Wolf of Shadows* may be rightly considered under the category of Realistic Animal Fiction (that is, if we are ready to admit it to the class of Realistic Fiction). Realistic Animal Fiction builds on the popularity that animal stories enjoy among young children. Such books as Marjory Flack's *The Story About Ping,* an amusing tale of a disobedient young duckling on the Yangtze River, or Robert McCloskey's *Make Way for Ducklings,* about a family of mallards making their home in downtown Boston, or Lynd Ward's beautifully illustrated *The Biggest Bear,* all treat their animal characters more or less realistically. They live as animals, they behave as animals, and they are not empowered with human speech (although some may argue they are given human emotions). Realistic Animal Stories for older readers follow similar patterns, with the authors depicting the animals as true to their species. For example, it might be logical for an author to depict an animal as hungry, protective of its young, or desperate for its survival, but it would make little sense to suggest that they engage in romantic entanglements or domestic arguments. Frequently these books focus on the relationship between an animal and a youthful human companion, such as in Marjorie Kinnan Rawlings's *The Yearling,* or Farley Mowatt's comical true-life adventures in *Owls in the Family.* Mowatt's book is found in the nonfiction section of the library, since it is autobiographical, and is an excellent example of the sometimes fine line that exists between fiction and reality. Marguerite Henry's books about horses, *Misty of Chincoteague, King of the Wind,* and others, remain among the best animal stories in the realistic tradition. Perhaps Sheila Burnford's *The Incredible Journey,* in which a cat and two dogs undertake a hazardous trip across the Canadian wilderness, oversteps the limits of credulity, for even though the events are related realistically, some readers feel that the animals assume too much of human nature to be totally believable animals.

Historical Realism

Historical Realism consists of realistic stories set in the past. It differs from Realistic Fiction set in contemporary times in that the writer of historical fiction incurs an obligation to portray the historical period faithfully. Many fine picture-books fit into the category of Historical Realism. (Children in preschool and early elementary school have not yet learned that history is supposed to be dull and dry—and with any luck they never will.) Brinton Turkle's *Thy Friend, Obadiah,* Cynthia Rylant's *When I Was Young in the Mountains,* and Donald Hall's *The Ox-Cart Man* are examples of Historical Realism for the very young. Wilder's *Little House* books, Carol Ryrie Brink's *Caddie Woodlawn,* and Jean Fritz's *The Cabin Faced West* are all suited for children of the middle years and all focus on family life in the early history of the United States. Also for readers in this age group is Marguerite de Angeli's lovely book *The Door in the Wall,* an adventure story set in thirteenth-century England. For older readers, we can cite the works of an American pioneer in historical fiction for youth, Howard Pyle's *Otto of the Silver Hand* and *Men of Iron,* both about the European Middle Ages.

The historical novel depends heavily on a believable and reasonably accurate setting and often includes actual historical personages, but it is *not* history. The events are creations of the author's imagination. We included Wilder's *Little House* series with Domestic Fiction, but these works serve as examples of Historical Realism as well. Unlike fiction set in contemporary times, Historical Realism must provide considerably more background for the novice reader. The more remote and unfamiliar the historical period, the more background the author must supply, including political and social history, customs, and even psychological attitudes (it is unlikely, for example, that an Egyptian slave or medieval peasant would wholeheartedly embrace a democratic way of life). Additionally, the writer must be aware of the state of science and technology during the period covered by the novel. For instance, an author of contemporary fiction need not explain modern methods of preserving food for us, because we all know about refrigerators and freezers. But when writing about the mid-nineteenth century, a writer might have to describe an ice house or the methods of preserving meat by salting or smoking.

On the other hand, readers are not reading the book primarily to learn about such things; the writer's task instead is to include such information as unobtrusively as possible. Joan Blos, herself a writer of some fine historical fiction (*A Gathering of Days* and *Brothers of the Heart*), has noted some of the pitfalls writers of historical fiction should avoid: overloading the text with historical background information, having characters reveal this information in an artificial and inappropriate fashion, or using language unsuited to the historical time ("The Overstuffed Sentence," 38–39). The apparatus of writing, in other words, should never get in the way of the story.

Historical Realism often fits into one of the other classes of fiction we have identified. For instance, it may be a domestic novel, such as Patricia MacLachlan's beautiful tale, *Sarah, Plain and Tall,* a unified work that sensitively explores the perceptions and feelings of a pioneer girl as she adjusts to a stepmother (an experience all too common in the old West). Or it may be a psychological novel, such as Elizabeth George Speare's *The Witch of Blackbird Pond* (about a young woman's integration into life in colonial New England). Or it may be an adventure story, such as Leon Garfield's *Smith* and *The Drummer Boy* or Rosemary Sutcliff's *Mark of the Horse Lord.* Or it may be suggestive of Social Realism, such as Irene Hunt's *Across Five Aprils* (about the hardships caused by the Civil War), or Yoshiko Uchida's *Journey to Topaz* (the story of the Japanese-American internment during World War II), or Paula Fox's *The Slave Dancer* (about American slave trade in the 1840s), or James and Christopher Collier's *My Brother Sam Is Dead,* and Esther Forbes's *Johnny Tremain* (both about the Revolutionary War). Historical fiction is a rich field and includes some of the finest writing for young people.

Multicultural Realism

Fiction that presents a sensitive and penetrating view of the world's vast cultural richness is essential in a well-balanced reading diet. We live in a global world, and that means we can no longer isolate ourselves from unfamiliar cultures and peoples. It is imperative that we take every opportunity to understand one another and thereby learn to accept one another. Multicultural Realism can present a view of an ethnic culture—its customs, its beliefs, its sorrows, its joys—in order that another cultural group might better understand the ways of the world and, through this knowledge, shed ignorant prejudices. Very young readers can discover the fascination of learning about foreign cultures in books such as Marie Hall Ets' *Nine Days to Christmas* (about a Mexican Christmas celebration) or Thomas Handforth's *Mei Li* (about the Chinese New Year customs). A book such as Lucille Clifton's *All Us Come Cross the Water* can illustrate to black and white Americans alike the historical origins of African-Americans.

These initial introductions to our multicultural world can be expanded upon as readers mature. Works such as Ann Nolan Clark's *The Secret of the Andes,* Elizabeth Foreman Lewis's *Young Fu of the Upper Yangtze,* and Armstrong Sperry's *Call It Courage* are all classic treatments of unfamiliar cultures. However, more recently, there has been an effort to educate Americans on the numerous cultures that make up their own diverse nation. Virginia Driving Hawk Sneve's *High Elk's Treasure* and Evelyn Sibley Lampman's *The Potlatch Family* both portray Native Americans (about which a great deal of ill-informed mythology has been promulgated, making books such as these even more important). In his *Dragonwings,* Laurence Yep writes of the troubles besetting the early Chinese immigrants to California, and the difficulties, generally, that face any culture trying to integrate into a widely different cultural system. Isaac Bashevis Singer writes of Judaic culture in *Yentl the Yeshiva Boy.* And the African-American culture has been explored by such writers as Mildred Taylor (*Roll of Thunder, Hear My Cry*) and Virginia Hamilton (*Zeely* and *M. C. Higgins, the Great*).

As with historical fiction, literature about ethnic groups may require the author to supply background information that is normally not required of writers of contemporary fiction. Also, as with historical fiction, Multicultural Realism may cross over into other categories. Paula Fox's *The Slave Dancer,* a grim portrayal of the 1840s slave trade between Africa and the United States, combines Historical Realism with Social Realism. Theodore Taylor's *The Cay,* the story of a white boy and an elderly black man shipwrecked on a deserted Caribbean island and the friendship that eventually results from their experiences, is actually an Adventure/Survival story. Nevertheless, it is important to single out those multicultural works precisely because they may help break down cultural barriers that have created misunderstanding and help them realize that beneath the external trappings, all people hunger and thirst, grieve and rejoice, fear and hope, hate and love in very much the same way.

REALISTIC FICTION AND THE YOUNG READER

It should be clear that the lines of distinction between the various types of realism are sometimes hazy and that many works will fit as nicely into one category as another. It is more important to realize that, regardless of the type, good Realistic Fiction depends upon its adherence to sound literary standards and upon its faithfulness to life as we know it. There seems to be no substitute for reading widely and voraciously all sorts of things, from the time-honored classics to modern experimental works (Robert Cormier's occasionally controversial works, such as *I Am the Cheese,* for example). The literary tastes of children and of teenagers are not yet established. They are still experimenting with literature of all sorts, both good and bad, and that is healthy. Perhaps the best we can do as adults is to make available to them the broadest possible selection. In these pages we have but scratched the surface of the rich store of literature available for young people. If we are patient and determined, we may be able to help even the most reluctant readers find books that they will cherish.

CRITICAL REFERENCES

Abrahamson, Jane. "Still Playing It Safe: Restricted Realism in Teen Novels." *School Library Journal* 22 (May 1976): 38–39.

Blos, Joan. "The Overstuffed Sentence and Other Means for Assessing Historical Fiction for Children." *School Library Journal* 31 (November 1985): 38–39.

Broderick, Dorothy M. *Image of the Black in Children's Fiction.* New York: Bowker, 1973.

Carlson, Ruth Kearney. *Emerging Humanity: Multi-Ethnic Literature for Children and Adolescents.* Dubuque, IA: Brown, 1972.

Dickinson, Peter. "In Defense of Rubbish." *Children's Literature in Education* 3 (November 1970): 7–10.

Ellis, Anne W. *The Family Story in the 1960's.* New York: Archon, 1970.

Hinton, S. E. "Teenagers Are for Real." *New York Times Book Review* (27 August 1967): 26–29.

Hipple, T., and B. Bartholomew. "The Novels College Freshmen Have Read." *ALAN Review* Winter 1982: 8–10.

Kingston, Carolyn. *The Tragic Mode in Children's Literature.* New York: Teachers College Press, 1974.

Lochhead, Marion. "Clio Junior: Historical Novels for Children." In *Only Connect.* 2d ed. Edited by Sheila Egoff, G. T. Stubbs, and L. F. Ashely. New York: Oxford University Press, 1980: 17–27.

Luecke, Fritz J., comp. *Children's Books: Views and Values.* Middletown, CT: Xerox Education Publications, 1973.

McDowell, Miles. "Fiction for Children and Adults: Some Essential Differences." *Children's Literature in Education* 10 (March 1973): 50–63.

Mertz, Maia Pank, and David A. England. "The Legitimacy of American Adolescent Fiction." *School Library Journal* 29 (October 1983): 119–123.

Moorman, Charles. *Kings & Captains: Variations on a Heroic Theme.* Louisville: University of Kentucky Press, 1971.

Moran, Barbara B., and Susan Stienfirst. "Why Johnny (and Jane) Read Whodunits in Series." *School Library Journal* March 1985: 113–117.

Nixon, Joan Lowry. "Clues to the Juvenile Mystery." *The Writer* 90 (February 1977): 23–26.

Nodelman, Perry. "How Typical Children Read Typical Books." *Children's Literature in Education* 12 (Winter 1981): 177–185.

Paterson, Katherine. *Gates of Excellence: On Reading and Writing Books for Children.* New York: Elsevier/Nelson, 1981.

Peck, Richard. "Some Thoughts on Adolescent Literature." *News from ALAN* September/October 1975: 4–7.

Rees, David. *The Marble in the Water.* Boston: The Horn Book: 1980.

————. *Painted Desert, Green Shade: Essays on Contemporary Writers for Children and Young Adults.* Boston: The Horn Book: 1984.

Rudman, Masha K. *Children's Literature: An Issues Approach.* 2d ed. New York: Longman, 1984.

Sims, Rudine. *Shadow & Substance: Afro-American Experience in Contemporary Children's Fiction.* Urbana, IL: National Council of Teachers of English, 1982.

Soderbergh, Peter A. "The Stratemeyer Strain: Educators and the Juvenile Series Book, 1900–1980." In *Only Connect.* 2d ed. Edited by Sheila Egoff, G. T. Stubbs, and L. F. Ashely. New York: Oxford University Press, 1980: 63–73.

Wilkin, Binnie Tate. *Survival Themes in Fiction for Children and Young People.* New York: Scarecrow Press, 1978.

A SELECTED BIBLIOGRAPHY OF REALISTIC FICTION

The following list is a representative sampling of realistic fiction classified according to the categories outlined in the chapter. It is necessary to remember that many books quite easily fit into more than one category. This is only a sampling; look for other books by these authors as well.

Domestic Realism

Alcott, Louisa May. *Little Women.* 1868–69. Various modern editions.
Burnett, Frances Hodgson. *The Secret Garden.* 1909. Various modern editions.
Cleary, Beverly. *Ramona the Pest.* New York: Morrow, 1968.
Enright, Elizabeth. *Thimble Summer.* New York: Holt, Rinehart and Winston, 1938.
Estes, Eleanor. *The Moffats.* New York: Harcourt Brace Jovanovich, 1941.
Fitzhugh, Louise. *Harriet the Spy.* New York: Harper, 1964.
Gates, Doris. *Blue Willow.* New York: Viking, 1940.
Hunt, Irene. *Up a Road Slowly.* New York: Follett, 1967.
L'Engle, Madeleine. *Meet the Austins.* New York: Vanguard Press, 1960.
Montgomery, L. L. *Anne of Green Gables.* Various modern editions.
Paterson, Katherine. *Jacob Have I Loved.* New York: Crowell, 1980.

Peck, Robert. *A Day No Pigs Would Die.* New York: Knopf, 1972.

Porter, Eleanor. *Pollyanna.* Various modern editions.

Sawyer, Ruth. *Roller Skates.* New York: Viking, 1936.

Sidney, Margaret. *The Five Little Peppers and How They Grew.* 1880. Varous modern editions.

Sorenson, Virginia. *Miracles on Maple Hill.* New York: Harcourt Brace Jovanovich, 1956.

Spyri, Johanna. *Heidi.* 1884. Various modern editions.

Voigt, Cynthia. *Dicey's Song.* New York: Atheneum, 1982.

Wiggin, Kate Douglas. *Rebecca of Sunnybrook Farm.* Various modern editions.

Social Realism

Bonham, Frank, *Durango Street.* New York: Dutton, 1965.

———. *The Nitty Gritty.* New York: Dutton, 1968.

Childress, Alice. *A Hero Ain't Nothin' but a Sandwich.* New York: Coward, McCann & Geoghegan, 1973.

Cleaver, Bill and Vera. *Where the Lilies Bloom.* Philadelphia: Lippincott, 1969.

Cormier, Robert. *Beyond the Chocolate War.* New York: Knopf, 1985.

———. *The Bumblebee Flies Anyway.* New York: Pantheon Books, 1983.

———. *The Chocolate War.* New York: Pantheon Books, 1974.

———. *I Am the Cheese.* New York: Pantheon Books, 1977.

Fox, Paula. *How Many Miles to Babylon?* Port Washington, NY: White, 1967.

Graham, Lorenz. *North Town.* New York: Crowell, 1965.

Hamilton, Virginia. *The Planet of Junior Brown.* New York: Macmillan, 1971.

Hinton, S. E. *The Outsiders.* New York: Viking, 1967.

Hunter, Kristen. *Soul Brothers and Sister Lou.* New York: Scribner, 1958.

Taylor, Mildred. *Roll of Thunder, Hear My Cry.* New York: Dial Press, 1976.

Zindel, Paul. *The Pigman.* New York: Harper, 1968.

The Problem Novel and the Psychological Novel

Blume, Judy. *Are You There, God? It's Me, Margaret.* New York: Bradbury, 1970.

———. *Tiger Eyes.* Scarsdale, NY: Bradbury, 1981.

Byars, Betsy. *Summer of the Swans.* New York: Viking, 1970.

Cleary, Beverly. *Dear Mr. Henshaw.* New York: Morrow, 1983.

Daly, Maureen. *Seventeenth Summer.* New York: Dodd, Mead, 1942.

Danziger, Paula. *The Cat Ate My Gymsuit.* New York: Dell (Delacorte Press), 1974.

Greene, Bette. *Philip Hall Likes Me. I Reckon Maybe.* New York: Dial Press, 1974.

———. *Summer of My German Soldier.* New York: Dial Press, 1973.

Klein, Norma. *Mom, the Wolfman and Me.* New York: Pantheon Books, 1972.

Konigsburg, E. L. *Jennifer, Hecate, Macbeth, William McKinley, and Me, Elizabeth.* New York: Atheneum, 1967.

Lipsyte, Robert. *One Fat Summer.* New York: Harper, 1977.

Lowry, Lois. *A Summer to Die.* Boston: Houghton Mifflin, 1977.

Oneal, Zibby. *In Summer Light.* New York: Viking, 1985.

———. *The Language of Goldfish.* New York: Random House, 1980.

Paterson, Katherine. *The Great Gilly Hopkins.* New York: Crowell, 1978.

Peck, Richard. *Secrets of the Shopping Mall.* New York: Dell (Delacorte Press), 1979.

Smith, Doris Buchanan. *A Taste of Blackberries.* New York: Crowell, 1973.

Voigt, Cynthia. *A Solitary Blue.* New York: Atheneum, 1983.

Adventure and Survival Fiction

Corcoran, Barbara. *A Star to the North*. Philadelphia: Lippincott, 1970.

George, Jean Craighead. *Julie of the Wolves*. New York: Harper, 1972.

———. *My Side of the Mountain*. New York: Dutton, 1959.

Holman, Felice. *Slake's Limbo*. New York: Scribner, 1974.

Houston, James. *Frozen Fire*. New York: Atheneum, 1977.

———. *Long Claw: An Arctic Adventure*. New York: Atheneum, 1981.

Konigsburg, E. L. *From the Mixed-Up Files of Mrs. Basil E. Frankweiler*. New York: Atheneum, 1967.

Mazer, Harry. *The Island Keeper*. New York: Dell (Delacorte Press), 1981.

———. *Snowbound*. New York: Dell, 1973.

O'Dell, Scott. *Island of the Blue Dolphins*. Boston: Houghton Mifflin, 1960.

Raskin, Ellen. *The Westing Game*. New York: Dutton, 1978.

Shecter, Ben. *Inspector Rose*. New York: Harper, 1969.

Sobol, Donald. *Encyclopedia Brown Saves the Day*. Nashville, TN: Nelson, 1970.

Speare, Elizabeth George. *The Sign of the Beaver*. Boston: Houghton Mifflin, 1983.

Stevenson, Robert Louis. *Treasure Island*. 1883. Various modern editions.

Strieber, Whitley. *Wolf of Shadows*. New York: Knopf, 1985.

Taylor, Theodore. *The Cay*. New York: Doubleday, 1969.

Twain, Mark. *The Adventures of Huckleberry Finn*. 1884. Various modern editions.

———. *The Adventures of Tom Sawyer*. Various modern editions.

Animal Realism

Burnford, Sheila. *The Incredible Journey*. Boston: Little, Brown, 1961.

Byars, Betsy. *The Midnight Fox*. New York: Viking, 1968.

Cleary, Beverly. *Socks*. New York: Morrow, 1973.

DeJong, Meindert. *Hurry Home, Candy*. New York: Harper, 1953.

Gates, Doris. *Little Vic*. New York: Viking, 1951.

George, Jean. *The Cry of the Crow*. New York: Harper, 1980.

Gipson, Fred. *Old Yeller*. New York: Harper, 1956.

Griffiths, Helen. *The Greyhound*. New York: Doubleday, 1964.

———. *The Wild Heart*. New York: Doubleday, 1963.

Henry, Marguerite. *King of the Wind*. New York: Rand McNally, 1948.

———. *Misty of Chincoteague*. New York: Rand McNally, 1947.

Kjelgaard, Jim. *Big Red*. New York: Holiday House, 1956.

James, Will. *Smoky, the Cow Horse*. New York: Scribner, 1926.

London, Jack. *The Call of the Wild*. 1903. Various modern editions.

Mowat, Farley. *Owls in the Family*. Boston: Little, Brown, 1962.

Mukerji, Dhan Gopal. *Gay-Neck*. New York: Dutton, 1927.

Rawlings, Marjorie Kinnan. *The Yearling*. New York: Scribner, 1938.

Rawls, Wilson. *Where the Red Fern Grows*. New York: Doubleday, 1961.

Historical Realism

Blos, Joan. *A Gathering of Days*. New York: Scribner, 1979.

Brink, Carol Ryrie. *Caddie Woodlawn*. 1936. Various modern editions.

Collier, James Lincoln, and Christopher Collier. *My Brother Sam Is Dead*. New York: Four Winds, 1974.

de Angeli, Marguerite. *The Door in the Wall*. New York: Doubleday, 1949.

Forbes, Esther. *Johnny Tremain*. Boston: Houghton Mifflin, 1946.

Fox, Paula. *The Slave Dancer*. New York: Bradbury, 1973.

Fritz, Jean. *The Cabin Faced West*. New York: Coward, McCann & Geoghegan, 1958.
Garfield, John. *Smith*. New York: Pantheon Books, 1967.
Haugaard, Erik Christian. *Orphans of the Wind*. Boston: Houghton Mifflin, 1966.
Hunt, Irene. *Across Five Aprils*. Chicago: Follett, 1964.
MacLachlan, Patricia. *Sarah, Plain and Tall*. New York: Harper, 1985.
Monjo, F. N. *The Sea Beggar's Son*. New York: Coward, McCann & Geoghegan, 1975.
Petry, Ann. *Tituba of Salem Village*. New York: Crowell, 1964.
Pyle, Howard. *Men of Iron*. 1890. Various modern editions.
———. *Otto of the Silver Hand*. 1888. Various modern editions.
Richter, Hans Peter. *Friedrich*. New York: Holt, Rinehart and Winston, 1970.
Serraillier, Ian. *The Silver Sword*. New York: Criterion, 1959.
Speare, Elizabeth George. *The Bronze Bow*. Boston: Houghton Mifflin, 1961.
Sutcliff, Rosemary. *The Lantern Bearers*. New York: Walck, 1959.
———. *The Mark of the Horse Lord*. New York: Walck, 1965.
Vining, Elizabeth Gray. *Adam of the Road*. New York: Viking, 1942.
Walsh, Jill Paton. *The Emperor's Winding Sheet*. New York: Farrar, 1978.
Wilder, Laura Ingalls. *Little House in the Big Woods*. 1932. New York: Harper, 1953.

Multicultural Fiction

Armer, Laura Adams. *Waterless Mountain*. New York: Longmans, Green (McKay), 1931. Native American.
Beskow, Elsa. *Pelle's New Suit*. New York: Harper, 1929. Swedish.
Bonham, Frank. *Viva Chicano*. New York: Dutton, 1970. Hispanic.
DeJong, Meindert. *The House of Sixty Fathers*. New York: Harper, 1956. Chinese.
———. *Journey from Peppermint Street*. New York: Harper, 1968. Dutch.
Guy, Rosa. *The Friends*. New York: Holt, Rinehart and Winston, 1973. African-American.
———. *Ruby*. New York: Viking, 1976. African-American.
Hamilton, Virginia. *The House of Dies Drear*. New York: Macmillan, 1968. African-American.
———. *M. C. Higgins, the Great*. New York: Macmillan, 1974. African-American.
———. *Zeely*. New York: Macmillan, 1967. African-American.
Kherdian, David. *The Road from Home: The Story of an Armenian Girl*. New York: Greenwillow (Morrow), 1979. Eastern European.
Krumgold, Joseph. *. . . And Now, Miguel*. New York: Crowell, 1953. Hispanic.
Lampman, Evelyn Sibley. *The Potlatch Family*. New York: Atheneum, 1976. Native American.
Lauritzen, Jonreed. *The Ordeal of the Young Hunter*. Boston: Little, Brown, 1954. Native American.
Lewis, Elizabeth Foreman. *Young Fu of the Upper Yangtze*. New York: Holt, Rinehart and Winston, 1932. Chinese.
Lord, Bette Bao. *In the Year of the Boar and Jackie Robinson*. New York: Harper, 1984. Chinese-American.
Mathis, Sharon Bell. *The Hundred Penny Box*. New York: Viking, 1975. African-American.
Potok, Chaim. *My Name Is Asher Lev*. New York: Knopf, 1972. Jewish.
Singer, Isaac Bashevis. *Yentl the Yeshiva Boy*. New York: Farrar, Straus & Giroux, 1962. Jewish.
Sneve, Virginia Driving Hawk. *High Elk's Treasure*. New York: Holiday House, 1972. Native American.
Snyder, Zilpha Keatley. *The Egypt Game*. New York: Atheneum, 1967. African-American.
Sperry, Armstrong. *Call It Courage*. New York: Macmillan, 1940. Pacific Islands.
Suhl, Yuri. *The Merrymaker*. New York: Four Winds, 1975. Jewish.
Uchida, Yoshiko. *Journey to Topaz*. New York: Scribner, 1971. Japanese-American.
Wojciechowska, Maia. *Shadow of a Bull*. New York: Atheneum, 1964. Spanish.
Yep, Laurence. *Child of the Owl*. New York: Harper, 1977. Chinese-American.
———. *Dragonwings*. New York: Harper, 1975. Chinese-American.

CHAPTER 11
Biography

DEFINITION

A biography is a nonfictional work describing the life—or part of the life—of an individual. (When a person writes the story of his or her own life, we call the work an autobiography.) Biographies are among the most popular of nonfiction books for young people. We separate our discussion of biographies from other nonfiction types primarily because biographies (and autobiographies), unlike other informational books, have traditionally been regarded as a sort of subgenre of literature. The biographer Paul Murray Kendall notes that biography lies between history and literature and has never been fully embraced by either (1985, 3). Nevertheless, biography is a very old genre; the Gospels, in fact, are among the earliest biographies, describing, as they do, the life of Jesus Christ. Through biographies we are reminded of the common thread of humanity that runs through us all. Biography can inspire us with portraits of the indomitable human spirit, or it can arouse us from complacency with portraits of human malice and insensitivity.

This century has seen many fine writers for both children and adults, earn their literary reputations as biographers. Esther Forbes, Jean Fritz, James Daugherty, and Ingri and Edgar Parin d'Aulaire, are just a few of the most famous. The field of biography has grown to yield a rich and varied harvest.

APPROACHES TO BIOGRAPHY

There are two widely recognized approaches to biography for children: one, the authentic biography, valuing faithful adherence to facts; the other, the fictionalized biography, valuing dramatic narrative. Each has its peculiar strengths and appeal.

Authentic Biography

If a biography attempts to convey factual information about a person's life and time faithfully, we call it an authentic biography. An authentic biography will not use any facts that cannot be supported by solid and reliable research. Consequently, if dialogue is used (which is not common in authentic biography) it must be dialogue that can be substantiated by historical documents (such as letters) or reliable personal recollections. Authentic biography attempts to be completely accurate in its presentation of the facts; however, we dare not forget that not even the most thorough and honest biographer is free from bias or wholly objective. By ignoring some facts and highlighting others, it is possible to slant even the most solid evidence, and readers need to be aware of such slanting.

James Daugherty was a pioneer of fine authentic biography for young people; his *Poor Richard* (a life of Benjamin Franklin), *Daniel Boone,* and *Abraham Lincoln* are justly celebrated. More recently, Russell Freedman's Newbery Award-winning *Lincoln: A Photobiography* has established still more exacting standards for young people's biography. This book should be a model for all future biographers for young people: careful research, including extraordinary illustration with photographs from the period; refusal to condescend to children in either vocabulary or selection of hard facts; honest and unsentimental portrayal of one of the great figures of American history; and avoidance of both debunking and deifying its subject.

Fictionalized Biography

In writing for young people, some biographers have found it inviting to dramatize certain events—to give characters dialogue or perhaps even to invent believable scenes—presumably to make the story come to life. These fictionalized biographies are readily recognizable by their dialogue. That is, if we are reading a biography of Benjamin Franklin and find extended conversations between young Franklin and his brother or his parents, we can be fairly certain that the author has invented these discussions, for it is unlikely that they are recorded with such detail in any surviving record. A true fictionalized biography will not invent scenes or events that did not happen, but rather dramatize specific scenes, speculating on the details. Naturally, since its boundaries between truth and fiction are not precisely defined, fictionalized biography is not as reliable as authentic biography, but it makes good reading. Jean Lee Latham's *Carry On, Mr. Bowditch* is a fine example of fictionalized biography. Most of this book consists of dramatized scenes depicting events that occurred in the late eighteenth century—scenes with dialogue to which no biographer could have been privy. Although she does not distort the essence of the life of the celebrated New England mathematician and navigator Nathaniel Bowditch, neither does she pretend that her book is authentic historical writing. We go to this sort of book purely for entertainment and not for accurate or complete information.

A third approach to biographical writing is biographical fiction, which is characterized by considerable fanciful invention and the great liberties it takes with the facts. Biographical fiction should properly be considered as fiction and is so classified in most libraries. Robert Lawson's wonderfully entertaining *Ben and Me,* for example, ostensibly describes the life of Benjamin Franklin as told by Amos, an irascible mouse that inhabits the great man's fur hat. Amos is an incurable egotist and takes most of the credit for Franklin's great works, describing how the Declaration of Independence was actually the work of mice fighting for their own liberty and how Amos was responsible for the "first" French Revolution—that of the French mice. It is all a great deal of fun, but it is not, by any stretch of the imagination, a biography of Franklin, and it is more appropriately evaluated by the standards of fantasy.

THE FORMS OF BIOGRAPHY

In addition to these differences in degree of authenticity, biographies also differ according to their content and, particularly, the extent of their coverage. Biographies may cover a subject's entire life or only a part of it. Biographies may also examine a subject's life with relationship to others who share some common ground. Of course, each of these types can be either authentic or fictionalized biographies.

Complete Biographies

For older readers, we can find a multitude of complete biographies, which, as the name suggests, examine the whole of the subject's life from cradle to grave. A complete biography may be simple, such as Aliki's charming picture-book biographies (*The Story of Johnny Appleseed*), or complex, such as Russell Freedman's *Lincoln: A Photobiography*. Jean Fritz has produced a number of very brief biographies, which are nonetheless complete in that they survey the entire life of the subject. Fritz has successfully distilled the essence of the lives of her subjects (all figures of the American Revolution) into works of under fifty pages, and she writes with a warm sense of humor that helps to bring her subjects closer to her readers. Since complete biographies necessitate bringing together a considerable amount of information that may be only loosely related, these are often the most difficult to unify. Still, the complete biography is what most readers think of when biography is mentioned.

Partial Biographies

Occasionally, biographies will appear that focus on only one part or one aspect of a subject's life. These partial biographies allow the author to focus more clearly on a specific theme. For example, Johanna Johnston's fictionalized biography of Harriet Beecher Stowe, *Harriet and the Runaway Book,* focuses chiefly on Mrs. Stowe's writing of *Uncle Tom's Cabin*. Esther Hautzig's autobiographical *The Endless Steppe: Growing Up in Siberia* recounts five years in the author's youth spent in forced labor. And, of course, one of the most famous of all partial autobiographical works is Anne Frank's *The Diary of a Young Girl*. Of necessity, biographies of living persons are technically partial biographies, since the life is not yet completed. However, the real point of the partial biography is to limit the writer's scope.

A whole series of books appeared in the 1940s and 1950s on the childhoods of famous Americans. Unfortunately, these were not generally well written, and they represented fictionalized biography at its worst, using made-up dialogue, for example, between young Thomas Jefferson and his friends that made them sound as if they were midwestern schoolchildren of the midtwentieth century. However, these books may remind us that young readers are often most interested in and can best identify with the events of childhood and adolescence. The activities of an accomplished adult—the usual subject of a biography—may not always be suitable or readily accessible material for young readers. Max Bolliger's *David,* which follows the life of King David up until he became King of Israel, is a good example of a partial biography for young readers that focuses on the subject's formative years. And Latham's already mentioned *Carry On, Mr. Bowditch,* covers only the first twenty-nine years of Bowditch's life, including his childhood and his adventures on the high seas. Latham undoubtedly concluded that young readers would be less enthusiastic about the last thirty-six years of his life, spent largely on scholarly pursuits.

Collective Biographies

Many biographical works briefly examine the lives of several people who are linked by a common thread—scientists, First Ladies, sports figures, and musicians, for example. Collective biographies may take two general forms. Most commonly, brief biographical sketches are provided for each individual included, forming a collection of biographies. Henrietta Buckminster's *Women Who Shaped History* deals with such influential women as Dorothea Dix, Harriet Tubman, and Mary Baker Eddy. One of the most famous of all collective biographies has been John F. Kennedy's *Profiles in Courage.* Occasionally we find biographies that weave into a single narrative the lives of two or more people who worked in collaboration. Jane Goodsell's biography of the founders of the famed clinic that bears their name, *The Mayo Brothers,* is an example.

The collective biography emphasizes above all the theme of an individual's life and work, and it further allows us to place that theme in a larger perspective. An additional benefit of the collective biography is that it can serve as a catalyst for further reading, prompting young readers to explore the life of one or more of the subjects involved, or perhaps to seek out biographies of others whose lives played on the same themes.

THE ELEMENTS OF BIOGRAPHICAL WRITING

Evaluating biography naturally requires a somewhat different set of criteria from fiction, since the two forms have quite different aims. Five basic elements of biographical writing deserve our special attention when we set about to judge a biography.

Subject

A subject's fame and glory are no guarantee that the biography will be interesting. Throughout the Middle Ages and the Renaissance, biographical writing generally focused on either saints or royalty, and in both cases the purpose was to glorify the subject. Only in the twentieth century has biography become truly democratized. Now it is possible to locate biographies of dancers, teachers, mathematicians, scoundrels, and slaves. There are really no limits when it comes to the choice of a biographical subject. The biographer's role is to present the subject in an interesting manner (by choosing the important facts and expressing them with grace and clarity). We expect a biography to convey a sense of the historical period and the geographic place in which the subject lived. Obviously, the more remote the historical period or the more distant and unfamiliar the place, the more background that is needed. And finally, the good biography not only reveals to us the life of the subject, but it contributes to our broader and deeper understanding of humankind. When we are finished reading the biography, we should not only feel that we know more about the person whose life was presented, but we should feel that we know something more about people in general. Otherwise, the biography becomes simply a vehicle for idle gossip.

Accuracy

The material of a good biography is both accurate and authentic. If it is a fictionalized biography, we expect the author to convey the true *essence* of the character if not always the specific details of the life. There should be evidence of careful research—Jean Fritz has shown us through her use of endnotes that this can be done even in biographies for younger readers. We expect that there be no glaring omissions that would distort the reader's view or understanding of the subject. (Naturally, we might expect biographies for younger readers to be discreet. For example, most biographers of Benjamin Franklin do not make a point of mentioning that his son was illegitimate, although Jean Fritz does point out in an endnote that we do not know who the son's mother was—a bold admission in a book for elementary school children.) The writer of a good biography avoids oversimplification, sentimentality, or overt didacticism, for any one of these would result in distortion.

The illustrations in a good biography pay careful attention to authenticity and are appropriately juxtaposed with the text. We can again turn to biographies of Benjamin Franklin for an example. Several biographies for young people include illustrations of the famous kite flying episode and depict a young boy, representing Franklin's son, accompanying Franklin in the storm. In fact, Franklin's son was a grown man of over twenty when the incident occurred. Careless illustration may cast doubt—rightly or wrongly—on the validity of the text.

It has only been in the last few years that biographers have begun to include apparatus in their books for young people—footnotes, endnotes, bibliographies, and indexes. Naturally, very young children will benefit little from such materials, but children in the middle and upper elementary grades are not too young to learn the uses of such supplementary information. The works of Milton Meltzer (not primarily a biographer but a social historian) and Russell Freedman (notably in his *Lincoln: A Photobiography*) are not only given added authority by their inclusion of supplementary materials, they also suggest that these writers have respect for their readers, seeing them as discerning and inquisitive individuals, who may want to learn more about the subject and his or her times.

Balance

Whereas early biographical writing tended to focus on the glorious exploits of "captains and kings," today we find biographies that reveal the human side of people, their errors in judgment, their personality flaws, their peculiar and eccentric habits, and so on. These inclusions generally do not cause us to think less of the individual, but rather they develop in us a greater capacity for sympathetic or empathetic understanding. Additionally, when a biographer presents an idealized portrait, there is the danger that young readers may come to believe that success is unattainable by ordinary people. We want to be able to believe in the characters, to see them as flesh and blood individuals. We enjoy being made to feel comfortable with our heroes.

This does not mean that we want our heroes debunked—a fault found often in popular biographies for adults (the perversions, sexual escapades, and criminal activities of public officials, sports heroes, movie stars, and so on). Young people want heroes and heroines to believe in. But at the same time young readers want to know that even heroes have their weaknesses, and that what sets them apart from others is that they are able to triumph in spite of these weaknesses. It is probably better for our egos if we learn that Patrick Henry achieved fame and respectability despite a streak of laziness, as Jean Fritz points out (*Where Was Patrick Henry on the 29th of May?*). We may suspect that there is hope for us.

Style

Some writers achieve what might have been thought the impossible—producing an incredibly dull book about an incredibly fascinating subject. A dull biography may result from an unwise selection of material, but more likely it is the result of a dry literary style. The good biographer writes with a style that is interesting, accessible, and appropriate to the subject. Necessary background material is carefully woven into the narrative, for young people prefer narrative or storytelling in their biographies. Dialogue, when it is used, is believable and authentic to the period. There is no reason for a biographer to depict young Tom Jefferson talking to his buddies as if he grew up in Detroit in the 1950s.

Naturally, the vocabulary and sentence structure of a good biography are suited to the intended audience, but need not be without reasonable challenge. Remember, boredom results either from the absence of any challenge at all or from an overwhelming and thus discouraging challenge. Another means of attracting and keeping the reader's interest is the use of humor. Jean Fritz effectively employs humor in her biographies without diminishing the stature of her subjects. Because humor is so important to the healthy human condition, it is difficult to understand why it appears so seldom in biography.

Theme

Finally, the theme of a good biography is both significant and sound. This is not to suggest that biography should be didactic, but without a theme to hold it together a biography is simply a loose collection of facts (something like a *Guinness Book of Records*—interesting to read in bits and pieces, but hardly a gripping story). Sometimes the theme is evident from the title. Jean Fritz's *The Double Life of Pocahontas* suggests the theme of a tragic woman caught between the conflicting values of two very different ways of life, that of her native Indian culture and that of her adoptive English culture. Milton Meltzer's *Benjamin Franklin: The New American* advances a rather standard view of Franklin as a man of rich and varied character with boundless physical energy and intellectual curiosity. The theme of a biography clarifies the writer's point of view concerning the character, and that may be to shed new light on what the author sees as old misunderstandings. Russell Freedman's portrait of Abraham Lincoln shows the sixteenth president as an extraordinarily complex and often troubled man, not without his significant shortcomings, but whose greatest strength was his sincere and warm humanity.

It is undoubtedly futile to hope that we have seen the last of the didactic biographies, those well-intentioned books that presume to teach us virtue through the examples of our heroes. But this is not to suggest that good biographies should contain no message for us whatever. On the contrary, the best biographies are built upon very profound themes— themes that speak to the strength and resilience of the human spirit, themes that remind us that the life well-lived is its own reward.

BIOGRAPHY AND YOUNG READERS

Not all young readers become enthralled with biography, but those who do become passionate about it. Just as there are science fiction buffs, there are biography buffs. Publishers have attempted to satisfy the appetites of these aficionados by producing the biography series. Dell has published its Famous Americans Series, consisting of very brief biographies, widely varying in quality, and lacking such apparatus as indexes or bibliographies. Puffin's Women of Our Time Series publishes some very fine authors, including Milton Meltzer on Betty Friedan and Patricia Reilly Giff on Mother Theresa. These are authentic biographies, but they still adopt the format of a fictional work, lacking apparatus. We may hope that some of the recent excellent contributions to the field will pave the way for more biographies of higher standards—biographies with uncompromising integrity and a healthy respect for the intellectual and emotional capacities of young readers.

BIBLIOGRAPHY OF CRITICAL STUDIES

Berry, Thomas Elliott, ed. *The Biographer's Craft.* New York: Odyssey, 1967.

Bowen, Catherine Drinker. *Biography: The Craft and the Calling.* Boston: Little, Brown, 1968.

Carr, Jo. "What Do We Do About Bad Biographies?" In *Beyond Fact.* Edited by Jo Carr. 119–128. Chicago: American Library Association, 1982.

Coolidge, Olivia. "My Struggle with Facts." *Wilson Library Bulletin,* October 1974, 146–151.

Fisher, Margery. "Life Course or Screaming Force." *Children's Literature in Education,* Autumn 1976, 107–127.

Forman, Jack. "Biography for Children: More Facts, Less Fiction." *Library Journal* 97 (September 15, 1972): 2968–2969.

Fritz, Jean. "George Washington, My Father, and Walt Disney." *Horn Book Magazine* 52 (April 1976): 191–198.

Groff, Patrick. "Biography: The Bad or the Bountiful." *Top of the News,* April 1973, 210–217.

Higgins, Judith. "Biographies They Can Read." *School Library Journal* 18 (April 1971): 33–34.

Jurich, Marilyn. "What's Left Out of Biography for Children?" *Children's Literature* 1 (1972): 143–151.

Kendall, Paul Murray. *The Art of Biography.* New York: Norton, 1985.

Marcus, Leonard. "Life Drawing: Some Notes on Children's Picture Book Biographies." *The Lion and the Unicorn* 4 (Summer 1980): 15–31.

Moore, Ann W. "A Question of Accuracy: Errors in Children's Biographies." *School Library Journal* 31 (February 1985): 34–35.

Segel, Elizabeth. "In Biographies for Young Readers, Nothing Is Impossible." *The Lion and the Unicorn* 4 (Summer 1980): 4–14.

Wilms, Denise M. "An Evaluation of Biography." In *Jump Over the Moon.* Edited by Pamela Barron and Jennifer Burley, pp. 220–225. New York: Holt, Rinehart and Winston, 1984.

A SELECTED BIBLIOGRAPHY OF BIOGRAPHIES

Since many writers specialize in biographical writing, look for other biographies by many of the writers represented on this list. If the subject of the biography is not obvious from the title, it has been supplied.

Adoff, Arnold. *Malcolm X.* Illustrated by John Wilson. New York: Crowell, 1970.

Aliki (pseudonym of Aliki Brandenburg). *The Story of Johnny Appleseed.* Englewood Cliffs, NJ: Prentice-Hall, 1963.

———. *A Weed Is a Flower: The Life of George Washington Carver.* Englewood Cliffs, NJ: Prentice-Hall, 1965.

Asimov, Isaac. *Breakthroughs in Science.* Boston: Houghton Mifflin, 1960. A collection of biographical sketches of famous scientists.

Blegvad, Erik. *Self-Portrait: Erick Blegvad.* Reading, MA: Addison-Wesley, 1979.

Bolliger, Max. *David.* Illustrated by Edith Schindler. New York: Dell (Delacorte), 1967. Biblical King of Israel.

Brooks, Polly Schoyer. *Queen Eleanor: Independent Spirit of the Medieval World.* Philadelphia: Lippincott, 1983.

Buckminster, Henrietta. *Women Who Shaped History.* New York: Macmillan, 1966.

Bulla, Clyde. *Songs of St. Francis.* Illustrated by Valenti Angelo. New York: Crowell, 1952. St. Francis of Assisi.

———. *Squanto, Friend of the Pilgrims.* Illustrated by Peter Burchard. New York: Crowell, 1954.

———. *Washington's Birthday.* Illustrated by Don Bolognese. New York: Crowell, 1957.

Clayton, Ed. *Martin Luther King: The Peaceful Warrior.* Englewood Cliffs, NJ: Prentice-Hall, 1968.

Coolidge, Olivia. *Tom Paine: Revolutionary.* New York: Scribner, 1969.

———. *Winston Churchill and the Story of Two World Wars.* Boston: Houghton Mifflin, 1960.

Cooper, Ilene. *Susan B. Anthony.* New York: Franklin Watts, 1984.

Daugherty, James. *Abraham Lincoln.* New York: Viking, 1943.

———. *Daniel Boone.* New York: Viking, 1939.

d'Aulaire, Ingri, and Edgar Parin d'Aulaire. *Abraham Lincoln.* New York: Doubleday, 1939.

Davidson, Margaret. *The Story of Eleanor Roosevelt.* New York: Four Winds, 1969.

De Trevino, Elizabeth Borton. *I, Juan de Pareja.* New York: Farrar, Straus & Giroux, 1965.

Eaton, Jeanette. *America's Own Mark Twain.* Illustrated by Leonard Everett Fisher. New York: Morrow, 1958.

Faber, Doris. *Eleanor Roosevelt: First Lady of the World.* New York: Viking, 1985.

Freedman, Russell. *Lincoln: A Photobiography.* Boston: Houghton Mifflin, 1987.

Fritz, Jean. *Can't You Make Them Behave, King George?* Illustrated by Tomie da Paola. New York: Coward, McCann & Geoghegan, 1977. King George III.

———. *The Double Life of Pocahontas.* New York: Putnam, 1983.

———. *Homesick: My Own Story.* New York: Putnam, 1982. Autobiography.

———. *Make Way for Sam Houston.* New York: Putnam, 1986.

———. *Where Was Patrick Henry on the 29th of May?* Illustrated by Margot Tomes. New York: Coward, McCann & Geoghegan, 1975.

Goodsell, Jane. *The Mayo Brothers.* New York: Crowell, 1972.

Greenfield, Eloise. *Mary McLeod Bethune.* New York: Crowell, 1977.

Hamilton, Virginia. *W. E. B. DuBois: A Biography.* New York: Crowell, 1972.

Hanff, Helene. *Queen of England: The Story of Elizabeth I.* New York: Doubleday, 1969.

Haskins, James. *The Story of Stevie Wonder.* New York: Lothrop, 1976.

Henry, Marguerite, and Wesley Dennis. *Benjamin West and His Cat Grimalkin.* Illustrated by Wesley Dennis. Indianapolis: Bobbs-Merrill, 1947. Early American artist Benjamin West.

Judson, Clara Ingram. *Abraham Lincoln, Friend of the People.* Chicago: Follett, 1950.

———. *Admiral Christopher Columbus.* Chicago: Follett, 1965.

Kennedy, John F. *Profiles in Courage.* New York: Harper, 1964. Abridged for young readers; stories of courageous Americans.

Kherdian, David. *The Road from Home: The Story of an Armenian Girl.* New York: Greenwillow (Morrow), 1979.

Komroff, Manuel. *Mozart.* Illustrated by Warren Chappell. New York: Knopf, 1956.

Lacy, Leslie Alexander. *Cheer the Lonesome Traveler: The Life of W. E. B. DuBois.* New York: Dial Press, 1970.

Latham, Jean Lee. *Carry On, Mr. Bowditch.* Boston: Houghton Mifflin, 1955.

Lawrence, Jacob. *Harriet and the Promised Land.* New York: Windmill (Simon & Schuster), 1968. One-time slave and heroine of the Underground Railroad Harriet Tubman.

McNeer, May. *America's Mark Twain.* Illustrated by Lynd Ward. Boston: Houghton Mifflin, 1962.

Mathis, Sharon Bell. *Ray Charles.* New York: Crowell, 1973.

Meigs, Cornelia. *Invincible Louisa.* Boston: Little, Brown, 1968.

Meltzer, Milton. *Benjamin Franklin: The New American.* New York: Watts, 1984.

———. *Dorothea Lange: Life Through the Camera.* New York: Viking, 1985.

———. *Langston Hughes: A Biography.* New York: Crowell, 1968.

Mitchison, Naomi. *African Heroes.* New York: Farrar, Straus & Giroux, 1969.

Monjo, F. N. *The One Bad Thing about Father.* New York: Harper, 1970. Theodore Roosevelt.

———. *Poor Richard in France.* New York: Holt, 1973. Benjamin Franklin.

Oneal, Zibby. *Grandma Moses: Painter of Rural America.* New York: Viking, 1986.

Provensen, Alice, and Martin Provensen. *The Glorious Flight: Across the Channel with Louis Blériot.* New York: Viking, 1983.

Raboff, Ernest. *Marc Chagall.* New York: Doubleday, 1968.

———. *Pablo Picasso.* New York: Doubleday, 1968.

Sandburg, Carl. *Abe Lincoln Grows Up.* Illustrated by James Daugherty. New York: Harcourt Brace Jovanovich, 1928.

Shiels, Barbara. *Winners: Women and the Nobel Prize.* Minneapolis: Dillon, 1985.

Shippen, Katherine. *Leif Eriksson: First Voyager to America.* New York: Harper, 1951.

Singer, Isaac Bashevis. *A Day of Pleasures: Stories of a Boy Growing Up in Warsaw.* New York: Farrar, Straus & Giroux, 1969. Autobiographical sketches.

Stoddard, Hope. *Famous American Women.* New York: Crowell, 1970.

Swift, Hildegarde. *From the Eagle's Wing: A Biography of John Muir.* Illustrated by Lynd Ward. New York: Morrow, 1962.

Tobias, Tobi. *Marian Anderson.* New York: Crowell, 1972.

Yates, Elizabeth. *Amos Fortune, Free Man.* New York: Dutton, 1950.

Zemach, Margot. *Self-Portrait: Margot Zemach.* Reading, MA: Addison-Wesley, 1978.

CHAPTER 12

Informational Books

DEFINITION

Biographies and history aside, informational books are not usually regarded as part of adult literature. Instead, nonfictional works are usually perceived as strictly functional and free from aesthetic demands. But this is not so in literature for young people, where there has always been a demand for quality in science books, travel books, how-to books, and so on. One of the reasons for this interest may be that children themselves do not clearly distinguish between fiction and nonfiction. Indeed, sometimes the lines are very hazy. Holling C. Holling's *Puddle-to-the-Sea,* for example, describes a fictional adventure of a little carved wooden canoe on its journey from Thunder Bay in the upper Great Lakes to the Atlantic Ocean. But aside from being an exciting adventure tale, this work is also a scientifically accurate book filled with a wealth of information especially about geography and natural science, and the text is accompanied by beautiful and meticulously detailed drawings.

As adults, we have unfortunately grown accustomed to expecting informational books to be merely utilitarian (and frequently dull), and we are pleasantly surprised when we find a stimulating history or geology or mathematics book. But children—who are quite tolerant when it comes to subject matter and theme—have little patience with dull books. Consequently, the writing of informational books for children requires both accuracy and creativity.

TYPES OF INFORMATIONAL BOOKS

For the purposes of this chapter, we shall take "informational books" to mean any works that deal exclusively with factual material and are clearly intended above all to instruct young readers. In Chapter 4 we briefly discussed the first informational books children are likely to encounter—the concept books. Now we will consider the wider realm of informational books, not only for toddlers and early elementary-school children but for older readers as well. There are informational books for young people on virtually every topic under the sun, but we shall attempt to simplify our discussion by grouping these works into four broad (and occasionally overlapping) subject categories.

Lands and Peoples

Think how many of our world's problems have resulted from our failure to understand and empathize with the multiplicity of cultures that share this planet. We only dimly understand our own culture, let alone those of distant foreign peoples. By being introduced to other cultures, other civilizations, we not only learn about them, but we discover a little more about ourselves. Additionally, tolerance is a happy by-product of expansive knowledge, and the books describing the history, governments, customs, and religions of societies around the world can help bring young readers this knowledge. One of the purposes of these books is to make the young readers aware that they are not the only people in the world, nor were they the first people in the world. As we all become more and more aware of the need for global understanding, the realization that what we do affects, in some way, everybody else on the planet, and that we cannot live isolated lives, these books are becoming increasingly important.

Through picture storybooks, such as Thomas Handforth's realistic piece, *Mei Lei,* or Gerald McDermott's re-creation of a Navajo folk myth, *Arrow to the Sun,* young children enjoy their earliest exposure to unfamiliar cultures. These are not, of course, strictly speaking informational books, but they do help young children realize that there are other ways of life on earth. Surely one of the great advantages of folktales from around the world is that they demonstrate at once the fundamental similarities of the human race and the manifold variations that societies offer. However, in addition to the fictional works, we can find some very fine informational books written especially for the very young. Aliki (pseudonym for Aliki Brandenburg) has been among the most consistently successful in bringing stories of lands and peoples to children in the lower grades (for example, *Mummies Made in Egypt,* in addition to accessible biographies of such people as Benjamin Franklin and George Washington Carver). The real flood of informational books comes for readers in the middle elementary years. Leonard Everett Fisher has created two outstanding series of first-rate informational books—one on colonial American crafts and one on nineteenth-century American commerce and industry. (His *Pumpers, Boilers, Hooks and Ladders* is suitable for a younger audience, and such works as *The Factories, The Railroads, The Schoolmasters, The Tanners, The Cabinetmakers,* and so on, are right for fourth, fifth, and sixth graders.) The hallmarks of his work are a clear text and powerful illustrations, two of the most important features of any informational book for young readers.

Among the outstanding works of Edwin Tunis are his *Frontier Living* (a Newbery Honor Book) and *Colonial Living,* both of which are examples of exhaustive research accompanied by meticulously accurate black-and-white line drawings by the author. Tunis's *Indians* was used as a text in Native American schools, and his *Weapons* served a similar purpose for the United States Air Force, even though both books were initially written for young readers.

Milton Meltzer has produced consistently high quality works on some rather complex facets of American history. His books include *In Their Own Words: A History of the American Negro; Brother Can You Spare a Dime? The Great Depression: 1929–1933;* and *Bread and Roses: The Struggle of American Labor, 1865–1915.* Meltzer's works are distinguished by their thorough scholarship. He treats his young readers with great respect, never condescending to them; he includes bibliographies and indexes (two features not necessarily found in informational books for young people), and he prefers to use period photographs to illustrate his works (a feature that gives them a great deal of authenticity). Meltzer's books are models of historical writing for young people.

In addition to his biographical writing mentioned in Chapter 11, Russell Freedman has written such historical works as *Cowboys of the Wild West,* presenting a fascinating history that corrects some of our misconceptions about cowboys. Through his use of photographs and an exciting writing style, Freedman suggests that the reality was even more compelling than the myth. Modern social concerns are documented in Brent Ashabranner's *Children of the Maya,* a photo-essay about Central American natives attempting to rebuild their lives in Florida after escaping from persecution in their homeland. History books for children have sometimes been notorious for their misinformation or their general inadequacy. The fact that for two centuries history textbooks virtually ignored the contributions of African-Americans and women is evidence of this careless attitude. There still remain strides to be made toward reliable, thorough, and honest historiography for children.

Science and Nature

Millicent Selsam, herself a fine science writer for children, tells us that "a good science book is not just a collection of facts" (1982, 62). That is the fault of many school textbooks, on all subjects not science alone—they provide voluminous, static facts, and overlook the more important total picture. Or, to cite an old but not inappropriate cliché, these books prevent us from seeing the forest because of the trees. A good science book, Selsam contends, demonstrates the workings of the scientific method as well as conveying "something of the beauty and excitement of science" (65).

As might be expected, nature books or books on natural history are among the most popular of the science books, particularly with younger readers. The current craze for dinosaur books is just one example (a recent traveling museum exhibit was aptly titled "Dinomania"), and we are told that the most frequently consulted entry in a young people's encyclopedia is "dogs." Jim Arnosky's *Secrets of a Wildlife Watcher* is a firsthand account of ways to locate and observe animals in the wild. This work is an example of how science writing can be brought to a practical level.

Nature books can lead us into a consideration of ecology, certainly one of the most crucial of current scientific issues. Laurence Pringle's *Living in a Risky World* encourages young readers to think about modern civilization and the implications of its life-style, particularly the effects of pollutants (acid rain, carcinogens, and other environmental hazards). A book such as this demonstrates that the scientific world is not divorced from the human world and from the complicated ethical issues that face humanity.

Science books date rather more rapidly than most publications, and there is the constant need for up-to-date works, as scientific discoveries reveal new facts, engender new theories, and provide for new technologies. Astronaut Sally Ride in *To Space and Back* (coauthored with Susan Okie) describes her experiences on the space shuttle flight, and this book serves a dual purpose of presenting up-to-date information of general interest and of dispelling feminine stereotyping in career choices. Franklyn M. Branley's *Uranus: The Seventh Planet* provides the latest information on that mysterious planet as supplied by Voyager 2's visit in 1986, an event that made obsolete all previous books on this great blue giant.

David Macaulay's monumental *The Way Things Work* explores the realms of the earth sciences—mechanics, physics (even nuclear physics), electronics, and chemistry. With amazing clarity and simplicity through hundreds of clever drawings, complex ideas and processes are revealed. This is a book with enormous appeal for adults as well as young people.

Fine and Applied Arts

The creative impulses of humanity have produced everything from architectural monuments (as illustrated by David Macaulay's carefully detailed *Cathedral* and *Castle*) to oil paintings (as presented in Ernest Raboff's series, Art for Children, on the major artists of the Western world) to such practical arts as the invention of writing (as graphically described in Leonard Everett Fisher's *Alphabet Art*). There is virtually no limit to the subject variety that can be found in these books. Dance (Arnold Haskell's *The Wonderful World of Dance*), music (Langston Hughes's *The First Book of Jazz*), gardening (Marc Brown's *Your First Garden Book*), and the theater (Walter Hodge's *Shakespeare's Theater*) only begin to scratch the surface of this field.

As with some of the science and nature books, there is occasional overlapping between this category and that of history. Macaulay's architecture books, mentioned above, and Judith St. George's *The Brooklyn Bridge: They Said It Couldn't Be Built* both focus on remarkable human achievements, as well as give us a historical sense. In a different vein is William Jaspersohn's *Magazine: Behind the Scenes at "Sports Illustrated."* This photo-essay is bound to appeal to sports buffs, but its focus is actually on the writing, editing, illustrating, and printing of a magazine. We also include books on sports, which can certainly be viewed as artistic expression (indeed, a skill such as ice skating, as described in Jonah and Laura Kalb's *The Easy Ice Skating Book,* has developed into a highly refined performing art). We should not forget the various craft and hobby books, such as Ferne Geller Cone's *Crazy Crocheting,* which describes a time-honored folk art form.

Human Development and Behavior

Books about human development and behavior include all those dealing with the cycle of life—especially birth, growth, sexuality, and death—and interpersonal relationships. These issues are treated frequently in picture storybooks (Martha Alexander's *Nobody Asked Me If I Wanted a Baby Sister,* and Judith Viorst's book about the death of a pet, *The Tenth Good Thing About Barney,* are two good examples). Technically, these cannot be considered *informational books,* but they do inform, and fiction is probably the most effective way of conveying complex psychological concepts to young readers. But for older readers, stories of human behavior often have a greater impact if they are factual.

Eda LeShan's *What Makes Me Feel This Way?* is written for upper-elementary children and deals with personal emotions. There are a growing number of informational books on personal responses to human predicaments. Jill Krementz specializes in writing frankly about difficult human problems. In . . . *How It Feels When Parents Divorce,* Krementz uses firsthand accounts from children of divorced parents. Appropriately, the book is illustrated with photographs, intensifying the reality of the subject.

Physical disabilities are too frequently ignored in books for children, and Ron Roy's *Move Over, Wheelchairs Coming Through!* is a welcome addition to informational books. Subtitled *Several Young People in Wheelchairs Talk about Their Lives,* this is a fascinating and moving account that provides an admirable combination of frankness and sensitivity.

EVALUATING INFORMATIONAL BOOKS

As with biographies, informational books must necessarily be evaluated by quite different standards from fiction, but an evaluation, nevertheless, is quite crucial. Readers, adults and children alike, have a tendency to accept unquestioningly whatever they see in print, particularly if the work purports to be informational. The following criteria may help in evaluating these books.

Purpose

The purpose of an informational book should be clear and manageable, and its subject treated thoroughly and objectively. Titles are important—most readers will prefer an unimaginative, but accurate, title to a vague showstopper that promises more than it delivers. All of us have at one time been sorely disappointed when a book's content did not live up to the hopes expressed in its title.

Naturally, the information should be appropriate to the age level of the intended audience. A good informational book ought to be challenging, but not threatening or over-whelming. Also, there should be a clear distinction made between fact and theory or supposition. Patricia Lauber, in *The Friendly Dolphins,* is quite careful to point out which details are known for sure about dolphins and which are still the best guesses of scientists. In this way children receive valuable critical training. It is good for us all to remember that few things are certain in this world.

We expect historians to avoid stereotypes and to present a balanced view of the infor-mation (history is more uncertain and far less objective than science). It is also important that information be up-to-date. Informational books, as we have noted, become rather quickly dated—Lauber's fine book on dolphins, for example, was written in 1963 and will obviously lack important discoveries about dolphins in the intervening quarter century. The copyright of an informational book carries far more significance than does that of a novel or poem.

Accuracy and Objectivity

A fictional writer must be a keen observer of human nature, but not necessarily an expert in any particular field of study. The author of an informational book, however, may need specialized training in the subject about which he or she is writing. This is less true for writers of picture concept books for preschoolers than it is for juvenile authors (one need not be a linguist to create a good alphabet book or a mathematician to create a good counting book).

Authors of informational books for older children tend to specialize—Milton Meltzer in social history, Leonard Everett Fisher in historical crafts and trades, David Macaulay in architecture, Millicent Selsam in natural history, Vicki Cobb in chemistry, to name a few. Interested readers begin to recognize familiar names and to seek out books by certain writers in a field. It is also not too soon for children in the middle elementary years to become aware of the authors behind the books and to learn about their qualifications. Sometimes biographical notes in the books themselves provide this information, but addi-tional information can be garnered from library card catalogs, books about writers (such as *Something About the Author*), and in books about children's literature. All this is not to suggest that a previously unknown writer cannot create a stunning informational book (or that a well-known writer cannot produce a bomb), but we ought to know something about the writer if we are going to take the information he or she gives us seriously.

Format and Organization

The format of the informational book is extremely important. The organization must be clear and logical, moving from simple to complex ideas, or developing chronologically. Organizational aids, such as headings and subheadings, and supplementary aids, such as a table of contents, a glossary, an index, and a bibliography, are especially desirable in books for adolescent readers (although surprisingly rare in older books).

Illustrations must be carefully placed in the text (preferably close to the material they are illustrating) and with captions if they are appropriate. We should expect illustrations both to increase our knowledge and to provide aesthetic pleasure. Photographs are frequently used to illustrate informational books, for they can provide a sense of reality and authenticity (particularly in history books, nature books, and books about people). However, we must be aware that photography is an art and that not just any photograph will do. Photographs well done can be beautiful and moving, serving more than simply to identify an object.

This is not to suggest that photographs are the only effective means of illustrating informational books. However, when graphic or painterly techniques are used to illustrate these works, they must not seem to trivialize the subject (can you imagine a cartoon book about divorce or the death of parent?) or to sentimentalize it unnecessarily. Leonard Everett Fisher opted for black-and-white scratchboard illustrations for his Colonial American Craftsmen series, for example, and they proved appropriately simple while conveying a sense of the hardship of eighteenth-century life. Regardless of the medium and style of the illustrative material, the important thing is that the illustrations contribute to the informational value of the book. There is no substitute for clear and accurate illustrations in an informational book.

Style

As was suggested above, high school and college textbooks are notoriously dull reading; too often these books simply rattle off facts without any attention to the reader's enjoyment. The first virtue of any informational book is clarity—without this, the book is a failure. But an informational book, not only through its choice of facts, but through its choice of words (diction) and sentence structure (syntax), can be stimulating reading. A good writer will suit both diction and syntax to the intended audience's age level. (We have already noted earlier in this text that boredom results from material being either too simple or too difficult for the reader.)

Where it is appropriate, humor can add enjoyment to informational books, so long as it neither mocks nor obscures an issue. Appropriate similes and metaphors (see Chapter 7) can not only make interesting reading, they can also clarify complicated or unfamiliar ideas. David Macaulay's *The Way Things Work* treats some extremely complicated concepts, but he ties the entire work together by using cartoon figures of woolly mammoths to demonstrate the various properties and scientific principles involved. For example, the mammoths are used to represent "force" or "effort." In this way, Macaulay makes use of both the metaphor, to illustrate an otherwise abstract concept, and humor, to make his explanations accessible and enjoyable. Humor can enable many people to learn concepts more quickly and to remember them more easily.

INFORMATIONAL BOOKS AS LITERATURE

The entire thrust of this chapter has been to suggest that informational books for young people can be (we would like to say "ought to be") works of art. They can be books that excite young readers to further reading, and books that young readers want to return to again and again—not only for information, but for enjoyment. It is quite right to expect that a nonfictional work be well-written, beautifully illustrated, imaginatively laid out, as well as up-to-date, accurate, and thought-provoking.

We ought to be uncompromising in our standards for nonfiction for young readers. In children's books there is no place for careless research, sloppy prose, indifferent illustrations, or uninviting formats—and this is true of fiction and nonfiction alike. The experiences of youth are deeply felt and long-lasting; we ought to make them when we can rich and stimulating as well. Today's youth are more fortunate than any in the past for the wealth of extraordinary literature available to them. But those are fortunate indeed who have been nurtured by adults who themselves know and love books. To pass that knowledge and love on to our children may very well be our most fruitful and enduring gift.

BIBLIOGRAPHY OF CRITICAL STUDIES

Bacon, Betty. "The Art of Nonfiction." *Children's Literature in Education* 14 (Spring 1981): 3–14.

Carr, Jo, ed. *Beyond Fact: Nonfiction for Children and Young People.* Chicago: American Library Association, 1982.

Chamberlain, Larry. "Enchantment Isn't Everything: A New Way of Looking at Lands and Peoples." *School Library Journal* (1978): 25–26.

Fisher, Margery. *Matters of Fact: Aspects of Non-Fiction for Children.* New York: Crowell, 1972.

Kobrin, Beverly. *Eyeopeners! How to Choose and Use Children's Books About Real People, Places, and Things.* New York: Viking, 1988.

Meltzer, Milton. "Where Do All the Prizes Go? The Case for Nonfiction." *Horn Book Magazine* 52 (February 1976): 17–23.

Norris, Lynn. "Extending Curiosity: Children's Informational Books." *Idaho Librarian,* October 1975, 126–128.

Selsam, Millicent E. "Writing about Science for Children." In *Beyond Fact: Nonfiction for Children and Young People.* Edited by Jo Carr. 61–65. Chicago: American Library Association, 1982.

Sutherland, Zena. "Information Pleases—Sometimes." *Wilson Library Journal* 49 (October 1974): 17–23.

———. "Science as Literature." *Literary Trends* 22:4 (April 1974): 485–489.

A SELECTED BIBLIOGRAPHY OF INFORMATIONAL BOOKS

The books in this list simply represent a cross section of the wealth of nonfictional reading available for young readers. The books in this list are categorized according to the four broad classifications outlined in this chapter; however, these are only general guidelines, and frequently books cross boundaries. For example, Franklyn Branley's *The Mystery of Stonehenge* may fit comfortably into both Lands and People as a historical work and into Science and Nature for its scientific explanation of that Stone Age phenomenon. This list is also in addition to those concept books listed at the end of Chapter 3.

Lands and Peoples

Aliki (pseudonym for Aliki Brandenburg). *Corn Is Maise—The Gift of the Indians.* New York: Crowell, 1976.

———. *A Medieval Feast.* New York: Crowell, 1983.

————. *Mummies Made in Egypt.* New York: Crowell, 1979.

Ashabranner, Brent. *Children of the Maya.* New York: Dodd, Mead & Co., 1986.

Baylor, Byrd. *When Clay Sings.* Illustrated by Tom Bakhi. New York: Scribner, 1972.

Bealer, Alex W. *Only the Names Remain: The Cherokees and the Trail of Tears.* Boston: Little, Brown, 1972.

Bontemps, Arna. *Story of the Negro.* 3d ed. New York: Knopf, 1958.

Branley, Franklyn. *The Mystery of Stonehenge.* New York: Crowell, 1969.

Caselli, Giovanni. *The First Civilizations.* New York: Bedrick, 1985.

Chaikin, Miriam, adapter. *Exodus.* Illustrated by Charles Mikolaycak. New York: Holiday House, 1987.

————. *Sound the Shofar: The Story and Meaning of Rosh Hashanah and Yom Kippur.* Boston: Houghton Mifflin, 1986.

Chubb, Thomas Caldecot. *The Byzantines.* Cleveland: World, 1959.

Commager, Henry Steele. *The First Book of American History.* Illustrated by Leonard Everett Fisher. New York: Watts, 1957.

Coolidge, Olivia. *Tales of the Crusades.* Boston: Houghton Mifflin, 1970.

Fisher, Leonard Everett. *The Factories.* New York: Holiday House, 1979.

————. *The Hospitals.* New York: Watts, 1980.

————. *The Peddlers.* New York: Watts, 1968.

————. *The Railroads.* New York: Holiday House, 1979.

————. *The Schoolmasters.* New York: Watts, 1967.

Foster, Genevieve. *The World of William Penn.* New York: Scribner, 1973.

————. *The Year of the Pilgrims—1620.* New York: Scribner, 1969.

Freedman, Russell. *Cowboys of the Wild West.* New York: Ticknor & Fields, 1985.

————. *Immigrant Kids.* New York: Dutton, 1980.

Hughes, Langston. *The First Book of Africa.* Rev. ed. New York: Watts, 1964.

Meltzer, Milton. *Brother Can You Spare Dime? The Great Depression: 1929–33.* New York: New American Library, 1977.

————. *The Hispanic Americans.* New York: Crowell, 1982.

Price, Christine. *Made in Ancient Egypt.* New York: Dutton, 1970.

Schwartz, Alvin. *The City and Its People: The Story of One City's Government.* New York: Dutton, 1967.

Tunis, Edwin. *Colonial Living.* Cleveland: World, 1957.

————. *Frontier Living.* Cleveland: World, 1961.

————. *Indians.* Cleveland: World, 1959.

————. *Weapons.* Cleveland: World, 1954.

Van Loon, Hendrik Willem. *The Story of Mankind.* Rev. ed. New York: Liveright, 1951.

Science and Nature

Arnosky, Jim. *Secrets of a Wildlife Watcher.* New York: Lothrop, 1983.

Branley, Franklyn. *Air Is All Around You.* New York: Crowell, 1986.

————. *Light and Darkness.* New York: Crowell, 1975.

————. *Uranus: The Seventh Planet.* New York: Crowell, 1975.

Cobb, Vicki. *The Scoop of Ice Cream.* Boston: Little, Brown, 1985.

————. *Sneakers Meet Your Feet.* Boston: Little, Brown, 1985.

George, Jean Craighead. *Spring Comes to the Ocean.* New York: Crowell, 1965.

Gross, Ruth Belov. *A Book about Pandas.* New York: Scholastic, 1974.

————. *Snakes.* New York: Four Winds, 1975.

Heller, Ruth. *The Reason for a Flower.* New York: Scholastic, 1983.

Lauber, Patricia. *The Friendly Dolphins.* New York: Random House, 1963.

————. *Tales Mummies Tell.* New York: Crowell, 1985.

Macaulay, David. *The Way Things Work.* Boston: Houghton Mifflin, 1988.

Mendoza, George. *The Digger Wasp.* New York: Dial Press, 1969.

Patent, Dorothy Hinshaw. *Where the Bald Eagles Gather.* Photos by William Munoz. Boston: Houghton Mifflin, 1984.

Pringle, Laurence. *City and Suburbs: Exploring Ecosystems.* New York: Macmillan, 1975.

——. *The Hidden World: Life Under a Rock.* New York: Macmillan, 1977.

——. *Living in a Risky World.* New York: Morrow, 1989.

Ride, Sally, and Susan Okie. *To Space and Back.* New York: Lothrop, 1986.

Fine and Applied Arts

Arnosky, Jim. *Sketching Outdoors in Spring.* New York: Lothrop, 1987.

Batterberry, Ariane, and Michael Batterberry. *The Pantheon Story of American Art for Young People.* New York: Pantheon Books, 1976.

Brown, Marc. *Your First Garden Book.* Boston: Little, Brown, 1981.

Bellville, Cheryl Walsh. *Theater Magic: Behind the Scenes at a Children's Theater.* Minneapolis: Carolrhoda, 1986.

Chase, Alice Elizabeth. *Famous Artists of the Past.* Bronx, NY: Platt & Munk, 1964.

Cone, Ferne Geller. *Crazy Crocheting.* Illustrated by Rachel Osterlof. Photos by J. Morton Cone. New York: Atheneum, 1981.

Cooper, Miriam. *Snap! Photography.* New York: Messner, 1981.

Fisher, Leonard Everett. *Alphabet Art.* New York: Four Winds, 1978.

——. *Calendar Art.* New York: Four Winds, 1987.

Haskell, Arnold. *The Wonderful World of Dance.* New York: Doubleday, 1969.

Hodges, C. Walter. *Shakespeare's Theatre.* New York: Coward, McCann & Geoghegan, 1964.

Hofsinde, Robert (Gray-Wolf). *Indian Arts.* New York: Morrow, 1971.

Hughes, Langston. *The First Book of Jazz.* New York: Watts, 1955.

Jaspersohn, William. *Magazine: Behind the Scenes at "Sports Illustrated."* Boston: Little, Brown, 1983.

Kalb, Jonah, and Laura Kalb. *The Easy Ice Skating Book.* Illustrated by Sandy Kossin. Boston: Houghton Mifflin, 1981.

Kohl, Herbert. *A Book of Puzzlements: Play and Invention with Language.* New York: Schocken, 1981.

Krementz, Jill. *A Very Young Rider.* New York: Knopf, 1977.

Lasky, Kathryn. *Puppeteer.* New York: Macmillan, 1985.

Marks, Mickey K. *OP-Tricks: Creating Kinetic Art.* Philadelphia: Lippincott, 1972.

Macaulay, David. *Castle.* Boston: Houghton Mifflin, 1977.

——. *Cathedral: The Story of Its Construction.* Boston: Houghton Mifflin, 1973.

——. *Pyramid.* Boston: Houghton Mifflin, 1975.

Raboff, Ernest. *Michelangelo Buonarroti.* New York: Harper, 1988.

——. *Pablo Picasso.* New York: Harper, 1987.

——. *Van Gogh.* New York: Harper, 1988.

St. George, Judith. *The Brooklyn Bridge: They Said It Couldn't Be Built.* New York: Putnam, 1982.

——. *The Panama Canal: Gateway to the World.* New York: Putnam, 1989.

Streatfeild, Noel. *A Young Person's Guide to Ballet.* London: Warne, 1985.

Tinkelman, Murray. *Rodeo: The Great American Sport.* New York: Greenwillow (Morrow), 1982.

Weiss, Harvey. *How to Make Your Own Books.* New York: Crowell, 1974.

Wolf, Diane. *Chinese Writing.* New York: Holt, Rinehart and Winston, 1975.

Human Development and Behavior

Bernstein, Joanne, and Stephen Gullo. *When People Die.* New York: Dutton, 1977.

Cole, Joanna. *The New Baby at Your House.* New York: Morrow, 1985.

Engel, Joel. *Handwriting Analysis Self-Taught.* New York: Elsevier/Nelson, 1980.

Giblin, James Cross. *From Hand to Mouth: Or How We Invented Knives, Forks, Spoons, and Chopsticks and the Table Manners to Go with Them.* New York: Crowell, 1987.

Jennes, Aylette. *Families: A Celebration of Diversity, Commitment, and Love.* Boston: Houghton Mifflin, 1990.

Kamien, Janet. *What If You Couldn't . . . ?* New York: Scribner, 1979.

LeShan, Eda. *What's Going to Happen to Me? When Parents Separate or Divorce.* New York: Four Winds, 1978.

————. *When a Parent Is Very Sick.* New York: Atlantic, 1986.

Meltzer, Milton. *The Landscape of Memory.* New York: Viking, 1987.

Perl, Lila. *The Great Ancestor Hunt: The Fun of Finding Out Who You Are.* Boston: Houghton Mifflin, 1989.

Rofes, Eric E. *The Kids' Book about Death and Dying.* Boston: Little, Brown, 1985.

Schwartz, Alvin. *Telling Fortunes: Love Magic, Dream Signs, and Other Ways to Learn the Future.* Philadelphia: Lippincott, 1987.

Terkel, Susan N., and Janice Rench. *Feeling Safe, Feeling Strong: How to Avoid Sexual Abuse and What to Do If It Happens to You.* Minneapolis: Lerner, 1984.

Appendix: Children's Book Awards

Every year numerous book awards are presented to works of children's literature, both for writing and for illustration. These awards are sponsored by various organizations, each with its own set of criteria. In addition, several awards are presented to individuals recognizing lifetime achievement in children's literature. Included below are some, but not all, of the more prestigious awards. The award-selection process is not infallible, and often some very excellent works have been overlooked whereas some award-winning works have not altogether successfully stood the test of time. In general, these lists can suggest—in addition to specific titles—authors and illustrators who produce works of high quality. But we should by no means be slaves to book award lists.

Included in the following lists are not only awards presented to writers in English, but some international awards. It is good that we make a concerted effort to acquaint ourselves not only with American and English children's authors, but with writers the world over. Perhaps in time, more of these foreign language books for children will be available in translation as we realize how important intercultural communication is to global understanding.

AMERICAN BOOK AWARDS

The Newbery Medal

The Newbery Medal was named for John Newbery, the British entrepreneur who pioneered children's book publishing in the eighteenth century. The award is, however, an American award, presented by the American Library Association to the most distinguished contribution to children's literature in a given year. Runners-up are termed Honor Books. As with any such award, there has not always been general agreement with the decisions. However, the list does include some of the finest of writing for young people over the last nearly seventy years.

1922   *The Story of Mankind* by Hendrik Willem van Loon, Liveright
       Honor Books: *The Great Quest* by Charles Hawes, Little, Brown; *Cedric the Forester* by Bernard Marshall, Appleton; *The Old Tobacco Shop: A True Account of What Befell a Little Boy in Search of Adventure* by William Bowen, Macmillan; *The Golden Fleece and the Heroes Who Lived before Achilles* by Padraic Colum, Macmillan; *Windy Hill* by Cornelia Meigs, Macmillan

1923   *The Voyages of Doctor Dolittle* by Hugh Lofting, Lippincott
       Honor Books: No record

1924   *The Dark Frigate* by Charles Hawes, Little, Brown
       Honor Books: No record

1925   *Tales from Silver Lands* by Charles Finger, Doubleday
       Honor Books: *Nicholas: A Manhattan Christmas Story* by Anne Carroll Moore, Putnam; *Dream Coach* by Anne Parrish, Macmillan

1926   *Shen of the Sea* by Arthur Bowie Chrisman, Dutton
       Honor Book: *Voyagers: Being Legends and Romances of Atlantic Discovery* by Padraic Colum, Macmillan

1927   *Smoky, the Cowhorse* by Will James, Scribner
       Honor Books: No record

1928   *Gayneck, The Story of a Pigeon* by Dhan Gopal Mukerji, Dutton
       Honor Books: *The Wonder Smith and His Son: A Tale from the Golden Childhood of the World* by Ella Young, Longmans; *Downright Dencey* by Caroline Snedeker, Doubleday

1929   *The Trumpeter of Krakow* by Eric P. Kelly, Macmillan
       Honor Books: *Pigtail of Ah Lee Ben Loo* by John Bennett, Longmans, Green (McKay); *Millions of Cats* by Wanda Gág, Coward, McCann & Geoghegan; *The Boy Who Was* by Grace Hallock, Dutton; *Clearing Weather* by Cornelia Meigs, Little, Brown; *Runaway Papoose* by Grace Moon, Doubleday; *Tod of the Fens* by Elinor Whitney, Macmillan

1930   *Hitty, Her First Hundred Years* by Rachel Field, Macmillan
       Honor Books: *Daughter of the Seine: The Life of Madame Roland* by Jeanette Eaton, Harper; *Pran of Albania* by Elizabeth Miller, Doubleday; *Jumping-off Place* by Marian Hurd McNeely, Longmans, Green (McKay); *Tangle-coated Horse and Other Tales: Episodes from the Fionn Saga* by Ella Young, Longmans, Green (McKay); *Vaino: A Boy of New England* by Julia Davis Adams, Dutton; *Little Blacknose* by Hildegarde Swift, Harcourt Brace Jovanovich

1931   *The Cat Who Went to Heaven* by Elizabeth Coatsworth, Macmillan
       Honor Books: *Floating Island* by Anne Parrish, Harper; *The Dark Star of Itza: The Story of a Pagan Princess* by Alida Malkus, Harcourt Brace Jovanovich; *Queer Person* by Ralph Hubbard, Doubleday; *Mountains Are Free* by Julia Davis Adams, Dutton; *Spice and the Devil's Cave* by Agnes Hewes, Knopf; *Meggy Macintosh* by Elizabeth Janet Gray, Doubleday; *Garram the Hunter: A Boy of the Hill Tribes* by Herbert Best, Doubleday; *Ood-Le-Uk the Wanderer* by Alice Lide and Margaret Johansen, Little, Brown

1932   *Waterless Mountain* by Laura Adams Armer, Longmans, Green (McKay)
       Honor Books: *The Fairy Circus* by Dorothy P. Lathrop, Macmillan; *Calico Bush*

by Rachel Field, Macmillan; *Boy of the South Seas* by Eunice Tietjens, Coward, McCann & Geoghegan; *Out of the Flame* by Eloise Lownsbery, Longmans, Green (McKay); *Jane's Island* by Marjorie Allee, Houghton Mifflin; *Truce of the Wolf and Other Tales of Old Italy* by Mary Gould Davis, Harcourt Brace Jovanovich

1933   *Young Fu of the Upper Yangtze* by Elizabeth Foreman Lewis, Winston
Honor Books: *Swift Rivers* by Cornelia Meigs, Little, Brown; *The Railroad to Freedom: A Story of the Civil War* by Hildegarde Swift, Harcourt Brace Jovanovich; *Children of the Soil: A Story of Scandinavia* by Nora Burglon, Doubleday

1934   *Invincible Louisa: The Story of the Author of "Little Women"* by Cornelia Meigs, Little, Brown
Honor Books: *The Forgotten Daughter* by Caroline Snedeker, Doubleday; *Swords of Steel* by Elsie Singmaster, Houghton Mifflin; *ABC Bunny* by Wanda Gág, Coward, McCann & Geoghegan; *Winged Girl of Knossos* by Erik Berry, Appleton; *New Land* by Sarah Schmidt, McBride; *Big Tree of Bunlahy: Stories of My Own Countryside* by Padraic Colum, Macmillan; *Glory of the Seas* by Agnes Hewes, Knopf; *Apprentice of Florence* by Ann Kyle, Houghton Mifflin

1935   *Dobry* by Monica Shannon, Viking
Honor Books: *Pageant of Chinese History* by Elizabeth Seeger, Longmans, Green (McKay); *Davy Crockett* by Constance Rourke, Harcourt Brace Jovanovich; *Day on Skates: The Story of a Dutch Picnic* by Hilda Van Stockum, Harper

1936   *Caddie Woodlawn* by Carol Ryrie Brink, Macmillan
Honor Books: *Honk, the Moose* by Phil Strong, Dodd, Mead; *The Good Master* by Kate Seredy, Viking; *Young Walter Scott* by Elizabeth Janet Gray, Viking; *All Sail Set: A Romance of the Flying Cloud* by Armstrong Sperry, Winston

1937   *Roller Skates* by Ruth Sawyer, Viking
Honor Books: *Phoebe Fairchild: Her Book* by Lois Lenski, Stokes; *Whistler's Van* by Idwal Jones, Viking; *Golden Basket* by Ludwig Bemelmans, Viking; *Winterbound* by Margery Bianco, Viking; *Audubon* by Constance Rourke, Harcourt Brace Jovanovich; *The Codfish Musket* by Agnes Hewes, Doubleday

1938   *The White Stag* by Kate Seredy, Viking
Honor Books: *Pecos Bill* by James Cloyd Bowman, Little, Brown; *Bright Island* by Mabel Robinson, Random House; *On the Banks of Plum Creek* by Laura Ingalls Wilder, Harper

1939   *Thimble Summer* by Elizabeth Enright, Holt, Rinehart and Winston
Honor Books: *Nino* by Valenti Angelo, Viking; *Mr. Popper's Penguins* by Richard and Florence Atwater, Little, Brown; *"Hello the Boat!"* by Phillis Crawford, Holt, Rinehart and Winston; *Leader by Destiny: George Washington, Man and Patriot* by Jeanette Eaton, Harcourt Brace Jovanovich; *Penn* by Elizabeth Janet Gray, Viking

1940   *Daniel Boone* by James Daugherty, Viking
Honor Books: *The Singing Tree* by Kate Seredy, Viking; *Runner of the Mountain Tops: The Life of Louis Agassiz* by Mabel Robinson, Random House; *By the*

Shores of Silver Lake by Laura Ingalls Wilder, Harper; *Boy with a Pack* by Stephen W. Meader, Harcourt Brace Jovanovich

1941   *Call It Courage* by Armstrong Sperry, Macmillan
Honor Books: *Blue Willow* by Doris Gates, Viking; *Young Mac of Fort Vancouver* by Mary Jane Carr, Crowell; *The Long Winter* by Laura Ingalls Wilder, Harper; *Nansen* by Anna Gertrude Hall, Viking

1942   *The Matchlock Gun* by Walter D. Edmonds, Dodd, Mead
Honor Books: *Little Town on the Prairie* by Laura Ingalls Wilder, Harper; *George Washington's World* by Genevieve Foster, Scribner; *Indian Captive: The Story of Mary Jemison* by Lois Lenski, Lippincott; *Down Ryton Water* by Eva Roe Gaggin, Viking

1943   *Adam of the Road* by Elizabeth Janet Gray, Viking
Honor Books: *The Middle Moffat* by Eleanor Estes, Harcourt Brace Jovanovich; *Have You Seen Tom Thumb?* by Mabel Leigh Hunt, Lippincott

1944   *Johnny Tremain* by Esther Forbes, Houghton Mifflin
Honor Books: *The Happy Golden Years* by Laura Ingalls Wilder, Harper; *Fog Magic* by Julia Sauer, Viking; *Rufus M.* by Eleanor Estes, Harcourt Brace Jovanovich; *Mountain Born* by Elizabeth Yates, Coward, McCann & Geoghegan

1945   *Rabbit Hill* by Robert Lawson, Viking
Honor Books: *The Hundred Dresses* by Eleanor Estes, Harcourt Brace Jovanovich; *The Silver Pencil* by Alice Dalgliesh, Scribner; *Abraham Lincoln's World* by Genevieve Foster, Scribner; *Lone Journey: The Life of Roger Williams* by Jeanette Eaton, Harcourt Brace Jovanovich

1946   *Strawberry Girl* by Lois Lenski, Lippincott
Honor Books: *Justin Morgan Had a Horse* by Marguerite Henry, Rand McNally; *The Moved-Outers* by Florence Crannell Means, Houghton Mifflin; *Bhimsa, the Dancing Bear* by Christine Weston, Scribner; *New Found World* by Katherine Shippen, Viking

1947   *Miss Hickory* by Carolyn Sherwin Bailey, Viking
Honor Books: *Wonderful Year* by Nancy Barnes, Messner; *Big Tree* by Mary and Conrad Buff, Viking; *The Heavenly Tenants* by William Maxwell, Harper; *The Avion My Uncle Flew* by Cyrus Fisher, Appleton; *The Hidden Treasure of Glaston* by Eleanore Jewett, Viking

1948   *The Twenty-One Balloons* by William Pene du Bois, Viking
Honor Books: *Pancakes-Paris* by Claire Huchet Bishop, Viking; *Le Lun, Lad of Courage* by Carolyn Treffinger, Abingdon; *The Quaint and Curious Quest of Johnny Longfoot, The Shoe-Kings Son* by Catherine Besterman, Bobbs-Merrill; *The Cow-tail Switch, and Other West African Stories* by Harold Courlander, Holt, Rinehart and Winston; *Misty of Chincoteague* by Marguerite Henry, Rand McNally

1949   *King of the Wind* by Marguerite Henry, Rand McNally
Honor Books: *Seabird* by Holling C. Holling, Houghton Mifflin; *Daughter of the Mountains* by Louise Rankin, Viking; *My Father's Dragon* by Ruth S. Gannett, Random; *Story of the Negro* by Arna Bontemps, Knopf

1950   *The Door in the Wall* by Marguerite de Angeli, Doubleday
Honor Books: *Tree of Freedom* by Rebecca Caudill, Viking; *The Blue Cat of Castle Town* by Catherine Coblentz, Longmans, Green (McKay); *Kildee House* by Rutherford Montgomery, Doubleday; *George Washington* by Genevieve Foster, Scribner; *Song of the Pines: A Story of Norwegian Lumbering in Wisconsin* by Walter and Marion Havighurst, Winston

1951   *Amos Fortune, Free Man* by Elizabeth Yates, Aladdin
Honor Books: *Better Known as Johnny Appleseed* by Mabel Leigh Hunt, Lippincott; *Gandhi, Fighter without a Sword* by Jeanette Eaton, Morrow; *Abraham Lincoln, Friend of the People* by Clara Ingram Judson, Follett; *The Story of Appleby Capple* by Anne Parrish, Harper

1952   *Ginger Pye* by Eleanor Estes, Harcourt Brace Jovanovich
Honor Books: *Americans before Columbus* by Elizabeth Baity, Viking; *Minn of the Mississippi* by Holling C. Holling, Houghton Mifflin; *The Defender* by Nicholas Kalashnikoff, Scribner; *The Light at Tern Rock* by Julia Sauer, Viking; *The Apple and the Arrow* by Mary and Conrad Buff, Houghton Mifflin

1953   *Secret of the Andes* by Ann Nolan Clark, Viking
Honor Books: *Charlotte's Web* by E. B. White, Harper; *Moccasin Trail* by Eloise McGraw, Coward, McCann & Geoghegan; *Red Sails to Capri* by Ann Weil, Viking; *The Bears on Hemlock Mountain* by Alice Dalgliesh, Scribner; *Birthdays of Freedom*, Vol. 1, by Genevieve Foster, Scribner

1954   *. . . and Now Miguel* by Joseph Krumgold, Crowell
Honor Books: *All Alone* by Claire Huchet Bishop, Viking; *Shadrach* by Meindert DeJong, Harper; *Hurry Home Candy* by Meindert DeJong, Harper; *Theodore Roosevelt, Fighting Patriot* by Clara Ingram Judson, Follett; *Magic Maize* by Mary and Conrad Buff, Houghton Mifflin

1955   *The Wheel on the School* by Meindert DeJong, Harper
Honor Books: *The Courage of Sarah Noble* by Alice Dalgliesh, Scribner; *Banner in the Sky* by James Ullman, Lippincott

1956   *Carry On, Mr. Bowditch* by Jean Lee Latham, Houghton Mifflin
Honor Books: *The Secret River* by Marjorie Kinnan Rawlings, Scribner; *The Golden Name Day* by Jennie Linquist, Harper; *Men, Microscopes, and Living Things* by Katherine Shippen, Viking

1957   *Miracles on Maple Hill* by Virginia Sorensen, Harcourt Brace Jovanovich
Honor Books: *Old Yeller* by Fred Gipson, Harper; *The House of Sixty Fathers* by Meindert DeJong, Harper; *Mr. Justice Holmes* by Clara Ingram Judson, Follett; *The Corn Grows Ripe* by Dorothy Rhoads, Viking; *Black Fox of Lorne* by Marguerite de Angeli, Doubleday

1958   *Rifles for Watie* by Harold Keith, Crowell
Honor Books: *The Horsecatcher* by Mari Sandoz, Westminster; *Gone-away Lake* by Elizabeth Enright, Harcourt Brace Jovanovich; *The Great Wheel* by Robert Lawson, Viking; *Tom Paine, Freedom's Apostle* by Leo Gurko, Crowell

1959   *The Witch of Blackbird Pond* by Elizabeth George Speare, Houghton Mifflin
Honor Books: *The Family under the Bridge* by Natalie Savage Carlson, Harper;

Along Came a Dog by Meindert DeJong, Harper; *Chucaro: Wild Pony of the Pampas* by Francis Kalnay, Harcourt Brace Jovanovich; *The Perilous Road* by William O. Steele, Harcourt Brace Jovanovich

1960   *Onion John* by Joseph Krumgold, Crowell
Honor Books: *My Side of the Mountain* by Jean George, Dutton; *America Is Born* by Gerald W. Johnson, Morrow; *The Gammage Cup* by Carol Kendall, Harcourt Brace Jovanovich

1961   *Island of the Blue Dolphins* by Scott O'Dell, Houghton Mifflin
Honor Books: *America Moves Forward* by Gerald W. Johnson, Morrow; *Old Ramon* by Jack Schaefer, Houghton Mifflin; *The Cricket in Times Square* by George Selden, Farrar, Straus & Giroux

1962   *The Bronze Bow* by Elizabeth George Speare, Houghton Mifflin
Honor Books: *Frontier Living* by Edwin Tunis, World; *The Golden Goblet* by Eloise McCraw, Coward, McCann & Geoghegan; *Belling the Tiger* by Mary Stolz, Harper

1963   *A Wrinkle in Time* by Madeleine L'Engle, Farrar, Straus & Giroux
Honor Books: *Thistle and Thyme: Tales and Legends from Scotland* by Sorche Nic Leodhas, Holt, Rinehart and Winston; *Men of Athens* by Olivia Coolidge, Houghton Mifflin

1964   *It's Like This, Cat* by Emily Cheney Neville, Harper
Honor Books: *Rascal* by Sterling North, Dutton; *The Loner* by Ester Wier, McKay

1965   *Shadow of a Bull* by Maia Wojciechowska, Atheneum
Honor Books: *Across Five Aprils* by Irene Hunt, Follett

1966   *I, Juan de Pareja* by Elizabeth Borten de Trevino, Farrar, Straus & Giroux
Honor Books: *The Black Cauldron* by Lloyd Alexander, Holt, Rinehart and Winston; *The Animal Family* by Randall Jarrell, Pantheon; *The Noonday Friends* by Mary Stolz, Harper

1967   *Up a Road Slowly* by Irene Hunt, Follett
Honor Books: *The King's Fifth* by Scott O'Dell, Houghton Mifflin; *Zlateh the Goat and Other Stories* by Isaac Bashevis Singer, Harper; *The Jazz Man* by Mark H. Weik, Atheneum

1968   *From the Mixed-Up Files of Mrs. Basil E. Frankweiler* by E. L. Konigsburg, Atheneum
Honor Books: *Jennifer, Hecate, Macbeth, William McKinley, and Me, Elizabeth* by E. L. Kongsiburg, Atheneum; *The Black Pearl* by Scott O'Dell, Houghton Mifflin; *The Fearsome Inn* by Isaac Bashevis Singer, Scribner; *The Egypt Game* by Zilpha Keatley Snyder, Atheneum

1969   *The High King* by Lloyd Alexander, Holt, Rinehart and Winston
Honor Books: *To Be a Slave* by Julius Lester, Dial Press; *When Shlemiel Went to Warsaw and Other Stories* by Isaac Bashevis Singer, Farrar, Straus & Giroux

1970   *Sounder* by William H. Armstrong, Harper
Honor Books: *Our Eddie* by Sulamith IshKishor, Pantheon Books; *The Many Ways of Seeing: An Introduction to the Pleasures of Art* by Janet Gaylord Moore, World; *Journey Outside* by Mary Q. Steele, Viking

1971   *Summer of the Swans* by Betsy Byars, Viking
        Honor Books: *Kneeknock Rise* by Natalie Babbitt, Farrar, Straus & Giroux; *Enchantress from the Stars* by Sylvia Louise Engdahl, Atheneum; *Sing Down the Moon* by Scott O'Dell, Houghton Mifflin

1972   *Mrs. Frisby and the Rats of NIMH* by Robert C. O'Brien, Atheneum
        Honor Books: *Incident at Hawk's Hill* by Allan W. Eckert, Little, Brown; *The Planet of Junior Brown* by Virginia Hamilton, Macmillan; *The Tombs of Atuan* by Ursula K. Le Guin, Atheneum; *Annie and the Old One* by Miska Miles, Little, Brown; *The Headless Cupid* by Zilpha Keatley Snyder, Atheneum

1973   *Julie of the Wolves* by Jean Craighead George, Harper
        Honor Books: *Frog and Toad Together* by Arnold Lobel, Harper; *The Upstairs Room* by Johanna Reiss, Crowell; *The Witches of Worm* by Zilpha Keatley Snyder, Atheneum

1974   *The Slave Dancer* by Paula Fox, Bradbury
        Honor Book: *The Dark Is Rising* by Susan Cooper, Atheneum

1975   *M. C. Higgins, the Great* by Virginia Hamilton, Macmillan
        Honor Books: *Figgs & Phantoms* by Ellen Raskin, Dutton; *My Brother Sam Is Dead* by James Lincoln Collier and Christopher Collier, Four Winds; *The Perilous Gard* by Elizabeth Marie Pope, Houghton Mifflin; *Philip Hall Likes Me. I Reckon Maybe* by Bette Greene, Dial Press

1976   *The Grey King* by Susan Cooper, Atheneum
        Honor Books: *The Hundred Penny Box* by Sharon Bell Mathis, Viking; *Dragonwings* by Lawrence Yep, Harper

1977   *Roll of Thunder, Hear My Cry* by Mildred D. Taylor, Dial Press
        Honor Books: *Abel's Island* by William Steig, Farrar, Straus & Giroux; *A String in the Harp* by Nancy Bond, Atheneum

1978   *Bridge to Terabithia* by Katherine Paterson, Crowell
        Honor Books: *Ramona and Her Father* by Beverly Cleary, Morrow; *Anpao: An American Indian Odyssey* by Jamake Highwater, Lippincott

1979   *The Westing Game* by Ellen Raskin, Dutton
        Honor Book: *The Great Gilly Hopkins* by Katherine Paterson, Crowell

1980   *A Gathering of Days: A New England Girl's Journal 1830–32* by Joan Blos, Scribner
        Honor Book: *The Road from Home: The Story of an Armenian Girl* by David Kherdian, Greenwillow (Morrow)

1981   *Jacob Have I Loved* by Katherine Paterson, Crowell
        Honor Books: *The Fledgling* by Jane Langton, Harper; *A Ring of Endless Light* by Madeleine L'Engle, Farrar, Straus & Giroux

1982   *A Visit to William Blake's Inn: Poems for Innocent and Experienced Travelers* by Nancy Willard, Harcourt Brace Jovanovich
        Honor Books: *Ramona Quimby, Age 8* by Beverly Cleary, Morrow; *Upon the Head of the Goat: A Childhood in Hungary, 1939–1944* by Aranka Siegal, Farrar, Straus & Giroux

1983   *Dicey's Song* by Cynthia Voigt, Atheneum
        Honor Books: *Blue Sword* by Robin McKinley, Morrow; *Dr. DeSoto* by William
        Steig, Farrar, Straus & Giroux; *Graven Images* by Paul Fleischman, Harper;
        Homesick: My Own Story by Jean Fritz, Putnam; *Sweet Whisper, Brother Rush*
        by Virginia Hamilton, Philomel (Putnam)

1984   *Dear Mr. Henshaw* by Beverly Cleary, Morrow
        Honor Books: *The Wish Giver* by Bill Brittain, Harper; *Sugaring Time* by Kathryn
        Lasky, Macmillan; *The Sign of the Beaver* by Elizabeth George Speare,
        Houghton Mifflin; *A Solitary Blue* by Cynthia Voigt, Atheneum

1985   *The Hero and the Crown* by Robin McKinley, Greenwillow (Morrow)
        Honor Books: *The Moves Make the Man* by Bruce Brooks, Harper; *One-Eyed
        Cat* by Paula Fox, Bradbury; *Like Jake and Me* by Mavis Jukes, Knopf

1986   *Sarah, Plain and Tall* by Patricia MacLachlan, Harper
        Honor Books: *Commodore Perry in the Land of the Shogun* by Rhoda Blumberg,
        Lothrop; *Dogsong* by Gary Paulsen, Bradbury

1987   *The Whipping Boy* by Sid Fleischman, Greenwillow (Morrow)
        Honor Books: *On My Honor* by D. Bauer, Clarion; *Volcano: The Eruption and
        Healing of Mount St. Helens* by Patricia Lauber, Bradbury; *A Fine White Dust*
        by Cynthia Rylant, Bradbury

1988   *Lincoln: A Photobiography* by Russell Freedman, Clarion/Houghton Mifflin
        Honor Books: *After the Rain* by Norma Fox Mazer, Morrow; *Hatchet* by Gary
        Paulsen, Bradbury

1989   *Joyful Noise: Poems for Two Voices* by Paul Fleischman, Harper
        Honor Books: *In the Beginning* by Virginia Hamilton, Harcourt Brace Jovanovich;
        Scorpions by Walter Dean Myers, Harper

1990   *Number the Stars* by Lois Lowry, Houghton Mifflin
        Honor Books: *Afternoon of the Elves* by Janet Taylor Lisle, Orchard Books/Watts;
        The Winter Room by Gary Paulsen, Orchard Books/Watts; *Shabanu: Daughter
        of the Wind* by Suzanne Fisher Staples, Knopf

The Caldecott Medal

Named for the British illustrator Randolph Caldecott, the Caldecott Medal has been
awarded annually since 1938 by the American Library Association to the most distinguished picture-book published in America. Runners up are given Honor Awards.
Although the passage of time has not always validated the awards and many fine books
have been overlooked, the awards list does provide a roll call of some of the best in
children's books. The Caldecott Award is given to the illustrator and honors the pictorial
art rather than the text.

1938   *Animals of the Bible* by Helen Dean Fish, illustrated by Dorothy P. Lathrop,
        Stokes
        Honor Books: *Seven Simeon: A Russian Tale* by Boris Artzybasheff, Viking;
        *Four and Twenty Blackbirds: Nursery Rhymes of Yesterday Recalled for
        Children of To-Day* by Helen Dean Fish, illustrated by Robert Lawson, Stokes

1939   *Mei Li* by Thomas Handforth, Doubleday
        Honor Books: *The Forest Pool* by Laura Adams Armer, Longmans, Green
        (McKay); *Wee Gillis* by Munro Leaf, illustrated by Robert Lawson, Viking;
        Snow White and the Seven Dwarfs by Wanda Gág, Coward, McCann &
        Geoghegan; *Barkis* by Clare Newberry, Harper; *Andy and the Lion: A Tale
        of Kindness Remembered or the Power of Gratitude* by James Daugherty, Viking

1940   *Abraham Lincoln* by Ingri and Edgar Parin d'Aulaire, Doubleday
        Honor Books: *Cock-a-Doodle Doo: The Story of a Little Red Rooster* by Berta
        and Elmer Hader, Macmillan; *Madeline* by Ludwig Bemelmans, Simon &
        Schuster; *The Ageless Story* by Lauren Ford, Dodd, Mead

1941   *They Were Strong and Good* by Robert Lawson, Viking
        Honor Book: *April's Kittens* by Clare Newberry, Harper

1942   *Make Way for Ducklings* by Robert McCloskey, Viking
        Honor Books: *An American ABC* by Maud and Miska Petersham, Macmillan;
        In My Mother's House by Ann Nolan Clark, illustrated by Velino Herrera,
        Viking; *Paddle-to-the-Sea* by Holling C. Holling, Houghton Mifflin; *Nothing
        at All* by Wanda Gág, Coward, McCann & Geoghegan

1943   *The Little House* by Virginia Lee Burton, Houghton Mifflin
        Honor Books: *Dash and Dart* by Mary and Conrad Buff, Viking; *Marshmallow*
        by Clare Newberry, Harper

1944   *Many Moons* by James Thurber, illustrated by Louis Slobodkin, Harcourt Brace
        Jovanovich
        Honor Books: *Small Rain: Verses from the Bible* selected by Jessie Orton Jones,
        illustrated by Elizabeth Orton Jones, Viking; *Pierre Pigeon* by Lee Kingman,
        illustrated by Arnold E. Bare, Houghton Mifflin; *The Mighty Hunter* by Berta
        and Elmer Hader, Macmillan; *A Child's Good Night Book* by Margaret Wise
        Brown, illustrated by Jean Charlot, W. R. Scott; *Good Luck Horse* by Chih-Yi
        Chan, illustrated by Plato Chan, Whittlesey

1945   *Prayer for a Child* by Rachel Field, illustrated by Elizabeth Orton Jones, Macmillan
        Honor Books: *Mother Goose: Seventy-Seven Verses with Pictures,* illustrated
        by Tasha Tudor, Walck; *In the Forest* by Marie Hall Ets, Viking; *Yonie Wonder-
        nose* by Marguerite de Angeli, Doubleday; *The Christmas Anna Angel* by Ruth
        Sawyer, illustrated by Kate Seredy, Viking

1946   *The Rooster Crows . . . ,* illustrated by Maud and Miska Petersham, Macmillan
        Honor Books: *Little Lost Lamb* by Golden MacDonald, illustrated by Leonard
        Weisgard, Doubleday; *Sing Mother Goose* by Opal Wheeler, illustrated by
        Marjorie Torrey, Dutton; *My Mother Is the Most Beautiful Woman in the World*
        by Becky Reyher, illustrated by Ruth Gannett, Lothrop; *You Can Write Chinese*
        by Kurt Wiese, Viking

1947   *The Little Island* by Golden MacDonald, illustrated by Leonard Weisgard,
        Doubleday
        Honor Books: *Rain Drop Splash* by Alvin Tresselt, illustrated by Leonard
        Weisgard, Lothrop; *Boats on the River* by Marjorie Flack, illustrated by Jay
        Hyde Barnum, Viking; *Timothy Turtle* by Al Graham, illustrated by Tony

Palazzo, Viking; *Pedro, The Angel of Olvera Street* by Leo Politi, Scribner; *Sing in Praise: A Collection of the Best Loved Hymns* by Opal Wheeler, illustrated by Marjorie Torrey, Dutton

1948   *White Snow, Bright Snow* by Alvin Tresselt, illustrated by Roger Duvoisin, Lothrop
Honor Books: *Stone Soup: An Old Tale* by Marcia Brown, Scribner; *McElligot's Pool* by Dr. Seuss, Random House; *Bambino the Clown* by George Schreiber, Viking; *Roger and the Fox* by Lavinia Davis, illustrated by Hildegard Woodward, Doubleday; *Song of Robin Hood* edited by Anne Malcolmson, illustrated by Virginia Lee Burton, Houghton Mifflin

1949   *The Big Snow* by Berta and Elmer Hader, Macmillan
Honor Books: *Blueberries for Sal* by Robert McCloskey, Viking; *All Around the Town* by Phyllis McGinley, illustrated by Helen Stone, Lippincott; *Juanita* by Leo Politi, Scribner; *Fish in the Air* by Kurt Wiese, Viking

1950   *Song of the Swallows* by Leo Politi, Scribner
Honor Books: *America's Ethan Allen* by Stewart Holbrook, illustrated by Lynd Ward, Houghton Mifflin; *The Wild Birthday Cake* by Lavinia Davis, illustrated by Hildegard Woodward, Doubleday; *The Happy Day* by Ruth Krauss, illustrated by Marc Simont, Harper; *Bartholomew and the Oobleck* by Dr. Seuss, Random House; *Henry Fisherman* by Marcia Brown, Scribner

1951   *The Egg Tree* by Katherine Milhous, Scribner
Honor Books: *Dick Whittington and His Cat* by Marcia Brown, Scribner; *The Two Reds* by William Lipkind, illustrated by Nicholas Mordvinoff, Harcourt Brace Jovanovich; *If I Ran the Zoo* by Dr. Seuss, Random House; *The Most Wonderful Doll in the World* by Phyllis McGinley, illustrated by Helen Stone, Lippincott; *T-Bone, the Baby Sitter* by Clare Newberry, Harper

1952   *Finders Keepers* by William Lipkind, illustrated by Nicholas Mordvinoff, Harcourt Brace Jovanovich
Honor Books: *Mr. T. W. Anthony Woo: The Story of a Cat and a Dog and a Mouse* by Marie Hall Ets, Viking; *Skipper John's Cook* by Marcia Brown, Scribner; *All Falling Down* by Gene Zion, illustrated by Margaret Bloy Graham, Harper; *Bear Party* by William Pene du Bois, Viking; *Feather Mountain* by Elizabeth Olds, Houghton Mifflin

1953   *The Biggest Bear* by Lynd Ward, Houghton Mifflin
Honor Books: *Puss in Boots* by Charles Perrault, illustrated and translated by Marcia Brown, Scribner; *One Morning in Maine* by Robert McCloskey, Viking; *Ape in a Cape: An Alphabet of Odd Animals* by Fritz Eichenberg, Harcourt Brace Jovanovich; *The Storm Book* by Charlotte Zolotow, illustrated by Margaret Bloy Graham, Harper; *Five Little Monkeys* by Juliet Kepes, Houghton Mifflin

1954   *Madeline's Rescue* by Ludwig Bemelmans, Viking
Honor Books: *Journey Cake, Ho!* by Ruth Sawyer, illustrated by Robert McCloskey, Viking; *When Will the World Be Mine?* by Miriam Schlein, illustrated by Jean Charlot, W. R. Scott; *The Steadfast Tin Soldier* by Hans Christian Andersen, illustrated by Marcia Brown, Scribner; *A Very Special House* by Ruth Krauss, illustrated by Maurice Sendak, Harper; *Green Eyes* by A. Birnbaum, Capitol

1955   *Cinderella, or the Little Glass Slipper* by Charles Perrault, translated and illustrated by Marcia Brown, Scribner

Honor Books: *Book of Nursery and Mother Goose Rhymes,* illustrated by Marguerite de Angeli, Doubleday; *Wheel on the Chimney* by Margaret Wise Brown, illustrated by Tibor Gergely, Lippincott; *The Thanksgiving Story* by Alice Dalgliesh, illustrated by Helen Sewell, Scribner

1956   *Frog Went A-Courtin* edited by John Langstaff, illustrated by Feodor Rojankovsky, Harcourt Brace Jovanovich

Honor Books: *Play with Me* by Marie Hall Ets, Viking; *Crow Boy* by Taro Yashima, Viking

1957   *A Tree Is Nice* by Janice May Udry, illustrated by Marc Simont, Harper

Honor Books: *Mr. Penny's Race Horse* by Marie Hall Ets, Viking; *1 Is One* by Tasha Tudor, Walck; *Anatole* by Eve Titus, illustrated by Paul Galdone, McGraw-Hill; *Gillespie and the Guards* by Benjamin Elkin, illustrated by James Daugherty, Viking; *Lion* by William Pene du Bois, Viking

1958   *Time of Wonder* by Robert McCloskey, Viking

Honor Books: *Fly High, Fly Low* by Don Freeman, Viking; *Anatole and the Cat* by Eve Titus, illustrated by Paul Galdone, McGraw-Hill

1959   *Chanticleer and the Fox* adapted from Chaucer and illustrated by Barbara Cooney, Crowell

Honor Books: *The House That Jack Built: A Picture Book in Two Languages* by Antonio Frasconi, Harcourt Brace Jovanovich; *What Do You Say, Dear?* by Sesyle Joslin, illustrated by Maurice Sendak, Scott; *Umbrella* by Taro Yashima, Viking

1960   *Nine Days to Christmas* by Marie Hall Ets and Aurora Labastida, illustrated by Marie Hall Ets, Viking

Honor Books: *Houses from the Sea* by Alice E. Goudey, illustrated by Adrienne Adams, Scribner; *The Moon Jumpers* by Janice May Udry, illustrated by Maurice Sendak, Harper

1961   *Baboushka and the Three Kings* by Ruth Robbins, illustrated by Nicolas Sidjakov, Parnassus

Honor Book: *Inch by Inch* by Leo Lionni, Obolensky

1962   *Once a Mouse . . .* by Marcia Brown, Scribner

Honor Books: *The Fox Went Out on a Chilly Night: An Old Song* by Peter Spier, Doubleday; *Little Bear's Visit* by Else Holmelund Minarik, illustrated by Maurice Sendak, Harper; *The Day We Saw the Sun Come Up* by Alice E. Goudey, illustrated by Adrienne Adams, Scribner

1963   *The Snowy Day* by Ezra Jack Keats, Viking

Honor Books: *The Sun Is a Golden Earring* by Natalia M. Belting, illustrated by Bernarda Bryson, Holt, Rinehart and Winston; *Mr. Rabbit and the Lovely Present* by Charlotte Zolotow, illustrated by Maurice Sendak, Harper

1964   *Where the Wild Things Are* by Maurice Sendak, Harper

Honor Books: *Swimmy* by Leo Lionni, Pantheon Books; *All in the Morning Early* by Sorche Nic Leodhas, illustrated by Evaline Ness, Holt, Rinehart and Winston; *Mother Goose and Nursery Rhymes* illustrated by Philip Reed, Atheneum

1965   *May I Bring a Friend?* by Beatrice Schenk de Regniers, illustrated by Beni Montresor, Atheneum
        Honor Books: *Rain Makes Applesauce* by Julian Scheer, illustrated by Marvin Bileck, Holiday; *The Wave* by Margaret Hodges, illustrated by Blair Lent, Houghton Mifflin; *A Pocketful of Cricket* by Rebecca Caudill, illustrated by Evaline Ness, Holt, Rinehart and Winston

1966   *Always Room for One More* by Sorche Nic Leodhas, illustrated by Nonny Hogrogian, Holt, Rinehart and Winston
        Honor Books: *Hide and Seek Fog* by Alvin Tresselt, illustrated by Roger Duvoisin, Lothrop; *Just Me* by Marie Hall Ets, Viking; *Tom Tit Tot* by Evaline Ness, Scribner

1967   *Sam, Bangs & Moonshine* by Evaline Ness, Holt, Rinehart and Winston
        Honor Book: *One Wide River to Cross* by Barbara Emberley, illustrated by Ed Emberley, Prentice-Hall

1968   *Drummer Hoff* by Barbara Emberley, illustrated by Ed Emberley, Prentice-Hall
        Honor Books: *Frederick* by Leo Lionni, Pantheon Books; *Seashore Story* by Taro Yashima, Viking; *The Emperor and the Kite* by Jane Yolen, illustrated by Ed Young, World

1969   *The Fool of the World and the Flying Ship* by Arthur Ransome, illustrated by Uri Shulevitz, Farrar, Straus & Giroux
        Honor Book: *Why the Sun and the Moon Live in the Sky: An African Folktale* by Elphinstone Dayrell, illustrated by Blair Lent, Houghton Mifflin

1970   *Sylvester and the Magic Pebble* by William Steig, Windmill (Simon & Schuster)
        Honor Books: *Goggles!* by Ezra Jack Keats, Macmillan; *Alexander and the Wind-Up Mouse* by Leo Lionni, Pantheon Books; *Pop Corn and Ma Goodness* by Edna Mitchell Preston, illustrated by Robert Andrew Parker, Viking; *Thy Friend, Obadiah* by Brinton Turkle, Viking; *The Judge: An Untrue Tale* by Harve Zemach, illustrated by Margot Zemach, Farrar, Straus & Giroux

1971   *A Story—A Story: An African Tale* by Gail E. Haley, Atheneum
        Honor Books: *The Angry Moon* by William Sleator, illustrated by Blair Lent, Little, Brown; *Frog and Toad Are Friends* by Arnold Lobel, Harper; *In the Night Kitchen* by Maurice Sendak, Harper

1972   *One Fine Day* by Nonny Hogrogian, Macmillan
        Honor Books: *If All the Seas Were One Sea* by Janina Domanska, Macmillan; *Moja Means One: Swahili Counting Book* by Muriel Feelings, illustrated by Tom Feelings, Dial Press; *Hildilid's Night* by Cheli Duran Ryan, illustrated by Arnold Lobel, Macmillan

1973   *The Funny Little Woman* retold by Arlene Mosel, illustrated by Blair Lent, Dutton
        Honor Books: *Anansi the Spider: A Tale from the Ashanti* adapted and illustrated by Gerald McDermott, Holt, Rinehart and Winston; *Hosie's Alphabet* by Hosea Tobias and Lisa Baskin, illustrated by Leonard Baskin, Viking; *Snow White and the Seven Dwarfs* translated by Randall Jarrell, illustrated by Nancy Ekholm Burkert, Farrar, Straus & Giroux; *When Clay Sings* by Byrd Baylor, illustrated by Tom Bahti, Scribner

1974   *Duffy and the Devil* by Harve Zemach, illustrated by Margot Zemach, Farrar, Straus & Giroux
        Honor Books: *Three Jovial Huntsmen* by Susan Jeffers, Bradbury; *Cathedral: The Story of Its Construction* by David Macaulay, Houghton Mifflin

1975   *Arrow to the Sun* adapted and illustrated by Gerald McDermott, Viking
        Honor Book: *Jambo Means Hello: A Swahili Alphabet Book* by Muriel Feelings, illustrated by Tom Feelings, Dial Press

1976   *Why Mosquitoes Buzz in People's Ears* retold by Verna Aardema, illustrated by Leo and Diane Dillon, Dial Press
        Honor Books: *The Desert Is Theirs* by Byrd Baylor, illustrated by Peter Parnall, Scribner; *Strega Nona* retold and illustrated by Tomie de Paola, Prentice-Hall

1977   *Ashanti to Zulu: African Traditions* by Margaret Musgrove, illustrated by Leo and Diane Dillon, Dial Press
        Honor Books: *The Amazing Bone* by William Steig, Farrar, Straus & Giroux; *The Contest* retold and illustrated by Nonny Hogrogian, Greenwillow (Morrow); *Fish for Supper* by M. B. Goffstein, Dial Press; *The Golem: A Jewish Legend* by Beverly Brodsky McDermott, Lippincott; *Hawk, I'm Your Brother* by Byrd Baylor, illustrated by Peter Parnall, Scribner

1978   *Noah's Ark* by Peter Spier, Doubleday
        Honor Books: *Castle* by David Macaulay, Houghton Mifflin; *It Could Always Be Worse* retold and illustrated by Margot Zemach, Farrar, Straus & Giroux

1979   *The Girl Who Loved Wild Horses* by Paul Goble, Bradbury
        Honor Books: *Freight Train* by Donald Crews, Greenwillow (Morrow); *The Way to Start a Day* by Byrd Baylor, illustrated by Peter Parnall, Scribner

1980   *Ox-Cart Man* by Donald Hall, illustrated by Barbara Cooney, Viking
        Honor Books: *Ben's Trumpet* by Rachel Isadora, Greenwillow (Morrow); *The Treasure* by Uri Shulevitz, Farrar, Straus & Giroux; *The Garden of Abdul Gasazi* by Chris Van Allsburg, Houghton Mifflin

1981   *Fables* by Arnold Lobel, Harper
        Honor Books: *The Bremen-Town Musicians* by Ilse Plume, Doubleday; *The Grey Lady and the Strawberry Snatcher* by Molly Bang, Four Winds; *Mice Twice* by Joseph Low, Atheneum; *Truck* by Donald Crews, Greenwillow (Morrow)

1982   *Jumanji* by Chris Van Allsburg, Houghton Mifflin
        Honor Books: *A Visit to William Blake's Inn: Poems for Innocent and Experienced Travelers* by Nancy Willard, illustrated by Alice and Martin Provensen, Harcourt Brace Jovanovich; *Where the Buffaloes Begin* by Olaf Baker, illustrated by Stephen Gammell, Warne; *On Market Street* by Arnold Lobel, illustrated by Anita Lobel, Greenwillow (Morrow); *Outside Over There* by Maurice Sendak, Harper

1983   *Shadow* by Blaise Cendrars, illustrated by Marcia Brown, Scribner
        Honor Books: *When I Was Young in the Mountains* by Cynthia Rylant, illustrated by Diane Goode, Dutton; *Chair for My Mother* by Vera B. Williams, Morrow

1984   *The Glorious Flight: Across the Channel with Louis Blériot July 25, 1909* by Alice and Martin Provenson, Viking
        Honor Books: *Ten, Nine, Eight* by Molly Bang, Greenwillow (Morrow); *Little Red Riding Hood* by Trina Schart Hyman, Holiday House

1985   *Saint George and the Dragon* by Margaret Hodges, illustrated by Trina Schart Hyman, Little, Brown
Honor Books: *Hansel and Gretel* by Rika Lesser, illustrated by Paul O. Zelinsky, Dodd, Mead; *The Story of the Jumping Mouse* by John Steptoe, Lothrop; *Have You Seen My Duckling?* by Nancy Tafuri, Greenwillow (Morrow)

1986   *The Polar Express* by Chris Van Allsburg, Houghton Mifflin
Honor Books: *The Relatives Came* by Cynthia Rylant, illustrated by Stephen Gammell, Bradbury; *King Bidgood's in the Bathtub* by Audrey Wook, illustrated by Don Wood, Harcourt Brace Jovanovich

1987   *Hey, Al* by Arthur Yorinks, illustrated by Richard Egielski, Farrar, Straus & Giroux
Honor Books: *The Village of Round and Square Houses* by Ann Grifalconi, Little, Brown; *Alphabatics* by Suse MacDonald, Bradbury; *Rumpelstiltskin* by Paul O. Zelinsky, Dutton

1988   *Owl Moon* by Jane Yolen, illustrated by John Schoenherr, Philomel (Putnam)
Honor Book: *Mufaro's Beautiful Daughter* by John Steptoe, Lothrop

1989   *Song and Dance Man* by Karen Ackerman, illustrated by Stephen Gammell, Knopf
Honor Books: *Goldilocks* by James Marshall, Dial Press; *The Boy of the Three-Year Nap* by Dianne Snyder, illustrated by Allen Say; *Mirandy and Brother Wind* by Patricia McKissack, illustrated by Jerry Pinkney, Knopf; *Free Fall* by David Wiesner, Lothrop

1990   *Lon Po Po: A Red-Riding Hood Story from China* by Ed Young, Philomel (Putnam)
Honor Books: *Hershel and the Hanukkah Goblins* by Eric Kimmel, illustrated by Trina Schart Hyman, Holiday; *Color Zoo* by Lois Ehlert, Lippincott; *Bill Peet: An Autobiography* by Bill Peet, Houghton Mifflin; *The Talking Eggs* retold by Robert D. San Souci, illustrated by Jerry Pinkney, Dial

Boston Globe–Horn Book Awards

Awarded annually since 1967 and sponsored jointly by the *Boston Globe* and *Horn Book Magazine,* two prizes originally were given—one to recognize the outstanding text and one the outstanding illustration. Beginning in 1976, the categories were redefined: Outstanding Fiction or Poetry, Outstanding Nonfiction, and Outstanding Illustration.

1967   Text: *The Little Fishes* by Erik Haugaard, Houghton Mifflin
Illustration: *London Bridge Is Falling Down* by Peter Spier, Doubleday

1968   Text: *The Spring Rider* by John Lawson, Crowell
Illustration: *Tikki Tikki Tembo* by Arlene Mosel, illustrated by Blair Lent, Holt, Rinehart and Winston

1969   Text: *A Wizard of Earthsea* by Ursula K. Le Guin, Houghton Mifflin
Illustration: *The Adventures of Paddy Pork* by John S. Goodall, Harcourt Brace Jovanovich

1970   Text: *The Intruder* by John Rowe Townsend, Lippincott
Illustration: *Hi, Cat!* by Ezra Jack Keats, Macmillan

1971   Text: *A Room Made of Windows* by Eleanor Cameron, Little, Brown
Illustration: *If I Built a Village* by Kazue Mizumura, Crowell

1972   Text: *Tristan and Iseult* by Rosemary Sutcliff, Dutton
Illustration: *Mr. Gumpy's Outing* by John Burningham, Holt, Rinehart and Winston

1973   Text: *The Dark Is Rising* by Susan Cooper, McElderry/Atheneum
Illustration: *King Stork* by Trina Schart Hyman, Little, Brown

1974   Text: *M. C. Higgins, the Great* by Virginia Hamilton, Macmillan
Illustration: *Jambo Means Hello* by Muriel Feelings, illustrated by Tom Feelings, Dial Press

1975   Text: *Transport 7-41-R* by T. Degens, Viking
Illustration: *Anno's Alphabet* by Mitsumasa Anno, Crowell

1976   Fiction: *Unleaving* by Jill Paton Walsh, Farrar, Straus & Giroux
Nonfiction: *Voyaging to Cathay: Americans in the China Trade* by Alfred Tamarin and Shirley Glubok, Viking
Illustration: *Thirteen* by Remy Charlip and Jerry Joyner, Parents

1977   Fiction: *Child of the Owl.* by Laurence Yep, Harper
Nonfiction: *Chance, Luck and Destiny* by Peter Dickinson, Little, Brown
Illustration: *Granfa' Grig Had a Pig and Other Rhymes* by Wallace Tripp, Little, Brown

1978   Fiction: *The Westing Game* by Ellen Raskin, Dutton
Nonfiction: *Mischling, Second Degree: My Childhood in Nazi Germany* by Ilse Koehn, Greenwillow (Morrow)
Illustration: *Anno's Journey* by Mitsumasa Anno, Philomel (Putnamt)

1979   Fiction: *Humbug Mountain* by Sid Fleischman, Little, Brown
Nonfiction: *The Road From Home: The Story of an Armenian Girl* by David Kherdian, Greenwillow (Morrow)
Illustration: *The Snowman* by Raymond Briggs, Random House

1980   Fiction: *Conrad's War* by Andrew Davies, Crown
Nonfiction: *Building: The Fight Against Gravity* by Mario Salvadori, McElderry/Atheneum
Illustration: *The Garden of Abdul Gasazi* by Chris Van Allsburg, Houghton Mifflin

1981   Fiction: *The Leaving* by Lynn Hall, Scribner
Nonfiction: *The Weaver's Gift* by Kathryn Lasky, Warne
Illustration: *Outside Over There* by Maurice Sendak, Harper

1982   Fiction: *Playing Beatie Bow* by Ruth Park, Atheneum
Nonfiction: *Upon the Head of the Goat: A Childhood in Hungary, 1939–1944* by Aranka Siegal, Farrar, Straus & Giroux
Illustration: *A Visit to William Blake's Inn: Poems for Innocent and Experienced Travelers* by Nancy Willard, illustrated by Alice and Martin Provenson

1983   Fiction: *Sweet Whispers, Brother Rush* by Virginia Hamilton, Philomel (Putnam)
Nonfiction: *Behind Barbed Wire: The Imprisonment of Japanese-Americans During World War II* by Daniel S. David, Dutton
Illustration: *A Chair for My Mother* by Vera B. Williams, Greenwillow (Morrow)

1984   Fiction: *A Little Fear* by Patricia Wrightson, McElderry/Atheneum
        Nonfiction: *The Double Life of Pocahontas* by Jean Fritz, Putnam
        Illustration: *Jonah and the Great Fish* retold and illustrated by Warwick Hutton,
        McElderry/Atheneum

1985   Fiction: *The Moves Make the Man* by Bruce Brooks, Harper
        Nonfiction: *Commodore Perry in the Land of the Shogun* by Rhoda Blumberg,
        Lothrop
        Illustration: *Mama Don't Allow* by Thatcher Hurd, Harper

1986   Fiction: *In Summer Light* by Zibby Oneal, Viking/Kestrel
        Nonfiction: *Auks, Rocks and the Odd Dinosaur* by Peggy Thompson, Crowell
        Illustration: *The Paper Crane* by Molly Bang, Greenwillow (Morrow)

1987   Fiction: *Rabble Starkey* by Lois Lowry, Houghton Mifflin
        Nonfiction: *Pilgrims of Plimouth* by Marcia Sewall, Atheneum
        Illustration: *Mufaro's Beautiful Daughters* by John Steptoe, Lothrop

1988   Fiction: *The Friendship* by Mildred Taylor, Dial Press
        Nonfiction: *Anthony Burns: The Defeat and Triumph of a Fugitive Slave* by
        Virginia Hamilton, Knopf
        Illustration: *The Boy of the Three-Year Nap* by Diane Snyder, Houghton Mifflin

1989   Fiction: *The Village by the Sea* by Paula Fox, Franklin Watts
        Nonfiction: *The Way Things Work* by David Macaulay, Houghton Mifflin
        Illustration: *Shy Charles* by Rosemary Wells, Dial

The Mildred L. Batchelder Award

Presented annually by the American Library Association, this award recognizes the most
outstanding children's book originally translated from a language other than English. (Unless
otherwise indicated, the author is also the translator.)

1968   *The Little Man* by Erich Kastner, translated by James Kirkup, illustrated by Rich
        Schreiter, Knopf, 1966

1969   *Don't Take Teddy* by Babbis Friis-Baastad, translated by Lise Somme McKinnon,
        Scribner, 1967

1970   *Wildcat under Glass* by Alki Zei, translated by Edward Fenton, Holt, Rinehart
        and Winston, 1968

1971   *In the Land of Ur: The Discovery of Ancient Mesopotamia* by Hans Baumann,
        Stella Humphries, illustrated by Hans Peter Renner, Pantheon Books, 1969

1972   *Friedrich* by Hans Peter Richter, translated by Edite Kroll, Holt, Rinehart and
        Winston, 1970

1973   *Pulga* by Siny Rose Van Iterson, translated by Alexander and Alison Gode,
        Morrow, 1971

1974   *Petros' War* by Alki Zei, translated by Edward Fenton, Dutton, 1972

1975   *An Old Tale Carved Out of Stone* by Aleksandr M. Linevski, translated by Maria
        Polushkin, Crown, 1973

1976   *The Cat and Mouse Who Shared a House* by Ruth Hurlimann, translated by Anthea Bell, Walck, 1974

1977   *The Leopard* by Cecil Bodker, illustrated by Gunnar Poulsen, Atheneum, 1975

1978   No award

1979   *Konrad* by Christine Nostlinger, translated by Anthea Bell, illustrated by Carol Nicklaus, Watts, 1977

        Rabbit Island by Jorg Steiner, translated by Ann Conrad Lammers, illustrated by Jorg Muller, Harcourt Brace Jovanovich, 1978

1980   *The Sound of Dragon's Feet* by Alki Zci, translated by Edward Fenton, Dutton, 1979

1981   *The Winter When Time Was Frozen* by Els Pelgrom, translated by Raphael and Maryka Rudnik, Morrow, 1980

1982   *The Battle Horse* by Harry Kullman, translated by George Blecher and Lone Thygesen-Blecher, Bradbury, 1981

1983   *Hiroshima no Pika* by Toshi Maruki, Lothrop, 1982

1984   *Ronia, the Robber's Daughter* by Astrid Lindgren, translated by Patricia Crampton, Viking, 1983

1985   *The Island on Bird Street* by Uri Orlev, translated by Hillel Halkin, Houghton Mifflin, 1984

1986   *Rose Blanche* by Christophe Gallaz and Roberto Innocenti, translated by Martha Coventry and Richard Graglia, illustrated by Roberto Innocenti, Creative Education, 1985

1987   *No Hero for the Kaiser* by Rudof Frank, translated by Patricia Crampton, illustrated by Klaus Steffans, Lothrop, 1986

1988   *If You Didn't Have Me* by Ulf Nilsson, illustrated by Eva Ericksson, translated by Lone Thygesen-Blecher and George Blecher, McElderry

1989   *Crutches* by Peter Hartling, Lothrop

1990   *Buster's World* by Branner og Korch, Dutton

The Laura Ingalls Wilder Award

Named in honor of the beloved author of the Little House books (who was also its first recipient), this award is presented by the Association of Library Service to Children of the American Library Association to the individual, either author or illustrator, whose work has over the years proved to be a significant contribution to children's literature. Originally awarded every five years, it has since 1980 been given every three years.

1954   Laura Ingalls Wilder

1960   Clara Ingram Judson

1965   Ruth Sawyer

1970   E. B. White

1975   Beverly Cleary

1980   Theodore Geisel (Dr. Seuss)

1983   Maurice Sendak

1986   Jean Fritz

1989   Elizabeth George Speare

National Council of Teachers of English Award for Excellence in Poetry for Children

This award is presented every three years (from 1977 through 1982 it was awarded annually) by the National Council of Teachers of English and was established to recognize a living poet's lifetime contribution to poetry for children.

1977   David McCord

1978   Aileen Fisher

1979   Karla Kuskin

1980   Myra Cohn Livingston

1981   Eve Merriam

1982   John Ciardi

1985   Lilian Moore

1988   Arnold Adoff

The Phoenix Award

Since 1985, the Children's Literature Association has annually presented this award to a book, published twenty years before, that did not receive any major award, but has proved, through the test of time, to be a work of enduring excellence.

1985   *Mark of the Horse Lord* by Rosemary Sutcliff, Walck

1986   *Queenie Peavy* by Robert Burch, Viking

1987   *Smith* by Leon Garfield, Constable

1988   *The Rider and His Horse* by Eric Christian Haugaard, Houghton Mifflin

1989   *The Night Watchman* by Helen Cresswell, Macmillan

1990   *Enchantress from the Stars* by Sylvia Engdahl, Macmillan

INTERNATIONAL AWARDS

The Hans Christian Andersen Award

This medal, named for the great Danish storyteller, is presented every two years by the International Board on Books for Young People to a living author and (since 1966) living illustrator whose works have made a significant, international contribution to children's literature.

1956   Eleanor Farjeon (Great Britain)

1958   Astrid Lindgren (Sweden)

1960   Erich Kastner (Germany)

1962   Meindert DeJong (United States)

1964   Rene Guillot (France)

1966   Author: Tove Jansson (Finland)
         Illustrator: Alois Carigiet (Switzerland)

1968   Authors: James Kruss (Germany) and Jose Maria Sanches-Silva (Spain)
         Illustrator: Jiri Trnka (Czechoslovakia)

1970   Author: Gianni Rodari (Italy)
         Illustrator: Maurice Sendak (United States)

1972   Author: Scott O'Dell (United States)
         Illustrator: Ib Spang Olsen (Denmark)

1974   Author: Maria Gripe (Sweden)
         Illustrator: Farsid Mesghali (Iran)

1976   Author: Cecil Bodker (Denmark)
         Illustrator: Tatjana Mawrine (USSR)

1978   Author: Paula Fox (United States)
         Illustrator: Otto S. Svend (Denmark)

1980   Author: Bohumil Riha (Czechoslovakia)
         Illustrator: Suekichi Akaba (Japan)

1982   Author: Lygia Gojunga Nunes (Brazil)
         Illustrator: Zbigniew Rychlicki (Poland)

1984   Author: Christine Nostlinger (Austria)
         Illustrator: Mitsumasa Anno (Japan)

1986   Author: Patricia Wrightson (Australia)
         Illustrator: Robert Ingpen (Australia)

1988   Author: Annie M. G. Schmidt (Netherlands)
         Illustrator: Dusan Kallay (Yugoslavia)

The Carnegie Medal

Awarded by the British Library Association to an outstanding book first published in the United Kingdom, this medal has been awarded annually since it was established in 1937 (the first award being presented to a book published in the preceding year).

1936   *Pigeon Post* by Arthur Ransome, Jonathan Cape

1937   *The Family from One End Street* by Eve Garnett, Muller

1938   *The Circus Is Coming* by Noel Streatfeild, Dent

1939   *Radium Woman* by Eleanor Doorly, Heinemann

1940   *Visitors from London* by Kitty Barne, Dent

1941   *We Couldn't Leave Dinah* by Mary Treadgold, Penguin Books

1942   *The Little Grey Men* by B. B., Eyre & Spottiswoode

1943   No award

1944   *The Wind on the Moon* by Eric Linklater, Macmillan

1945   No award

1946   *The Little White Horse* by Elizabeth Goudge, Brockhampton Press

1947   *Collected Stories for Children* by Walter de la Mare, Faber

1948   *Sea Change* by Richard Armstrong, Dent

1949   *The Story of Your Home* by Agnes Allen, Transatlantic

1950   *The Lark on the Wind* by Elfrida Vipont Foulds, Oxford University Press

1951   *The Wool-Pack* by Cynthia Harnett, Methuen

1952   *The Borrowers* by Mary Norton, Dent

1953   *A Valley Grows Up* by Edward Osmond, Oxford University Press

1954   *Knight Crusader* by Ronald Welch, Oxford University Press

1955   *The Little Bookroom* by Eleanor Farjeon, Oxford University Press

1956   *The Last Battle* by C. S. Lewis, Bodley Head

1957   *A Grass Rope* by William Mayne, Oxford University Press

1958   *Tom's Midnight Garden* by Philippa Pearce, Oxford University Press

1959   *The Lantern Bearers* by Rosemary Sutcliff, Oxford University Press

1960   *The Making of Man* by I. W. Cornwall, Phoenix

1961   *A Stranger at Green Knowe* by Lucy Boston, Faber

1962   *The Twelve and the Genii* by Pauline Clarke, Faber

1963   *Time of Trial* by Hester Burton, Oxford University Press

1964   *Nordy Banks* by Sheena Porter, Oxford University Press

1965   *The Grange at High Force* by Philip Turner, Oxford University Press

1966   No award

1967   *The Owl Service* by Alan Garner, Collins

1968   *The Moon in the Cloud* by Rosemary Harris, Faber

1969   *The Edge of the Cloud* by K. M. Peyton, Oxford University Press

1970   *The God Beneath the Sea* by Leon Garfield and Edward Blishen, Kestrel

1971   *Josh* by Ivan Southall, Angus & Robertson

1972   *Watership Down* by Richard Adams, Rex Collings

1973   *The Ghost of Thomas Kempe* by Penelope Lively, Heinemann

1974   *The Stronghold* by Mollie Hunter, Hamilton

1975   *The Machine-Gunners* by Robert Westall, Macmillan

1976   *Thunder and Lightnings* by Jan Mark, Kestrel

1977   *The Turbulent Term of Tyke Tiler* by Gene Kemp, Faber

1978   *The Exeter Blitz* by David Rees, Hamish Hamilton

1979   *Tulku* by Peter Dickinson, Dutton

1980   *City of Gold* by Peter Dickinson, Gollancz

1981   *The Scarecrows* by Robert Westall, Chatto & Windus

1982   *The Haunting* by Margaret Mahy, Dent

1983   *Handles* by Jan Mark, Kestrel

1984   *The Changeover* by Margaret Mahy, Dent

1985   *Storm* by Kevin Crossley-Holland, Heinemann

1986   *Granny Was a Buffer Girl* by Berlie Doherty, Methuen

1987   *The Ghost Drum* by Susan Price, Faber

1988   *A Pack of Lies* by Geraldine McCaughrean, Oxford University Press

The Kate Greenaway Medal

Named for the celebrated nineteenth-century children's illustrator, this medal is awarded annually by the British Library Association to the most distinguished illustrated work for children first published in the United Kindgom during the preceding year. (Unless otherwise noted, the author is also the illustrator.)

1956   *Tim All Alone* by Edward Ardizzone, Oxford University Press

1957   *Mrs. Easter and the Storks* by V. H. Drummond, Faber

1958   No award

1959   *Kashtanka and a Bundle of Ballads* by William Stobbs, Oxford University Press

1960   *Old Winkle and the Seagulls* by Elizabeth Rose, illustrated by Gerald Rose, Faber

1961   *Mrs. Cockle's Cat* by Philippa Pearce, illustrated by Anthony Maitland, Kestrel

1962   *Brian Wildsmith's ABC* by Brian Wildsmith, Oxford University Press

1963   *Borka* by John Burningham, Jonathan Cape

1964   *Shakespeare's Theatre* by C. W. Hodges, Oxford University Press

1965   *Three Poor Tailors* by Victor Ambrus, Hamilton

1966   *Mother Goose Treasury* by Raymond Briggs, Hamilton

1967   *Charlie, Charlotte & the Golden Canary* by Charles Keeping, Oxford University Press

1968   *Dictionary of Chivalry* by Grant Uden, illustrated by Pauline Baynes, Kestrel

1969   *The Quangle-Wangle's Hat* by Edward Lear, illustrated by Helen Oxenbury, Heinemann
        Dragon of an Ordinary Family by Margaret May, illustrated by Helen Oxenbury, Heinemann

1970   *Mr. Gumpy's Outing* by John Burningham, Jonathan Cape

1971   *The Kingdom under the Sea* by Jan Pienkowski, Jonathan Cape

1972   *The Woodcutter's Duck* by Krystyna Turska, Hamilton

1973   *Father Christmas* by Raymond Briggs, Hamilton

1974   *The Wind Blew* by Pat Hutchins, Bodley Head

1975   *Horses in Battle* by Victor Ambrus, Oxford University Press
        Mishka by Victor Ambrus, Oxford University Press

1976   *The Post Office Cat* by Gail E. Haley, Bodley Head

1977   *Dogger* by Shirley Hughes, Bodley Head

1978   *Each Peach Pear Plum* by Janet and Allan Ahlberg, Kestrel

1979   *Haunted House* by Jan Pienkowski, Dutton

1980   *Mr. Magnolia* by Quentin Blake, Jonathan Cape

1981   *The Highwayman* by Alfred Noyes, illustrated by Charles Keeping, Oxford University Press

1982   *Long Neck and Thunder Foot* by Michael Foreman, Kestrel
Sleeping Beauty and Other Favorite Fairy Tales by Michael Foreman, Gollancz

1983   *Gorilla* by Anthony Browne, Julia McRae Books

1984   *Hiawatha's Childhood* by Errol LeCain, Faber

1985   *Sir Gawain and the Loathly Lady* by Selina Hastings, illustrated by Juan Wijngaard, Walker

1986   *Snow White in New York* by Fiona French, Oxford University Press

1987   *Crafty Chameleon* by Adrienne Kennaway, Hodder & Stoughton

1988   *Can't You Sleep, Little Bear?* by Martha Waddell, illustrated by Barbara Firth, Walker

Australian Children's Book of the Year Award

This has been awarded annually since 1946 to the most distinguished children's book by an Australian citizen. Occasionally, more than one book in a given year will be so honored, and occasionally no award is presented.

1946   *Karrawingi, the Emu* by Leslie Rees, Sands

1947   No award

1948   *Shackleton's Argonauts* by Frank Hurley, Angus & Robertson

1949   *Whalers of the Midnight Sun* by Alan Villiers, Angus & Robertson

1950   No award

1951   *Verity of Sydney Town* by Ruth Williams, Angus & Robertson

1952   *The Australia Book* by Eve Pownall, Sands

1953   *Aircraft of Today & Tomorrow* by J. H. and W. D. Martin, Angus & Robertson
Good Luck to the Rider by Joan Phipson, Angus & Robertson

1954   *Australian Legendary Tales* by K. L. Parker, Angus & Robertson

1955   *The First Walkabout* by H. A. Lindsay and N. B. Tindale, Kestrel

1956   *The Crooked Snake* by Patricia Wrightson, Angus & Robertson

1957   *The Boomerang Book of Legendary Tales* by Enid Moodie-Heddle, Kestrel

1958   *Tiger in the Bush* by Nan Chauncy, Oxford University Press

1959   *Devil's Hill* by Nan Chauncy, Oxford University Press
Sea Menace by John Gunn, Constable

1960   *All the Proud Tribesmen* by Kylie Tennant, Macmillan

1961   *Tangara* by Nan Chauncy, Oxford University Press

1962   *The Racketty Street Gang* by H. L. Evers, Hodder & Stoughton
Rafferty Rides a Winner bvy Joan Woodbery, Parrish

1963   *The Family Conspiracy* by Joan Phipson, Angus & Robertson

1964   *The Green Laurel* by Eleanor Spence, Oxford University Press

1965   *Pastures of the Blue Crane* by Hesba F. Brinsmead, Oxford University Press

1966   *Ash Road* by Ivan Southall, Angus & Robertson

1967   *The Min Min* by Mavis Thorpe Clark, Landsdowne

1968   *To the Wild Sky* by Ivan Southall, Angus & Robertson

1969   *When Jays Fly to Barbmo* by Margaret Balderson, Oxford University Press

1970   *Uhu* by Annette Macarther-Onslow, Ure Smith

1971   *Bread and Honey* by Ivan Southall, Angus & Robertson

1972   *Longtime Passing* by Hesba F. Brinsmead, Angus & Robertson

1973   *Family at the Lookout* by Noreen Shelly, Oxford University Press

1974   *The Nargun and the Stars* by Patricia Wrightson, Hutchinson

1975   No award

1976   *Fly West* by Ivan Southall, Angus & Robertson

1977   *The October Child* by Eleanor Spence, Oxford University Press

1978   *The Ice Is Coming* by Patricia Wrightson, Hutchinson

1979   *The Plum-Rain Scroll* by Ruth Manley, Hodder & Stoughton

1980   *Displaced Person* by Lee Harding, Hyland House

1981   *Playing Beatie Bow* by Ruth Park, Nelson

1982   *The Valley Between* by Colin Thiele, Rigby

1983   *Master of the Grove* by Victor Kelleher, Penguin Books

1984   *A Little Fear* by Patricia Wrighton, Hutchinson

1985   *The True Story of Lillie Stubeck* by James Aldridge, Hyland House

1986   *The Green Wind* by Thurley Fowler, Rigby

1987   *All We Know* by Simon French, Angus & Robertson

        Pigs Might Fly by Emily Rodda, illustrated by Noela Young, Angus & Robertson

Australian Picture Book of the Year

Beginning in 1956, an additional award was established for the most distinguished Australian picture-book of the year. Unless otherwise indicated, the author is also the illustrator.

1956   *Wish the Magic Nut* by Peggy Barnard, illustrated by Shelia Hawkins, Sands

1957   No award

1958   *Piccaninny Walkabout* by Axel Poignant, Angus & Robertson

1959–1964   No awards

1965   *Hugo's Zoo* by Elisabeth MacIntyre, Angus & Robertson

1966–1968   No awards

1969   *Sly Old Wardrobe* by Ivan Southall, illustrated by Ted Greenwood, Cheshire

1970   No award

1971   *Waltzing Matilda* by A. B. Paterson, illustrated by Desmond Digby, Collins

1972–1973   No awards

1974	*The Bunyip of Berkeley's Creek* by Jenny Wagner, illustrated by Ron Brooks, Kestrel
1975	*The Man from Ironbark* by A. B. Paterson, illustrated by Quentin Hole, Collins
1976	*The Rainbow Serpent* by Dick Roughsey, Collins
1977	*ABC of Monsters* by Deborah Niland, Hodder & Stoughton
1978	*John Brown, Rose and the Midnight Cat* by Jenny Wagner, illustrated by Ron Brooks, Kestrel
1979	*The Quinkins* by Percy Trezise and Dick Roughsey, Collins
1980	*One Dragon's Dream* by Peter Pavey, Nelson
1981	No award
1982	*Sunshine* by Jan Ormerod, Kestrel
1983	*Who Sank the Boat?* by Pamela Allen, Nelson
1984	*Bertie and the Bear* by Pamela Allen, Nelson
1985	(Commended) *Home in the Sky* by Jeannie Baker and Junko Morimoto (retelling by Helen Smith), Collins
1986	*Felix and Alexander* by Terry Denton, Oxford University Press
1987	*Kojuro and the Bears* adapted by Helen Smith, illustrated by Junko Morimoto, Collins

The Canadian Library Award

Presented by the Canadian Library Association since 1947, this award recognizes the most distinguished children's book by a Canadian citizen. Beginning in 1956, an additional award has been presented to a distinguished work published in French. The association also has presented, since 1971, the Amelia Frances Howard-Gibbon Medal for outstanding illustration by a Canadian illustrator in a children's book published in Canada. In some years no award may be given.

1947	*Starbuck Valley Winter* by Roderick Haig-Brown, Collins
1948	*Kristi's Trees* by Mabel Dunham, Hale
1949	No award
1950	*Franklin of the Arctic* by Richard S. Lambert, McClelland & Stewart
1951	No award
1952	*The Sun Horse* by Catherine Anthony Clarke, Macmillan of Canada
1953	No award
1954	*Mgr. de Laval* by Emile S. J. Gervais, Comité des Fondateurs de l'Église Canadienne
1955	No awards
1956	*Train for Tiger Lily* by Louise Riley, Macmillan of Canada
1957	*Glooskap's Country* by Cyrus Macmillan, Oxford University Press
1958	*Lost in the Barrens* by Farley Mowat, Little, Brown
	The Chevalier du Roi by Beatrice Clement, Les Éditions de l'Atelier

1959   *The Dangerous Cove* by John F. Hayes, Copp Clark
        Un Drôle de Petit Cheval by Helen Flamme, Editions Lemeac

1960   *The Golden Phoenix* by Marius Barbeau and Michael Hornyansky, Walck
        L'Été Enchanté by Paule Daveluy, Les Éditions de l'Atelier

1961   *The St. Lawrence* by William Toye, Oxford University Press
        Plantes Vagabondes by Marcelle Gauvreau, Centre de Psychologie et de Pedagogie

1962   *Les Îles du Roi Maha Maha II* by Claude Aubry, Les Éditions du Pelican

1963   *The Incredible Journey* by Sheila Burnford, Little, Brown
        Drôle d'Automne by Paule Daveluy, Les Éditions du Pelican

1964   *The Whale People* by Roderick Haig-Brown, William Collins of Canada
        Feerie by Cecile Chabot, Librairie Beauchemin Ltée

1965   *Tales of Nanabozho* by Dorothy Reid, Oxford University Press
        Le Loup de Noel by Claude Aubry, Centre de Psychologie de Montreal

1966   *Tikta'Liktak* by James Houston, Kestrel
        Le Chêne des Tempêtes by Andre Mallet-Hobden, Fides
        The Double Knights by James McNeal, Walck
        Le Wapiti by Monique Corriveau, Jeunesse

1967   *Raven's Cry* by Christie Harris, McClelland & Stewart

1968   *The White Archer* by James Houston, Kestrel
        Legendes Indiennes du Canada by Claude Melancon, Éditions du Jour

1969   *And Tomorrow the Stars* by Kay Hill, Dodd, Mead

1970   *Sally Go Round the Sun* by Edith Fowke, McClelland & Stewart
        Le Merveilleuse Histoire de la Naissance by Lionel Gendron, Les Éditions de
        l'Homme

1971   *Cartier Discovers the St. Lawrence* by William Toye, Oxford University Press
        La Surprise de Dame Chenille by Henriette Major, Centre de Psychologie de
        Montreal

1972   *Mary of Mile 18* by Ann Blades, Tundra

1973   *The Marrow of the World* by Ruth Nichols, Macmillan of Canada
        Le Petit Sapin Qui A Pousse sur une Étoile by Simone Bussieres, Presses
        Laurentiennes

1974   *The Miraculous Hind* by Elizabeth Cleaver, Holt, Rinehart and Winston of Canada

1975   *Alligator Pie* by Dennis Lee, Macmillan of Canada

1976   *Jacob Two-Two Meets the Hooded Fang* by Mordecai Richler, Knopf

1977   *Mouse Woman and the Vanished Princess* by Christie Harris, McClelland &
        Stewart

1978   *Garbage Delight* by Dennis Lee, Macmillan

1979   *Hold Fast* by Kevin Major, Clarke, Irwin

1980   *River Runners: A Tale of Hardship and Bravery* by James Houston, McClelland
        & Stewart

1981   *The Violin Maker's Gift* by Donn Kushner, Macmillan of Canada

1982   *The Root Cellar* by Janet Lunn, Lester & Orpen Dennys

1983   *Up to Low* by Brian Doyle, Groundwood

1984   *Sweetgrass* by Jan Hudson, Tree Frog Press

1985   *Mama's Going to Buy a Mockingbird* by Jean Little, Penguin Books

1986   *Julie* by Cora Taylor, Western

1987   *Shadow in Hawthorn Bay* by Janet Lunn, Scribner

1988   *A Handful of Time* by Kit Pearson, Viking

1989   *Easy Avenue* by Brian Doyle, Groundwood

Amelia Frances Howard-Gibbon Medal

Awarded since 1971 by the Canadian Library Association, this medal honors excellence in children's illustration in a book published in Canada. The award must go to a citizen or resident of Canada. Unless otherwise indicated, the author is also the illustrator.

1971   *The Wind Has Wings,* edited by Mary Alice Downie and Barbara Robertson, illustrated by Elizabeth Cleaver, Oxford University Press

1972   *A Child in Prison Camp* by Shizuye Takashima, Tundra

1973   *Au Delà du Soleil/Beyond the Sun* by Jacques de Roussan, Tundra

1974   *A Prairie Boy's Winter* by William Kurelek, Tundra

1975   *The Sleighs of My Childhood/Les Traineaux de Mon Enfance* by Carlos Italiano, Tundra

1976   *A Prairie Boy's Summer* by William Kurelek, Tundra

1977   *Down by Jim Long's Stage: Rhymes for Children and Young Fish* by Al Pittman, illustrated by Pam Hall, Breakwater

1978   *The Loon's Necklace* by William Toye, illustrated by Elizabeth Cleaver, Oxford University Press

1979   *A Salmon for Simon* by Betty Waterton, illustrated by Ann Blades, Douglas & McIntyre

1980   *The Twelve Dancing Princesses* by Laszlo Gal, Methuen

1981   *The Trouble with Princesses* by Douglas Tait, McClelland & Stewart

1982   *Ytek and the Arctic Orchid: An Innuit Legend* by Heather Woodall, Douglas & McIntyre

1983   *Chester's Barn* by Lindee Climo, Tundra

1984   *Zoom at Sea* by Tim Wynne-Jones, illustrated by Ken Nutt, Douglas & McIntyre

1985   *Chin Chiang and the Dragon's Dance* by Ian Wallace, Groundwood

1986   *Zoom Away* by Tim Wynne-Jones, illustrated by Ken Nutt, Douglas & McIntyre

1987   *Moonbeam on a Cat's Ear* by Marie-Louise Gay, Stoddard

1988   *Rainy Day Magic* by Marie-Louise Gay, Hodder & Stoughton

1989   *Amos's Sweater* by Janet Lunn, illustrated by Kim LaFaye, Douglas & McIntyre

Index